Backbone.js Blueprints

Understand Backbone.js pragmatically by building seven different applications from scratch

Andrew Burgess

BIRMINGHAM - MUMBAI

Backbone.js Blueprints

Copyright © 2014 Packt Publishing

All rights reserved. No part of this book may be reproduced, stored in a retrieval system, or transmitted in any form or by any means, without the prior written permission of the publisher, except in the case of brief quotations embedded in critical articles or reviews.

Every effort has been made in the preparation of this book to ensure the accuracy of the information presented. However, the information contained in this book is sold without warranty, either express or implied. Neither the author, nor Packt Publishing, and its dealers and distributors will be held liable for any damages caused or alleged to be caused directly or indirectly by this book.

Packt Publishing has endeavored to provide trademark information about all of the companies and products mentioned in this book by the appropriate use of capitals. However, Packt Publishing cannot guarantee the accuracy of this information.

First published: May 2014

Production Reference: 1130514

Published by Packt Publishing Ltd.
Livery Place
35 Livery Street
Birmingham B3 2PB, UK.

ISBN 978-1-78328-699-7

www.packtpub.com

Cover Image by Duraid Fatouhi (duraidfatouhi@yahoo.com)

Credits

Author
Andrew Burgess

Reviewers
Marc D. Bodley
Ivano Malavolta
Lorenzo Pisani

Commissioning Editor
Gregory Wild

Acquisition Editor
Gregory Wild

Content Development Editors
Balaji Naidu
Larissa Pinto

Technical Editors
Miloni Dutia
Siddhi Rane

Copy Editors
Sayanee Mukherjee
Deepa Nambiar
Laxmi Subramanian

Project Coordinator
Wendell Palmer

Proofreaders
Simran Bhogal
Ameesha Green

Indexer
Hemangini Bari

Graphics
Yuvraj Mannari

Production Coordinator
Aparna Bhagat

Cover Work
Aparna Bhagat

About the Author

Andrew Burgess writes code and writes about code. While he dabbles with around half a dozen different programming languages, JavaScript is his favorite and is also his first love. He's been writing tutorials for Nettuts+ since 2009, and he has been creating screencasts for Tuts+ since 2012. He's written a few small e-books on other web development topics; some of them are:

- *Getting Good with Git*, Rockable Press
- *Getting Good with JavaScript*, Rockable Press
- *Getting Good with PHP*, Rockable Press

> I'd like to thank Gregory Wild, Wendell Palmer, Larissa Pinto, and all the other great people from Packt Publishing, for making the book-writing process such a breeze. Thanks have to go to Jeremy Ashkenas for creating the amazing Backbone and Underscore libraries.
> Finally, and most importantly, I must thank my family for being so understanding with the crazy schedule that writing a book gives you.

About the Reviewers

Marc D. Bodley is a passionate User Experience Engineer and a jack-of-all-trades developer with over eight years of experience within JavaScript and frontend technologies. He is excited to see JavaScript being adopted as more of a mainstream development language and not just an accessory to development. He is equally excited to see the structure and thought process of more conventional, strongly typed languages being applied to JavaScript to bring order to what is potentially a large and disorganized JS-driven code base. He has worked on large- and small-scale applications for a range of organizations, from Belk.com, to start-up style data-heavy applications, and continues to look for, learn, and enforce JavaScript and programming best practices. He is grateful to be a contributor towards this effort.

Ivano Malavolta is postdoctoral researcher at the Gran Sasso Science Institute, Italy. He has a PhD in Computer Science from the University of L'Aquila, Italy. Currently, his research activity is positioned in three main fields: software architecture, Model-Driven Engineering, and mobile-enabled systems. He has co-authored scientific publications in international journals, and international conferences, and workshops in using these themes. He is a program committee member and reviewer of international conferences and journals in his fields of interest. Ivano is an instructor at the University of L'Aquila, and he is teaching these topics in dedicated courses for both the Bachelor's and Master's degree students.

He is a strong advocate of applying academic research results in real scenarios, and he is working on projects that have been awarded as the most innovative solutions in both national and international venues. He is a member of the ACM and the IEEE.

Lorenzo Pisani is a software engineer with over a decade of experience in developing applications with PHP, MySQL, and JavaScript. As a huge advocate of open source software, he publishes just about everything he builds, outside of work, to his GitHub profile (https://github.com/Zeelot) for others to use and learn from.

www.PacktPub.com

Support files, eBooks, discount offers, and more

You might want to visit www.PacktPub.com for support files and downloads related to your book.

Did you know that Packt offers eBook versions of every book published, with PDF and ePub files available? You can upgrade to the eBook version at www.PacktPub.com and as a print book customer, you are entitled to a discount on the eBook copy. Get in touch with us at service@packtpub.com for more details.

At www.PacktPub.com, you can also read a collection of free technical articles, sign up for a range of free newsletters and receive exclusive discounts and offers on Packt books and eBooks.

http://PacktLib.PacktPub.com

Do you need instant solutions to your IT questions? PacktLib is Packt's online digital book library. Here, you can access, read, and search across Packt's entire library of books.

Why Subscribe?

- Fully searchable across every book published by Packt
- Copy and paste, print, and bookmark content
- On demand and accessible via web browser

Free Access for Packt account holders

If you have an account with Packt at www.PacktPub.com, you can use this to access PacktLib today and view nine entirely free books. Simply use your login credentials for immediate access.

Table of Contents

Preface	**1**
Chapter 1: Building a Simple Blog	**7**
Setting up the application	7
Starting with the server	9
Creating the template	11
Adding the public folder	12
Beginning the Backbone code	13
Creating a model and collection	13
Performing a quick and dirty test	15
Writing some views	16
The PostListView class	17
The PostsListView class	18
Using our views	19
Creating a router	20
Viewing a post	23
Creating new posts	26
Adding comments	28
Serving comments	29
Comment views	30
Summary	34
Chapter 2: Building a Photo-sharing Application	**37**
Creating user accounts	37
Creating our application navigation	45
Uploading photos	48
Sending photos from the server to the client	54
Creating profile pages	55
Creating the individual photo page	58

Following users	62
Displaying a followed user's photos	67
Summary	69

Chapter 3: Building a Live Data Dashboard — 71

Planning our application	72
Setting up precompiled templates	72
Creating the models	74
Creating controls	76
Including Bootstrap	78
Starting the router	78
Building the CreateEventView class	80
Creating the events table	84
Deleting a record	88
Editing event records	89
Making it live	94
Sorting events	96
Summary	100

Chapter 4: Building a Calendar — 101

Planning our application	101
Creating the model and collection	102
Creating the month view	106
Building the week row	108
Building the day cells	112
Creating the individual day screen	116
Writing the server code	132
Summary	134

Chapter 5: Building a Chat Application — 135

Outlining the application	135
Setting up the application	136
Preparing our template	137
A word about Socket.IO	137
Creating modules	138
Creating users	140
Building the layout	142
Starting the router	144
Letting users join the fun	146
Joining a room	152
Building the chat module	158
Back to the controller	161

Adding some other routes	162
Writing CSS	164
Summary	167
Chapter 6: Building a Podcast Application	**169**
What are we building?	169
Building user accounts	170
Subscribing to and storing podcasts	174
Preparing index.ejs	182
Creating our models and collections	183
Building the navigation	185
Displaying podcasts	186
Creating a layout	189
Beginning the router	190
Subscribing to new podcasts	190
Displaying the list of episodes	193
Displaying episodes	198
Summary	200
Chapter 7: Building a Game	**201**
What are we building?	201
User accounts	202
Templates	203
Creating the game data	205
Writing the models	207
Splitting up words	208
Writing the tokens view	211
Views of the clues	215
Creating the guess view	218
Building the info view	224
Wrapping our views in a GameView class	228
Starting the router	229
Creating the home view	230
Building a scoreboard	232
Writing the navigation	235
Adding new words	236
Summary	238
Index	**239**

Preface

There was a time when if you wanted to build a web application, you were pretty much on your own. You had to start from scratch and figure it all out on your own. However, now there are plenty of libraries and frameworks that you can use to build amazing web apps that are full of features; Backbone is just one of those libraries.

Backbone is a client-side library that offers models to manage data records, collections to use when working with sets of models, and views to display that data. Strictly speaking, it's not an MVC library, it's a relatively loose toolbox that you can use in many different ways.

This book is not an introduction to Backbone. We won't be going through every feature in the library as if it were a friendly version of the documentation. Instead, we'll be looking at Backbone in the context of building an entire web application from start to finish. This means that there are a few features of Backbone—a few obscure methods or properties—that we won't use at all. If you want to learn every nook and cranny of Backbone, you should read the documentation at `http://backbonejs.org/`.

This book has two goals. The first is to teach you how to use Backbone to build complete web applications. A complete web application will have a lot more than just JavaScript that runs in the browser. There's HTML and CSS to consider, and of course, every application needs a server. In each chapter of this book, we'll build a different application from scratch, and we'll need to create all these components. Of course, these will be applications with heavy client sides, so most of the code we will write will use Backbone. However, because we're building complete applications, you'll get to see how our Backbone code will work in tandem with the rest of the code.

Preface

The other goal of this book is to teach you how Backbone thinks. As we build an application, we'll use as many different techniques as we possibly can. While there are many Backbone conventions, most of them are not actually necessary for your code to work. By learning what is required, you can fulfill those requirements and write the rest of your code as you see fit, following convention or not.

What this book covers

Chapter 1, *Building a Simple Blog*, introduces you to each of the main components of Backbone and how they work together. If you haven't used Backbone before, this is important groundwork; if you have, this will be your refresher on the purpose of each Backbone piece.

Chapter 2, *Building a Photo-sharing Application*, shows you how to build a photo sharing website similar to Instagram. Among other things, you'll learn how to customize the way Backbone models are sent to and received from the server. This is because we'll be using a Backbone model to upload files.

Chapter 3, *Building a Live Data Dashboard*, takes things to the next level by building an application that continually polls the server for changes to a dataset, effectively creating a *live* application. We'll also look at better code organization.

Chapter 4, *Building a Calendar*, will continue the theme of building apps with well-organized code. We'll also learn about properly distributing application functionality.

Chapter 5, *Building a Chat Application*, goes in a different direction by using Socket.IO to control the transfer of data between the client and the server. Also, we'll use the Marionette framework to make our jobs a little easier.

Chapter 6, *Building a Podcast Application*, shows that not every Backbone application is client-side code, some applications will have a lot of server code. We'll also look at building some custom infrastructure to work with Backbone.

Chapter 7, *Building a Game*, wraps up the book with a fun project. We'll review all the main components of Backbone, as well as building non-Backbone pages to create a more complete web application. Of course, we'll also have to write the game logic.

What you need for this book

Since this book is mostly about client-side code, the main tools are a text editor and a browser. However, there are a few others you'll need. You'll have to install Node.js (http://nodejs.org), which comes with npm, the Node package manager. If you're on a Mac, that's all you'll need. However, if you are on Windows, you'll also want to have a version of Python 2 (preferably 2.7.3) and Express 2013 for Windows Desktop; you'll need these to install the bcrypt Node.js package for some of the chapters.

Who this book is for

This book is written for anyone who wants to learn the Backbone library proficiently; by building seven very different applications, you'll quickly learn all the ins and outs of Backbone. Hopefully, you'll also improve your coding skills, for both client and server coding.

Of course, you'll need to know a few things before we get started. You should have a decent working knowledge of JavaScript. More nuanced language features will be explained in the text, but you should be able to hold your own most of the time. Also, all the server code we write will be in Node.js, so you'll want to be familiar with that. If you understand that Node.js code is often asynchronous and that's why it uses callbacks, you'll be fine. You'll want to be familiar with HTML and CSS; while they will not feature heavily, they will have their parts to play.

You might wonder if you need to be familiar with Backbone at all to benefit from this book. You'll probably be a little more comfortable with it all if you understand the basics of Backbone, and what the general purposes of its main components are. However, if you've not used it, don't worry. The very first chapter will introduce you to all the parts of Backbone by using them in a simple application.

Conventions

In this book, you will find a number of styles of text that distinguish between different kinds of information. Here are some examples of these styles, and an explanation of their meaning.

Code words in text, database table names, folder names, filenames, file extensions, pathnames, dummy URLs, user input, and Twitter handles are shown as follows: "Next, we can create a file named app.js in the public directory."

Preface

A block of code is set as follows:

```
var Posts = Backbone.Collection.extend({
  model: Post,
  url: "/posts"
});
```

When we wish to draw your attention to a particular part of a code block, the relevant lines or items are set in bold:

```
var User = Backbone.Model.extend({
  url: function () {
    return '/user-' + this.get('id') + '.json';
  }
});
```

Any command-line input or output is written as follows:

```
npm install passport --save
```

New terms and **important words** are shown in bold. Words that you see on the screen, in menus or dialog boxes for example, appear in the text like this: "Type in a name and click on **Join**, and the name will appear above in the list."

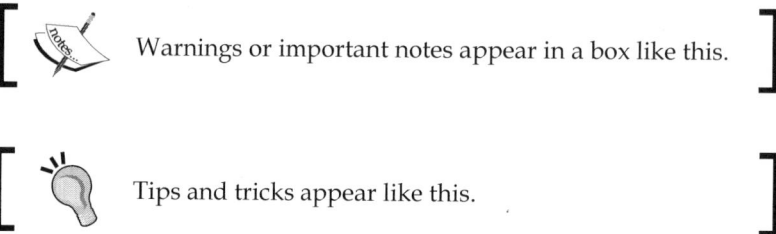

> Warnings or important notes appear in a box like this.

> Tips and tricks appear like this.

Reader feedback

Feedback from our readers is always welcome. Let us know what you think about this book—what you liked or may have disliked. Reader feedback is important for us to develop titles that you really get the most out of.

To send us general feedback, simply send an e-mail to feedback@packtpub.com, and mention the book title via the subject of your message.

If there is a topic that you have expertise in and you are interested in either writing or contributing to a book, see our author guide on www.packtpub.com/authors.

Customer support

Now that you are the proud owner of a Packt book, we have a number of things to help you to get the most from your purchase.

Downloading the example code

You can download the example code files for all Packt books you have purchased from your account at http://www.packtpub.com. If you purchased this book elsewhere, you can visit http://www.packtpub.com/support and register to have the files e-mailed directly to you.

Errata

Although we have taken every care to ensure the accuracy of our content, mistakes do happen. If you find a mistake in one of our books—maybe a mistake in the text or the code—we would be grateful if you would report this to us. By doing so, you can save other readers from frustration and help us improve subsequent versions of this book. If you find any errata, please report them by visiting http://www.packtpub.com/submit-errata, selecting your book, clicking on the **errata submission form** link, and entering the details of your errata. Once your errata are verified, your submission will be accepted and the errata will be uploaded on our website, or added to any list of existing errata, under the Errata section of that title. Any existing errata can be viewed by selecting your title from http://www.packtpub.com/support.

Piracy

Piracy of copyright material on the Internet is an ongoing problem across all media. At Packt, we take the protection of our copyright and licenses very seriously. If you come across any illegal copies of our works, in any form, on the Internet, please provide us with the location address or website name immediately so that we can pursue a remedy.

Please contact us at copyright@packtpub.com with a link to the suspected pirated material.

We appreciate your help in protecting our authors, and our ability to bring you valuable content.

Questions

You can contact us at questions@packtpub.com if you are having a problem with any aspect of the book, and we will do our best to address it.

1
Building a Simple Blog

We're going to begin by assuming that your experience in Backbone is very minimal; in fact, even if you've never used Backbone before, you should still be able to follow along just fine. The application we're going to build in this chapter is a very simple blog. As blogs go, it's going to have very few features; there will be posts that viewers can read and make comments on. However, it will introduce you to every major feature in the Backbone library, get you comfortable with the vocabulary, and how these features work together in general.

By the end of this chapter, you'll know how to:

- Use Backbone's model, collection, and view components
- Create a Backbone router that controls everything the user sees on the screen
- Program the server side with Node.js (and Express.js) to create a backend for our Backbone app

So let's get started!

Setting up the application

Every application has to be set up, so we'll begin with that. Create a folder for your project—I'll call mine `simpleBlog`—and inside that, create a file named `package.json`. If you've used Node.js before, you know that the `package.json` file describes the project; lists the project home page, repository, and other links; and (most importantly for us) outlines the dependencies for the application.

Here's what the `package.json` file looks like:

```
{
  "name": "simple-blog",
  "description": "This is a simple blog.",
```

Building a Simple Blog

```
      "version": "0.1.0",
      "scripts": {
        "start": "nodemon server.js"
      },
      "dependencies": {
        "express": "3.x.x",
        "ejs"     : "~0.8.4",
        "bourne"  : "0.3"
      },
      "devDependencies": {
        "nodemon": "latest"
      }
    }
```

> **Downloading the example code**
>
> You can download the example code files for all Packt books you have purchased from your account at http://www.packtpub.com. If you purchased this book elsewhere, you can visit http://www.packtpub.com/support and register to have the files e-mailed directly to you.

This is a pretty bare-bones package.json file, but it has all the important bits. The name, description, and version properties should be self-explanatory. The dependencies object lists all the npm packages that this project needs to run: the key is the name of the package and the value is the version. Since we're building an ExpressJS backend, we'll need the express package. The ejs package is for our server-side templates and bourne is our database (more on this one later).

The devDependencies property is similar to the dependencies property, except that these packages are only required for someone working on the project. They aren't required to just use the project. For example, a build tool and its components, such as Grunt, would be development dependencies. We want to use a package called nodemon. This package is really handy when building a Node.js backend: we can have a command line that runs the nodemon server.js command in the background while we edit server.js in our editor. The nodemon package will restart the server whenever we save changes to the file. The only problem with this is that we can't actually run the nodemon server.js command on the command line, because we're going to install nodemon as a local package and not a global process. This is where the scripts property in our package.json file comes in: we can write simple script, almost like a command-line alias, to start nodemon for us. As you can see, we're creating a script called start, and it runs nodemon server.js. On the command line, we can run npm start; npm knows where to find the nodemon binary and can start it for us.

[8]

So, now that we have a `package.json` file, we can install the dependencies we've just listed. On the command line, change to the current directory to the project directory, and run the following command:

```
npm install
```

You'll see that all the necessary packages will be installed. Now we're ready to begin writing the code.

Starting with the server

I know you're probably eager to get started with the actual Backbone code, but it makes more sense for us to start with the server code. Remember, good Backbone apps will have strong server-side components, so we can't ignore the backend completely.

We'll begin by creating a `server.js` file in our project directory. Here's how that begins:

```
var express = require('express');
var path    = require('path');
var Bourne  = require("bourne");
```

If you've used Node.js, you know that the `require` function can be used to load Node.js components (`path`) or npm packages (`express` and `bourne`). Now that we have these packages in our application, we can begin using them as follows:

```
var app      = express();
var posts    = new Bourne("simpleBlogPosts.json");
var comments = new Bourne("simpleBlogComments.json");
```

The first variable here is `app`. This is our basic Express application object, which we get when we call the `express` function. We'll be using it a lot in this file.

Next, we'll create two `Bourne` objects. As I said earlier, `Bourne` is the database we'll use in our projects in this book. This is a simple database that I wrote specifically for this book. To keep the server side as simple as possible, I wanted to use a document-oriented database system, but I wanted something serverless (for example, SQLite), so you didn't have to run both an application server and a database server. What I came up with, `Bourne`, is a small package that reads from and writes to a JSON file; the path to that JSON file is the parameter we pass to the constructor function. It's definitely not good for anything bigger than a small learning project, but it should be perfect for this book. In the real world, you can use one of the excellent document-oriented databases. I recommend MongoDB: it's really easy to get started with, and has a very natural API. Bourne isn't a drop-in replacement for MongoDB, but it's very similar. You can check out the simple documentation for Bourne at https://github.com/andrew8088/bourne.

Building a Simple Blog

So, as you can see here, we need two databases: one for our blog posts and one for comments (unlike most databases, Bourne has only one table or collection per database, hence the need for two).

The next step is to write a little configuration for our application:

```
app.configure(function () {
  app.use(express.json());
  app.use(express.static(path.join(__dirname, 'public')));
});
```

[handwritten annotations: "middleware", "method chooses mw"]

This is a very minimal configuration for an Express app, but it's enough for our usage here. We're adding two layers of middleware to our application; they are "mini-programs" that the HTTP requests that come to our application will run through before getting to our custom functions (which we have yet to write). We add two layers here: the first is `express.json()`, which parses the JSON requests bodies that Backbone will send to the server; the second is `express.static()`, which will statically serve files from the path given as a parameter. This allows us to serve the client-side JavaScript files, CSS files, and images from the `public` folder.

You'll notice that both these middleware pieces are passed to `app.use()`, which is the method we call to choose to use these pieces.

> You'll notice that we're using the `path.join()` method to create the path to our public assets folder, instead of just doing `__dirname` and `'public'`. This is because Microsoft Windows requires the separating slashes to be backslashes. The `path.join()` method will get it right for whatever operating system the code is running on. Oh, and `__dirname` (two underscores at the beginning) is just a variable for the path to the directory this script is in.

The next step is to create a route method:

```
app.get('/*', function (req, res) {
  res.render("index.ejs");
});
```

In Express, we can create a route calling a method on the app that corresponds to the desired HTTP verb (get, post, put, and delete). Here, we're calling `app.get()` and we pass two parameters to it. The first is the route; it's the portion of the URL that will come after your domain name. In our case, we're using an asterisk, which is a catchall; it will match any route that begins with a forward slash (which will be all routes). This will match every GET request made to our application. If an HTTP request matches the route, then a function, which is the second parameter, will be called.

This function takes two parameters; the first is the request object from the client and the second is the response object that we'll use to send our response back. These are often abbreviated to `req` and `res`, but that's just a convention, you could call them whatever you want.

So, we're going to use the `res.render` method, which will render a server-side template. Right now, we're passing a single parameter: the path to the template file. Actually, it's only part of the path, because Express assumes by default that templates are kept in a directory named `views`, a convention we'll be using. Express can guess the template package to use based on the file extension; that's why we don't have to select EJS as the template engine anywhere. If we had values that we want to interpolate into our template, we would pass a JavaScript object as the second parameter. We'll come back and do this a little later.

Finally, we can start up our application; I'll choose to use the port `3000`:

```
app.listen(3000);
```

We'll be adding a lot more to our `server.js` file later, but this is what we'll start with. Actually, at this point, you can run `npm start` on the command line and open up `http://localhost:3000` in a browser. You'll get an error because we haven't made the view template file yet, but you can see that our server is working.

Creating the template

All web applications will have templates of some kind. Most Backbone applications will be heavy on the frontend templates. However, we will need a single server-side template, so let's build that.

While you can choose from different template engines, many folks (and subsequently, tutorials) use Jade (`http://jade-lang.com/`), which is like a Node.js version of the Ruby template engine Haml (`http://haml.info/`). However, as you already know, we're using EJS (`https://github.com/visionmedia/ejs`), which is similar to Ruby's ERB. Basically, we're writing regular HTML with template variables inside `<%= %>` tags.

As we saw earlier, Express will be looking for an `index.ejs` file in the `views` folder, so let's create that and put the following code inside it:

```
<!DOCTYPE html>
<html>
  <head>
    <title> Simple Blog </title>
  </head>
  <body>
```

Building a Simple Blog

```
            <div id="main"></div>
            <script src="/jquery.js"></script>
            <script src="/underscore.js"></script>
            <script src="/backbone.js"></script>
            <script src="/app.js"></script>
    </body>
</html>
```

At this point, if you still have the server running (remember `npm start` on the command line), you should be able to load `http://localhost:3000` without getting an error. The page will be blank, but you should be able to view the source and see the HTML code that we just wrote. That's a good sign; it means we're successfully sending stuff from the server to the client.

Adding the public folder

Since Backbone is a frontend library, it's something we'll need to be serving to the client. We've set up our Express app to statically serve the files in our `public` directory, and added several script tags to the `index.ejs` file, but we haven't created these things yet.

So, create a directory named `public` in your project directory. Now download the latest versions of Underscore (`http://underscorejs.org`), Backbone (`http://backbonejs.org`), and jQuery (`http://jquery.com`) and put them in this folder. It's very likely that newer versions of these libraries have come out since this book was written. Since updates to these projects could change the way they work, it's best to stick to the following versions:

- Backbone: Version 1.1.2
- Underscore: Version 1.6.0
- jQuery: Version 2.0.3

I will mention here that we're including Underscore and jQuery because Backbone depends on them. Actually, it only really depends on Underscore, but including jQuery does give us a few extra features that we'll be happy to have. If you need to support older versions of Internet Explorer, you'll also want to include the `json2.js` library (`https://github.com/douglascrockford/JSON-js`), and switch to a version of jQuery 1 (jQuery 2 doesn't support older versions of IE).

 Everything up to this point will be the same for each of the applications we are going to build in this book. In the downloaded files for this book, you can start each chapter by copying the template folder and working from there.

[12]

Beginning the Backbone code

Once you have these three files in the `public` folder, you're ready to create the `app.js` file. In most of our Backbone applications, this is where the major portion of the work is going to be done. Now that everything else is in place, we can begin the app-specific code.

Creating a model and collection

When building a Backbone app, the first thing I like to think about is this: what data will I be working with? This is my first question because Backbone is very much a data-driven library: almost everything the user will see and work will in some way be related to a piece of data. This is especially true in the simple blog we're creating; every view will either be for viewing data (such as posts) or creating data (such as comments). The individual pieces of data that your application will work on (such as titles, dates, and text) will be grouped into what are usually called **models**: the posts and comments in our blog, the events in a calendar app, or the contacts in an address book. You get the idea.

To start with, our blog will have a single model: the post. So, we create the appropriate Backbone model and collection classes. The code snippet for our model is as follows:

```
var Post = Backbone.Model.extend({});
var Posts = Backbone.Collection.extend({
  model: Post,
  url: "/posts"
});
```

There's actually a lot going on in these five lines. First, all the main Backbone components are properties of the global variable `Backbone`. Each of these components is a class. JavaScript does not actually have proper classes; the prototype-backed functions pass for classes in JavaScript. They also have an extend method, which allows us to create subclasses. We pass an object to this `extend` method, and all properties or methods inside that object will become part of the new class we're creating, along with the properties and methods that make up the class we're extending.

> I want to mention early in the book that a lot of the similar code you see between Backbone apps is just convention. That's one of the reasons I love Backbone so much; there's a strong set of conventions to use, but you can totally work outside that box just as easily. Throughout the book, I'm going to do my best to show you not only the common conventions, but also how to break them.

Building a Simple Blog

In this code, we're creating a model class and a collection class. We actually don't need to extend the model class at all for now; just a basic Backbone model will do. However, for the collection class, we'll add two properties. First, we need to associate this collection with the appropriate model. We do this because a collection instance is basically just a glorified array for a bunch of model instances. The second property is `url`: this is the location of the collection on the server. What this means is that if we do a GET request to `/posts`, we'll get back a JSON array of the posts in our database. This also means that we will be able to send a POST request to `/posts` and store a new post in our database.

At this point, now that we have our data-handling classes on the frontend, I'd like to head back to the `server.js` file to create the routes required by our collection. So, in the file, add the following piece of code:

```
app.get("/posts", function (req, res) {
  posts.find(function (results) {
    res.json(results);
  });
});
```

First off, I'll mention that it's important that this call to `app.get` goes above our `/*` route. This is because of the fact that Express sends the requests through our routes sequentially and stops (by default, anyway) when it finds a matching one. Since `/posts` will match both `/posts` and `/*`, we need to make sure it hits the `/posts` route first.

Next, you'll recall our `posts` database instance, which we made earlier. Here, we're calling its `find` method with only a callback, which will pass the callback an array of all the records in the database. Then, we can use the response object's `json` method to send that array back as JSON (the `Content-Type` header will be `application/json`). That's it!

While we're here in the `server.js` file, we add the POST method for the same route: this is where the post data will come in from the browser and be saved to our database. The following is the code snippet for the `post()` method:

```
app.post("/posts", function (req, res) {
  posts.insert(req.body, function (result) {
    res.json(result);
  });
});
```

The `req` object has a body property, which is the JSON data that represents our post data. We can insert it directly into the `posts` database. When Backbone saves a model to the server in this way, it expects the response to be the model it sent with an ID added to it. Our database will add the ID for us and pass the updated model to the callback, so we only have to send it as a response to the browser, just as we did when sending all the posts in the previous method using `res.json`.

Of course, this isn't very useful without a form to add posts to the database, right? We'll build a form to create new posts soon, but for now we can manually add a post to the `simpleBlogPosts.json` file; this file may not exist yet because we haven't written any data, so you'll have to create it. Just make sure the file you create has the right name, that is, the same name as the parameter we passed to the `Bourne` constructor in our `server.js` file. I'm going to put the following code in that file:

```
[
  {
    "id": 1,
    "pubDate": "2013-10-20T19:42:46.755Z",
    "title": "Lorem Ipsum",
    "content": "<p>Dolor sit amet . . .</p>"
  }
]
```

Of course, you can make the `content` field longer; you get the idea. This is the JSON field that will be sent to our `Posts` collection instance and become a set of the `Post` model instance (in this case, a set of only one).

Performing a quick and dirty test

We've actually written enough code at this point to test things out. Head to `http://localhost:3000` in your browser and pop open a JavaScript console; I prefer Chrome and the Developer tools but use whatever you want. Now try the following lines:

```
var posts = new Posts();
posts.length // => 0
```

We can create a `Posts` collection instance; as you can see, it's empty by default. We can load the data from the server by running the following line:

```
posts.fetch();
```

Building a Simple Blog

A collection instance's `fetch` method will send a GET request to the server (in fact, if your in-browser tools allow you to see a network request, you'll see a GET request to `/posts`). It will merge the models that it receives from the server with the ones already in the collection. Give a second to get a response and then run the following lines:

```
posts.length // => 1
var post = posts.get(1);
post.get("title"); // Lorem Ipsum
```

Every collection instance has a `get` method; we pass it an ID and it will return the model instance with that ID (note that this is the `id` field from the database, and not the index number in the collection). Then, each model instance has a `get` method that we can use to get properties.

Writing some views

In simple applications like the one we're creating in this chapter, most of the Backbone code that we write will be in views. I think it's fair to say that views can be the most challenging part of a Backbone app, because there are so many ways that almost everything can be done.

It's important to understand that a `Backbone.View` instance and a screen full of web apps aren't the same thing. One view in the browser may actually be many Backbone views. The first view that we want to create is a list of all the posts; these will be links to individual post pages. We could do this in two ways: as one big view or as multiple smaller views put together. In this instance, we're going to be using multiple views. Here's how we'll break it down: each list item will be generated by its own view instance. Then, the wrapper around the list items will be another view. You can picture it as looking something like this:

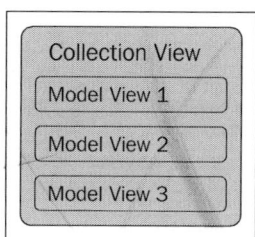

The PostListView class

Let's start with the child views. We'll call this `PostListView` class. Naming views can be a little tricky. Often, we'll have a view for the collection and a view for the model, and we'll just append `View` to the end of their names, for example, `PostView` and `PostsView`. However, a model or collection will have multiple views. The one we're about to write is to list our models. That's why we're calling it `PostListView`:

```
var PostListView = Backbone.View.extend({
  tagName: "li",
  template: _.template("<a href='/posts/{{id}}'>{{title}}</a>"),
  render: function () {
    this.el.innerHTML = this.template(this.model.toJSON());
    return this;
  }
});
```

Just like `Backbone.Model` and `Backbone.Collection`, we create a view class by extending `Backbone.View`. We have three properties in the extending object that make up our `PostListView`. The first one to look at is the `template` property; this property holds the template that our view will render. There are plenty of ways to create a template; in this case, we're using the Underscore's `template` function; we pass a string to `_.template`, and it returns a function which we can use to generate the correct HTML. Take a look at this template string: it's regular HTML with variables placed within double curly braces.

Next, let's look at the `render` method. By convention, this is the method that we call to actually render the view. Every view instance has a property named `el`. This is the base element for the view instance: all other elements for this view go inside it. By default, this is a `div` element, but we've set the `tagName` property to `li`, which means we'll get a list item instead. By the way, there's also a `$el` property, which is a jQuery object wrapping the `el` property; this only works if we have jQuery included in our application.

So, inside our `render` function, we need to fill in this element. In this case, we'll do that by assigning the `innerHTML` property. To get the HTML output, we use the template we just wrote. That's a function, so we call it, and pass `this.model.toJSON()`. The `this.model` portion comes from when we instantiate this view: we'll pass it a model. Every model has a `toJSON` method, which returns a raw object with just the attributes of the model. Since our model will have the `id` and `title` attributes, passing this to our template function will return a string with those values interpolated into the template string we wrote.

Building a Simple Blog

We end our `render` function by returning the view instance. Again, this is just convention. Because of this, we can use the convention where we get the element for this view via `view.render().el`; this will render the view and then get the `el` property. Of course, there's no reason you couldn't return `this.el` directly from render.

There's one more thing to address here, but it's about Underscore and not Backbone. If you've used the Underscore's `template` function before, you know that curly braces aren't its normal delimiters. I've switched from the default `<%= %>` delimiters, because those are the delimiters for our server-side template engine. To change Underscore's delimiters, just add the following code snippet to the top of our `app.js` file:

```
_.templateSettings = {
  interpolate: /\{\{(.+?)\}\}/g
};
```

Of course, you realize that we could make the delimiters whatever we want, as long as a regular expression can match it. I like the curly braces.

The PostsListView class

Now that we have the view for our list items, we need the parent view that wraps those list items:

```
var PostsListView = Backbone.View.extend({
  template: _.template("<h1>My Blog</h1><ul></ul>"),
  render: function () {
    this.el.innerHTML = this.template();
    var ul = this.$el.find("ul");
    this.collection.forEach(function (post) {
      ul.append(new PostListView({
        model: post
      }).render().el);
    });
    return this;
  }
});
```

As views go, this is pretty simple, but we can learn a few new things from it. First, you'll notice that our template doesn't actually use any variables, so there's no reason for us to actually use a template. We could directly assign that HTML string as `this.el.innerHTML`; however, I like to do the little template dance anyway because I might change the template string to include some variables in the future.

Notice the second line of the `render` function: we're finding an `ul` element; the same `ul` element that we just made as a child element of our root element, `this.el`. However, instead of using `this.el`, we're using `this.$el`.

[18]

Next, we're looping over each item in the collection that we'll associate with this view (when we instantiate it). For each post in the collection, we will create a new `PostListView` class. We pass it an `options` object, which assigns the view's model as the current post. Then, we render the view and return the view's element. This is then appended to our `ul` object.

We'll end by returning the view object.

Using our views

We're almost ready to actually display some content in the browser. Our first stop is back in the `server.js` file. We need to send the array of posts from the database to our `index.ejs` template. We do this by using the following code snippet:

```
app.get('/*', function (req, res) {
  posts.find(function (err, results) {
    res.render("index.ejs", { posts: JSON.stringify(results) });
  });
});
```

Just as we do in the `/posts` route, we call `posts.find`. Once we get the results back, we render the view as before. But this time, we pass an object of values that we want to be able to use inside the template. In this case, that's only the posts. We have to run the results through `JSON.stringify`, because we can't serve an actual JavaScript object to the browser; we need a string representation (the JSON form) of the object.

Now, in the `index.ejs` file of the `views` folder, we can use these posts. Create a new script tag under the other ones we created before. This time, it will be an inline script:

```
<script>
  var posts = new Posts(<%- posts %>);
  $("#main").append(new PostsListView({
    collection: posts
  }).render().el);
</script>
```

The first line creates our posts collection; notice our use of the template tags. This is how to interpolate our `posts` array into the template. There's no typo there by the way; you might have expected an opening tag of `<%=`, but that opening tag will escape any possible characters in the string, which wrecks the quotes in our JSON code. So, we use `<%-`, which doesn't escape characters.

Building a Simple Blog

The next line should be pretty straightforward. We're using jQuery to find our main element and appending the element of a new `PostsListView` instance. In the `options` object, we'll set the collection for this view. We then render it and find the element to append.

Now, make sure your server is running, and go to `http://localhost:3000` in the browser. You should see the following screenshot:

You're using the three main Backbone components—collection, models, and views—to create a mini-application! That's great, but we've only just got started.

Creating a router

Go ahead and click on the link that we've just rendered. You'll find that the URL changes and the page refreshes, but the content is still the same. This is because of a choice we've made in how our application works, that is, we made a catchall route that matches every GET request to our server. This means that `/`, `/posts/1`, and `/not/a/meaningful/link` show us the same content. This is what's often called a **single-page** web application, that is, as much as possible is done on the client side, with JavaScript doing the heavy lifting, and not a different language on the server. With this kind of application, the whole thing could work off a single URL that never changes. However, this makes it hard to bookmark parts of the application. So, we want to make sure our application uses good URLs. To do this, we need to create a Backbone router as follows:

```
var PostRouter = Backbone.Router.extend({
  initialize: function (options) {
    this.posts = options.posts;
    this.main  = options.main;
  },
  routes: {
    '': 'index',
    'posts/:id': 'singlePost'
  },
  index: function () {
    var pv = new PostsListView({ collection: this.posts }
    this.main.html(pv.render().el);
  },
  singlePost: function (id) {
```

```
        console.log("view post " + id);
    }
});
```

Here's the first version of our `PostRouter`. You should see a familiar pattern as we begin: we extend the component `Backbone.Router`. The next important piece is the `initialize` method. We never add one of these to our model, collection, or views, but they can all take an `initialize` method. This is the constructor function for our router. In good old Backbone convention, we expect to get a single `options` parameter. We'll expect this object to have two properties: `posts` and `main`. These should be the posts collection and the `div#main` element, respectively. We'll assign these as properties on our router instance.

> Technically, the `initialize` function isn't the constructor function. It's a function that is called by the constructor function. To completely replace the default behavior, write a method called `constructor`, not `initialize`.

The next important part is the `routes` object. In this object, the keys are routes and the values are the router methods to call when those routes are used. So, the same page will be loaded from the server, but then the client-side router will look at exactly what URL was requested and show the right content.

The first route is an empty string; this is the / route (but it's best practice not to include the slash in the front, so that the router will work with both hash URLs and the pushState API). When we load that route, we'll run the router's `index` function.

So what does this function do? It should look familiar; it's like what we put in our `index.ejs` file as a quick test. It creates our `PostsListView` instance and puts it on the page. Notice that we're using the `this.posts` and `this.main` properties that we just created.

The other route we're creating here is `/posts/:id`, which runs the `singlePost` function. The colon-label portion of that route will catch the content after that slash and pass it to the route method as a parameter. Right now, all we're doing in the `singlePost` method is logging a message to the console, but there's more to come.

Now that we've written a router, we need to start using it. You know that inline script in the `index.ejs` file? Replace its content with the following code:

```
var postRouter = new PostRouter({
    posts: new Posts(<%- posts %>),
    main: $("#main")
});
Backbone.history.start({pushState: true});
```

Building a Simple Blog

Once again, we're creating the `posts` collection and the references to the main `<div>` element. This time, however, they're properties of the router. We actually don't have to do anything with the router instance, just create it. However, we do have to start the history tracking: that's what the last line does. Remember, we're using a single-page app, so our URLs are not actual routes on the server. This used to be done with a hash in the URL, but the better and more modern way to do this is with the `pushState` API, which is a browser API that let's you change the URL in the browser's address bar without actually changing the contents of the page. So, that's what we do with the `options` object, where we set `pushState` to `true`.

If you browse your way over to `http://localhost:3000/`, you'll see our post listing. Now, click on the post link, and well, the page still reloads. However, on the new link, you see no page content but a line logged to the console. So, the router is working but it isn't stopping the reload. When the page reloads, the router sees the new route and runs the right method.

So the question now is, how do we keep the page from refreshing, but still change the URL? To do this, we have to prevent the default behavior of the link that we clicked on. To do this, we need to add the following pieces to our `PostListView` (in the `app.js` file):

```
events: {
  'click a': 'handleClick'
},
handleClick: function (e) {
  e.preventDefault();
  postRouter.navigate($(e.currentTarget).attr("href"),
    {trigger: true});
}
```

The `events` property is important here, as it handles any DOM events that happen within the base element of our view. The keys in this object should follow the pattern `eventName selector`. Of course, `eventName` can be any DOM event. The selector should be a string that jQuery can match. Part of the beauty of this selector is that it only matches elements within this view, so you often don't have to make it very specific. In our case, just `'a'` is good enough.

The value of each `events` property is the name of the method to call when this event occurs. The next step is to write this method as another property of this same view; it gets the jQuery event object as a parameter. Inside the `handleClick` method, we're calling `e.preventDefault` to keep the default behavior from happening. Since this is an anchor element, the default behavior is switching to the linked-to page. Instead, we perform that navigation inside our Backbone application: that's the next line.

What we're doing here isn't a completely good idea, but it will work for now. We're referencing the `postRouter` variable, which isn't created in this file; in fact, it's created after this file is loaded on the client. We can get away with this because this function won't be called until after the `postRouter` variable is created. However, in a more serious application, we would probably want better code decoupling. However, for our skill level, this is okay.

We're calling the router's `navigate` method. The first parameter is the route to navigate to: we get this from the anchor element. We also pass an `options` object, which sets `trigger` to `true`. If we don't trigger the navigation, the URL will change in the browser's location bar, but nothing else will change. Since we are triggering the navigation, the appropriate router method will be called, if one exists. One does in our case, `singlePost`, so you should see our message printed to the JavaScript console in the browser.

Viewing a post

Now that we have the right URL for a post page, let's make a view for individual posts:

```
var PostView = Backbone.View.extend({
  template: _.template($("#postView").html()),
  events: {
    'click a': 'handleClick'
  },
  render: function () {
    var model = this.model.toJSON();
    model.pubDate = new
      Date(Date.parse(model.pubDate)).toDateString();
    this.el.innerHTML = this.template(model);
    return this;
  },
  handleClick: function (e) {
    e.preventDefault();
    postRouter.navigate($(e.currentTarget).attr("href"),
      {trigger: true});
    return false;
  }
});
```

Building a Simple Blog

This view should mark an important milestone in your Backbone education: you understand most of the conventions that you're looking at in this code. You should recognize all the properties of the view, as well as most of the method content. I want to point out here there's much more convention going on than you may realize. For example, the `template` property is only ever referred to inside the `render` method, so you could call it something different, or put it inside the `render` method, as shown in the following line of code:

```
var template = _.template($("#postView").html());
```

Even the `render` method is only used by us when rendering the view. It's convention to call it `render`, but really, nothing will break if you don't. Backbone never calls it internally.

> You might wonder why we follow these Backbone conventions if we don't have to. I think it's partly because they are very sensible defaults, and because it makes reading other people's Backbone code much easier. However, another good reason to do it is because there are many third-party Backbone components that depend on these conventions. When using them, conventions become expectations that are required for things to work.

However, there are a few things in this view that will be new to you. First, instead of putting the template text in a string that gets passed directly to `_.template`, we're putting it in the `index.ejs` file and using jQuery to pull it in. This is something you'll see often; it's handy to do because most applications will have larger templates, and it's hard to manage a lot of HTML in JavaScript strings. So, put the following code in your `index.ejs` file related to your "actual" script tags:

```
<script type="text/template" id="postView">
  <a href='/'>All Posts</a>
  <h1>{{title}}</h1>
  <p>{{pubDate}}</p>
  {{content}}
</script>
```

It's important to give your script tag a `type` attribute, so the browser doesn't try to execute it as JavaScript. What that type is doesn't really matter; I use `text/template`. We also give it an `id` attribute, so we can reference it from the JavaScript code. Then, in our JavaScript code, we use jQuery to get the element, and then get its content using the `html` method.

Chapter 1

The other different piece of this view is that we're not passing `this.model.toJSON()` directly to the `render` method. Instead, we're saving it to the `model` variable, so that we can format the `pubDate` property. When stored as JSON, dates aren't very pretty. We use a few built-in `Date` methods to fix this up and reassign it to the model. Then, we pass the updated `model` object to the `render` method.

If you're wondering why we're using `events` and `handleClick` to override the anchor action again, notice the **All Posts** link in our template; this will be displayed above our post content. However, I hope you notice the flaw in this pattern: this will sabotage all links that might be in the content of our post, which might lead outside our blog. This is another reason why, as I said earlier, this pattern of view-changing isn't that great; we'll look at improvements on this in future chapters.

Now that we've created this view, we can update the `singlePost` method in our router:

```
singlePost: function (id) {
  var post = this.posts.get(id);
  var pv = new PostView({ model: post });
  this.main.html(pv.render().el);
}
```

Instead of just logging the ID to the console, we find the post with that ID in our `this.posts` collection. Then, we create a `PostView` instance, giving it that post as a model. Finally, we replace the content of the `this.main` element with the rendered content of the post view.

If you do a simple click-through test now, you should be able to go to our home page, click on the post's title, and see this:

> All Posts
>
> **Lorem Ipsum**
>
> Sun Oct 20 2013
>
> Dolor sit amet, consectetur adipiscing
> diam eget libero egestas mattis sit amet

You should be congratulated! You've just built a complete Backbone application (albeit an application with an extremely low level of functionality but an application nonetheless).

Creating new posts

Now that we can show posts, let's create a form to make new posts. It's important to realize that we're just going to create a form. There's no user account and no authentication, just a form that anyone could use to make new posts. We'll start with the template, which we'll put in the `index.ejs` file:

```
<script type="text/template" id="postFormView">
  <a href="/">All Posts</a><br />
  <input type="text" id="postTitle" placeholder="post title" />
  <br />
  <textarea id="postText"></textarea>
  <br />
  <button id="submitPost"> Post </button>
</script>
```

It's a very basic form, but it will do. So now, we need to create our view; use the following code:

```
var PostFormView = Backbone.View.extend({
  tagName: 'form',
  template: _.template($("#postFormView").html()),
  initialize: function (options) {
    this.posts = options.posts;
  },
  events: {
    'click button': 'createPost'
  },
  render: function () {
    this.el.innerHTML = this.template();
    return this;
  },
  createPost: function (e) {
    var postAttrs = {
      content: $("#postText").val(),
      title: $("#postTitle").val(),
      pubDate: new Date()
    };
    this.posts.create(postAttrs);
    postRouter.navigate("/", { trigger: true });
    return false;
  }
});
```

It's pretty big, but you should be able to understand most of it. We start by making the view a `<form>` element through the `tagName` property. We fetch the template we just created in the `template` property. In the `initialize` method, we take a `Posts` collection as an option and assign it as a property, much like we did in the router. In the `events` property, we listen for a click event on the button. When that happens, we call the `createPost` method. Rendering this view is pretty simple. Actually, the real complexity here is in the `createPost` method, but even that is pretty simple. We create a `postAttrs` object that has all the properties of our post: the content and the text from the form and a date that we add.

After creating this `postAttrs` object, we pass it to the `Posts` collection's `create` method. This is a convenience method, really, that creates the `Post` model instance, saves it to the server, and adds it to the collection. If we wanted to do this "manually", we'd do something similar to the following lines of code:

```
var post = new Post(commentAttrs);
this.posts.add(post);
post.save();
```

Every Backbone model constructor takes an object, which is a hash of attributes. We can add that model to the collection using the `add` method. Then, every model instance has a `save` method, which sends the model to the server.

> In this case, it's important to add the model to the collection before saving it, because our model class doesn't know the server route to POST to on its own. If we wanted to be able to save model instances that aren't in a collection, we'd have to give the model class a `urlRoot` property:
>
> ```
> urlRoot: "/posts",
> ```

Finally, we navigate back to the home page.

The next step is to add a new route to the router. In the `routes` property of the router class, add the following line:

```
'posts/new': 'newPost'
```

Then, we add the `newPost` method, which is very simple:

```
newPost: function () {
  var pfv = new PostFormView({ posts: this.posts });
  this.main.html(pfv.render().el);
},
```

That's all! Like I said, this isn't how you'd really do blog posting in a proper blog, but it shows us how to send model data back to the server.

Adding comments

Let's take things one step further, shall we? Let's add some (very primitive) commenting functionality.

Once again, we should start by thinking about the data. It's obvious, in this case: our basic data object, if you will, is the comment. However, we also need to think about how our data needs to interact with other data in the application, that is, every post that we have needs to be able to have multiple comments connected to it. Backbone doesn't have any conventions for inter-model-and-collection relationships, so we'll come up with something on our own.

We start with model and collection, as shown in the following code:

```
var Comment = Backbone.Model.extend({});
var Comments = Backbone.Collection.extend({
  initialize: function (models, options) {
    this.post = options.post;
  },
  url: function () {
    return this.post.url() + "/comments";
  }
});
```

You remember the `initialize` function, right? This will run when we instantiate the collection. Conventionally, it takes two parameters: an array of models and an options object. We'll expect a collection of comments to be related to a single post, and we get that post as an option.

In our `Posts` collection, `url` was a string property; however, it can also be a function that returns a string if we need a more dynamic URL. This is exactly what we need for our `Comments` collection because the URL is dependent upon the post. As you can see, the server location of a collection of comments is the URL for the post, plus `/comments`. So, for a post with ID 1, it's `/posts/1/comments`. For a post with ID 42, it's `/posts/42/comments`, and so on.

> The `url` method on a model instance checks to see whether our model class has the property `urlRoot`; if so, it will use that. Otherwise, it uses its collection's `url` property. In either case, it will append its `id` property to the `url` property to get its own unique URL.

The next step is to loosely connect the `Comments` collection to the `Post` model. We need to add an `initialize` method to our `Post` model as shown here:

```
var Post = Backbone.Model.extend({
  initialize: function () {
    this.comments = new Comments([], { post: this });
  }
});
```

I say "loosely" because there's no actual relation here between a post and its own comments (apart from setting `post: this` in the `options` object, which helps set the current URL); all this does is create a new `Comments` collection whenever a post is created. It's important to realize that this `comments` property is not like the other properties of a model. To be specific, it's a regular JavaScript property of the object, but not an attribute of the post model itself. We can't get it with the model's `get` method.

Serving comments

The next step is to prepare the server to send and receive comments. Sending comments to the client is actually pretty; see here:

```
app.get("/posts/:id/comments", function (req, res) {
  comments.find(
    { postId: parseInt(req.params.id, 10) },
    function (err, results) {
      res.json(results);
    }
  );
});
```

Just like in the Backbone router routes, we can use colon-target-style tokens in our Express routes to take a variable. However, instead of showing up as function parameters, we can get them as a subproperty of the request object `req.param`.

We're using the `comments` database object we created previously. The database has a `find` method, which takes a query object as the first parameter. In this case, we just want to find all comment records that have a `postId` property that matches the `id` parameter from the URL. Since the `id` parameter is a string, we'll need to use `parseInt` to convert it to a number. When we get the records, we'll send them back as JSON, just like we did with the posts.

Building a Simple Blog

What about saving comments? These will be POSTed back to the server as the request body, and they're POSTed to the same URL, you can see in the following code:

```
app.post("/posts/:id/comments", function (req, res) {
  comments.insert(req.body, function (err, result) {
    res.json(result);
  });
});
```

Since we're parsing the request body as JSON (see the middleware we added), we can insert it directly into our database. In our callback, we're taking a `result` parameter and sending it back to the client as JSON. This is important, because the `id` property on Backbone models should be set on the server. Our database does this automatically, so the result we send back is the same object we received with a new `id` property. This is the response Backbone expects.

Comment views

Now, we're ready to create the comment views. This could be done in many ways, but we're going to do it with three view classes. The first is to display individual comments. The second is the form to create new comments. The third wraps these two views and adds some important functionality.

The first is the simplest, so let's start with it:

```
var CommentView = Backbone.View.extend({
  template: _.template($("#commentView").html()),
  render: function () {
    var model = this.model.toJSON();
    model.date = new Date(Date.parse(model.date)).toDateString();
    this.el.innerHTML = this.template(model);
    return this;
  }
});
```

We're formatting the date, as we did previously, for posts. Also, we're once again putting the template content in a script tag. Here's the script tag that goes in the `index.ejs` file:

```
<script type="text/template" id="commentView">
  <hr />
  <p><strong>{{name}}</strong> said on {{date}}: </p>
  <p>{{text}}</p>
</script>
```

Pretty straightforward, isn't it?

Next up is the `CommentFormView` class. This is the form that viewers will use to add a comment to post. We'll start with the template this time by using the following code:

```html
<script type="text/template" id="commentFormView">
  <input type="text" id="cmtName" placeholder="name" /><br />
  <textarea id="cmtText"></textarea><br />
  <button id="submitComment"> Submit </button>
</script>
```

Nothing too special: a textbox for the name, a text area for the text, and a submit button. A very basic form, you'll agree. Now we have the class itself:

```js
var CommentFormView = Backbone.View.extend({
  tagName: "form",
  initialize: function (options) {
    this.post = options.post;
  },
  template: _.template($("#commentFormView").html()),
  events: {
    'click button': 'submitComment'
  },
  render: function () {
    this.el.innerHTML = this.template();
    return this;
  },
  submitComment: function (e) {
    var name = this.$("#cmtName").val();
    var text = this.$("#cmtText").val();
    var commentAttrs = {
      postId: this.post.get("id"),
      name: name,
      text: text,
      date: new Date()
    };
    this.post.comments.create(commentAttrs);
    this.el.reset();
  }
});
```

Building a Simple Blog

This form view is long, but pretty similar to the other form, the one for creating posts. The `tagName` property sets the view's base element to a form. Since the comments this form makes need to be related to a post, we set the post as a property via the `options` object in the `initialize` method.

> Instead of creating a `post` property on this view, we could use the `model` property. As you may have noticed, this is a specially-named property that gets assigned automatically when it's part of the `options` object (so we wouldn't need an `initialize` method). However, that property is usually the model that is displayed in this view. Since that's not what we're using here, I prefer to make a custom property, so someone reading this code wouldn't misunderstand the purpose of the post model in this view.

Of course, we'll need to capture the `click` event on the **Submit** button. When that happens, the `submitComment` method will be run. The first portion of this method is simple; we're getting the values from the textbox and text area. Then, we're putting together a `commentAttrs` object with four properties: the ID of the post this comment belongs to, the name of the commenter, the text, and the date and time of the comment's creation (right now).

After creating this `commentAttrs` object, we pass it to the post's comment collection's `create` method, just as we did in the `PostFormView`. The final line in the `submitComment` method is a built-in DOM method that resets the form; it clears all fields.

The last view is `CommentsView`, which pulls these two view classes together, as shown here:

```
var CommentsView = Backbone.View.extend({
  initialize: function (options) {
    this.post = options.post;
    this.post.comments.on('add', this.addComment, this);
  },
  addComment: function (comment) {
    this.$el.append(new CommentView({
      model: comment
    }).render().el);
  },
  render: function () {
    this.$el.append("<h2> Comments </h2>");
```

```
    this.$el.append(new CommentFormView({
      post: this.post
    }).render().el);
    this.post.comments.fetch();
    return this;
  }
});
```

Just like `CommentFormView`, this view will be given a `Post` instance when it's created. In the `render` method, we first append a heading to the view element, and then we render and append our comment form. All this should look relatively familiar, but the rest is new. The second-last line in `render` calls the `fetch` method of the post's comments collection. This makes a GET request to the server and fills the collection with the comments that are returned from the server.

Now, look back at the `initialize` method; the last line is the first we've seen of Backbone's event capabilities. As we perform different tasks and call different methods of Backbone objects, different events are triggered, and we can listen for those events and react when they occur. In this case, we're listening for the comment collection's `add` event. This event occurs whenever we add a new model to this collection. If you think about the code we've written, you'll see that there are two places where we add models to this collection:

- When calling `comments.create` in the `submitComment` method in `CommentFormView`
- When calling `comments.fetch` in the `render` method in this view

So, whenever a model is added to our collection, we want to call the `this.addComment` method. Notice that we're passing a third parameter to the `on` method: `this`. This is the context for the function we want to call. By default, there will be no value for `this` inside functions called by the `on` method, so we want to tell it to use this view instance as context.

The `addComment` method takes the freshly-added comment as a parameter (the collections object and an `options` object are also passed to functions that are responding to an `add` event, but we don't need them here). We can then create a `CommentView` instance for this model and append its element to our view element.

Well, it's all there now. You can go ahead and give it a try, that is, load a post page and add a few comments. Each time, you should see the comment appear below the form. Then, if you refresh the page, the comments you made will again appear under the post. You might notice a little delay in the loading of the comments. This is because we aren't loading them with the initial page load. Instead, they are loaded during the rendering of `CommentsView`. Granted, this is milliseconds after the page load, but you might see a quick flash. You will see the following on your screen:

Summary

This brings us to the end of the first chapter. If you hadn't dug into Backbone much before this, I hope that you're starting to feel comfortable with the basics of the library.

In this chapter, we looked briefly at all the main components of Backbone. We saw how models and collections are the homes for our data records, and how they drive the web application. We made a handful of views, some to display individual model instances, some to display a collection, and some to display other page components or wrap other views. We created a router and used it to direct almost all the traffic on our web application. We even got a little taste of Backbone's robust events API.

Besides the nitty-gritty of the Backbone API, I hope you picked up some of the bigger ideas. One of these is the `options` object, as almost every Backbone component constructor function takes an `options` object as the final parameter, and many functions that interact with the server do as well. There are some magic property names—such as `model` or `collection`—that Backbone handles automatically, but you can also pass your own options and work with them inside the classes.

The other big takeaway from this chapter is the balance between convention and choice when coding. Compared to the other similar libraries, Backbone is incredibly light and flexible and enforces very few coding patterns. The good part is that the few conventions that Backbone does strongly support are actually really great ideas that it makes sense to follow. Of course, it's just one programmer's opinion, but I've found that Backbone engenders an almost perfect balance of convention to follow and freedom to code however you want. We'll learn more about this balance when we build a photo-sharing application in the next chapter.

2
Building a Photo-sharing Application

You've done a great job of understanding the most basic Backbone features. I think you're ready to level up and build something a little bigger, a little tougher. So in this chapter, we'll be building an Instagram clone of sorts; users will be able to create accounts, upload photos, follow other users, and comment on photos. We'll use a lot of the features that we used in the last chapter, but we'll also look at a bunch of new ones. We'll cover the following topics:

- How user accounts affect a Backbone application
- Writing your own model sync function
- Alternate uses for models
- Uploading files via AJAX

Creating user accounts

We're going to start with the application template that we created in the first part of the last chapter. So, in the code download that comes with this book, find the `template` folder and make a copy of it. You'll need to install the necessary Node.js packages, of course; so, run `npm install` in the terminal.

Building a Photo-sharing Application

The main difference between this application and the one we wrote in the last chapter is that this app has a much more significant server component; we want to be able to create user accounts and allow users to log in and log out. In fact, that's where we have to start. There's a really great Node.js package called Passport (http://passportjs.org/), which makes authentication easy. We'll begin by installing the library, as well as the bcrypt package, which we'll use to encrypt users' passwords. Do this with these commands:

```
npm install passport --save
npm install passport-local --save
npm install bcrypt --save
```

The --save flag will add these packages to the package.json file.

There are several dozen lines of setup for this, so we're going to put them in their own file. In the project folder, create a signin.js file. The first step is to pull in the libraries that we need:

```
var bcrypt = require("bcrypt");
var LocalStrategy = require("passport-local").Strategy;
var salt = bcrypt.genSaltSync(10);
```

A strategy, in the Passport terminology, is a method of authentication. We're authenticating locally, as opposed to using Twitter or Facebook. The salt variable will be used when we encrypt a user's password; it's a good practice in encryption to ensure our user's passwords are stored safely.

Next, we'll create our strategy object, like so:

```
exports.strategy = function (db) {
  return new LocalStrategy(function (username, password, done) {
    db.findOne({ username: username }, function (err, user) {
      if (!user) {
        done(null, false, { message: "Incorrect username." });
      } else if(!bcrypt.compareSync(password,user.passwordHash)) {
        done(null, false, { message: "Incorrect password." });
      } else {
        done(null, user);
      }
    });
  });
};
```

Chapter 2

First things first: we're assigning a property to an `exports` object. This is a Node.js module's object that can be exported from this file. When we require this file from the `server.js` file, anything that is a property of the `exports` object will be a property of the object returned from our `require` call.

Now, about the code here: this might look a little weird to you, but hang on. We can't just create the `strategy` method, because we need to use the database inside the `strategy` object. So, instead, we create a function that will take the database and return a `strategy` object. The `strategy` object constructor takes a function that will do the authentication and that function takes three parameters: the username, the password, and a callback function, which we call `done`.

Inside the function, we search the database for a user with the username we received as a parameter. Inside the callback, we first check to see if the user exists; if not, we call the `done` method by passing three parameters. The first is any error that occurred: that can just be `null`, because there's no error. Second is `false`; would be a user object, but we pass `false` because there isn't one. The last parameter is a message that we could display to the user.

However, if we do find a user, we'll need to match the password that we were given. When we begin creating users in the database, we'll use the `bcrypt` package to convert the plaintext password to a hash, so we don't store the plaintext version. Then, here, we can compare the results using the `bcrypt.compareSync` method; it takes the password we're comparing and the `user.passwordHash` property from the user object we got out of the database. Finally, if that comparison doesn't fail, we'll authenticate the user by sending the user object back in the `done` method.

This is a lot to start with, but it's important to begin with the authentication. We'll also need the `serialize` and `deserialize` methods; these will be used by the Passport's session feature to keep the user object available over page refreshes. The methods:

```
exports.serialize = function (user, done) {
  done(null, user.id);
};

exports.deserialize = function (db) {
  return function (id, done) {
    db.findOne({ id: id }, function (user) {
      done(null, user);
    });
  };
};
```

Building a Photo-sharing Application

The `serialize` method will send only the user's ID; in the `deserialize` method, we pull the same trick that we did with the `strategy` object, because we need the database inside the `deserialize` function. We return the function, which takes the ID, and send the user object to the `done` method.

One final piece for the module; when creating a user account, we'll need to convert the plaintext password to the hashed version. To do this, we'll use the `bcrypt.hashSync` method:

```
exports.hashPassword = function (password) {
  return bcrypt.hashSync(password, salt);
};
```

Our function will take a single parameter—the plaintext password—and will hash it. Don't forget to pass the `salt` object we created as the second parameter to the `hashSync` method.

Now, we're ready to go to the `server.js` file and start things in there. We start by pulling in the Passport library and our `signin.js` file, as shown in the following code:

```
var passport = require("passport");
var signin   = require("./signin");
```

If you're not familiar with requesting local Node.js modules, we can just pass a relative path to the `require` function, as you see here. We don't need to include the `.js` extension.

We also need to create the database instances that we'll need for the application; we do that like this:

```
var users = new Bourne("users.json");
var photos = new Bourne("photos.json");
var comments = new Bourne("comments.json");
```

Next, we need to set up the passport functions that we put in the `signin.js` file. Use this code to do that:

```
passport.use(signin.strategy(users));
passport.serializeUser(signin.serialize);
passport.deserializeUser(signin.deserialize(users));
```

We pass the function that creates our strategy to `passport.use`. Then, we set the `serialize` and `deserialize` functions. Notice that `strategy` and `deserialize` take the `users` database as arguments and return the correct function.

[40]

The next step is to prepare the middleware for the application. In our previous application, we didn't need much middleware, because we weren't doing that much on the server. But this time, we have to manage users' sessions. So here's what we have:

```
app.configure(function () {
  app.use(express.urlencoded());
  app.use(express.json());
  app.use(express.multipart());
  app.use(express.cookieParser());
  app.use(express.session({ secret: 'photo-application' }));
  app.use(passport.initialize());
  app.use(passport.session());
  app.use(express.static('public'));
});
```

All the extra pieces of middleware—the ones that we didn't use in the previous chapter—are here for managing the user session. Actually, most of Express's middleware comes from the Connect library (https://github.com/senchalabs/connect); it might seem like we're adding a lot of middleware pieces here, but the truth is that they're broken into many small pieces, so you can choose exactly what you need. You can find out more about each individual piece on the Connect website (http://www.senchalabs.org/connect/), but here are the pieces of middleware in this application that we haven't used before:

- `urlencoded`: This method parses `x-ww-form-urlencoded` request bodies, providing the parsed object as `req.body`
- `multipart`: This method parses multipart/form-data request bodies, providing the parsed object as `req.body` and `req.files`
- `cookieParser`: This method parses the cookie header and provides that data as `req.cookies`
- `session`: This method sets up the session store with the given options
- `passport.initialize`: This method sets up Passport
- `passport.session`: This method sets up persistent logins with Passport

Now that these pieces are in place, we're ready to start writing some routes. We'll start with the routes that are specifically related to logging a user in and out. Here's the route for logging in:

```
app.get("/login", function (req, res) {
  res.render("login.ejs");
});
```

Building a Photo-sharing Application

The first one is simple; at the `/login` route, we'll render the `login.ejs` template. More on the content of this file soon. However, you can probably guess that there's going to be a form on that page. The users will put in their usernames and passwords; when they submit the form, the data will be posted back to this URL. So, we'll need to accept POST requests on the same URL. So, here's the `post` method version:

```
app.post('/login', passport.authenticate('local', {
  successRedirect: '/',
  failureRedirect: '/login'
}));
```

You'll notice something different about this route; we're not writing our own function. Instead, we're calling the `passport.authenticate` function. As you saw earlier, we're using a local strategy, so that's the first parameter. After that, we have an object with two properties. It defines the routes to which the user will be redirected, depending on whether the user is authenticated or not. Obviously, if the user is successfully logged in, they will be sent to the root route; otherwise, they'll be sent back to the login page. The `get` method is given in the following code:

```
app.get("/logout", function (req, res) {
  req.logout();
  res.redirect('/');
});
```

This one's simple too: to log out, we'll just call the `logout` method that Passport adds to the request object, and then redirect to the root route again.

Let's take care of the `login.ejs` file now. This will have to go in the `view` folder:

```
<h1> Sign In </h1>
<form method="post" action="/login">
  <p>Username: <input name='username' type='text' /></p>
  <p>Password: <input name='password' type='password' /></p>
  <button> Login </button>
</form>
<h1> Create Account </h1>
<form method="post" action="/create">
  <p>Username: <input name='username' type='text' /></p>
  <p>Password: <input name='password' type='password' /></p>
  <button> Create </button>
</form>
```

We have two forms here: one for logging in, and one for creating users. Really, they're pretty much identical, but they'll be posted to different routes. We've already written the route for the first one, but we don't yet have a route for creating new users. So, guess what's next?

```
app.post('/create', function (req, res, next) {
  var userAttrs = {
    username: req.body.username,
    passwordHash: signin.hashPassword(req.body.password),
    following: []
  };
  users.findOne({ username: userAttrs.username }, function
    (existingUser) {
    if (!existingUser) {
      users.insert(userAttrs, function (user) {
        req.login(user, function (err) {
          res.redirect("/");
        });
      });
    } else {
      res.redirect("/");
    }
  });
});
```

In this route's function, we start by creating the `userAttrs` object. We'll get the username and the password from the `req.body` object, making sure we use the `hashPassword` method to hash the password. We'll also include an empty array called `following`; we'll be storing the list of IDs of the users that they are following in this array.

Next, we'll search our database to see if another user has that username. If not, we can insert the user attribute objects we just created. Once we've stored the user, we can set the session up by using the `req.login` method that Passport gives us. Once they're logged in, we can redirect them to the root route.

That pretty much completes our user accounts feature. I should point out that I've left out some bits that would be important in a production application; for example, there will be no helpful messages for the user if they mistype their usernames or passwords when logging in, or try to create a user account with a username that already exists. They'll just be directed back to the forms. Of course, this as well as other important account-related features could be implemented (such as, changing a password); but we want to get to the Backbone code. That's what you're here for, right?

As we've seen, a user will be directed back to the root route once they are logged in. We actually don't have the root route method yet, so let's create it now, as shown in the following code:

```
app.get('/*', function (req, res) {
  if (!req.user) {
    res.redirect("/login");
    return;
  }
  res.render("index.ejs", {
    user: JSON.stringify(safe(req.user))
  });
});
```

It's actually not just the root route; it will collect many routes. The first step is to check for the `req.user` object, to see if the user is logged in. Remember the `deserialize` method we wrote? Passport will be using that behind the scenes to make sure that this `req.user` object is exactly the record we have in our database. If that isn't set, we'll send the user to the `/login` route. Otherwise, things can continue.

Right now, we're keeping things very simple; we're just rendering the `index.ejs` template. The only piece of data we're sending into that is the user. We already know why we need to wrap it in `JSON.stringify`, but what's the `safe` function? This is something we're about to write: the idea here is that we don't want to send the whole user record back to the browser; we want to remove some classified properties, such as `passwordHash`. Here is the `safe` function:

```
function safe(user){
  var toHide = ['passwordHash'],
    clone = JSON.parse(JSON.stringify(user));

  toHide.forEach(function (prop) {
    delete clone[prop];
  });
  return clone;
}
```

It's very basic; we have an array of property names we want to remove. We start by cloning the `user` parameter. Then, we loop over the `toHide` variable, and delete those properties on the clone. Finally, we return the safe `user` object.

Well, things are really coming together here on the server. We're finally ready to turn our attention to the client-side code. We'll start with the `index.ejs` file.

Chapter 2

Creating our application navigation

We've already got a basic version of this from the template. However, we need to adjust the script tags at the bottom. After the tag for `backbone.js`, but before the tag for `app.js`, you'll want to add the following line:

```
<script>var USER = <%- user %>;</script>
```

This is the `user` object that is the user that is currently logged in. We'll need to be able to work with some of its properties inside our application components, which is why we need to load it before the `app.js` file.

Speaking of the `app.js` file, that's our next stop. This time, we're going to begin with a router:

```
var AppRouter = Backbone.Router.extend({
  initialize: function (options) {
    this.main = options.main;
    this.navView = new NavView();
  },
  routes: {
    '': 'index'
  },
  index: function () {
    this.main.html(this.navView.render().el);
  }
});
```

This is very similar to the router from our previous application. Any options—such as DOM elements, models, or collections—that we'll want to use inside our application will be passed into the router constructor. As you can see, we're prepared for the `main` element (mother of all that's displayed to the user). We'll also create a `navView` property. You can probably guess that this will display some navigation; our app will have several important links, and we want to make it simple for our users to get around. We'll write this view next.

> You might wonder why we've made USER a global variable instead of a property of our router. After all, as we saw last time, those properties are data from the server that we need inside views here on the browser, right? There's really no reason you couldn't, but I prefer to do it this way because our application isn't really about manipulating user records. While we will have a User class, it will just be for convenience. User records are not created or modified on the client side.

In our `routes` object, we're setting up our index route. Right now, we will only be rendering the navigation in that `index` method, but it's a good start.

Let's write the navigation view. It's the simplest view we have in this application, which is created by the following code:

```
var NavView = Backbone.View.extend({
  template: _.template($("#navView").html()),
  render: function () {
    this.el.innerHTML = this.template(USER);
    return this;
  }
});
```

This code is pretty standard view code. Notice that we're using the `USER` object as the data for this template. Here's the template content, which goes in the `index.ejs` file:

```
<script type="text/template" id="navView">
  <ul>
    <li><a href="/">Home</a></li>
    <li><a href="/users">All Users</a></li>
    <li><a href="/users/{{id}}">My Profile</a></li>
    <li><a href="/upload">Add Photo</a></li>
    <li>Logged in as <strong>{{ username }}</strong></li>
    <li><a href="/logout">Log out</a></li>
  </ul>
  <hr />
</script>
```

We've got enough here to give this a try. In the `index.ejs` file, make sure we're creating and starting the router by using the following code:

```
var r = new AppRouter({
  main: $("#main")
});
Backbone.history.start({ pushState: true });
```

Start up the server (`npm start`) and head to `http://localhost:3000`. You should see something like the following screenshot:

Go ahead and create a new user account by putting a username and password into the bottom form. When you click on the **Create** button, you'll be sent to a screen like this:

That's great! Things are shaping up.

As you work through building this application, you're going to find something annoying; every time you make a change, `nodemon` will restart the server, and the session that keeps you logged in will disappear. You'll have to log in again, every time. To get around this, I added the following code at the top of the `server.js` file:

```
var requser = {
  username: "andrew",
  id: 1
};
```

Then, everywhere that you use `req.user`, use `requser` instead. It's easy to do a search and replace on this, and it will keep you logged in over server refreshes. I'll continue to use `req.user` in the code snippets ahead. However, this convenience hack isn't perfect. When we get to the feature of following other users, you'll have to remove this `requser` variable, or things won't make sense.

Uploading photos

Let's tackle the file uploads next. This is a photo sharing website, so it's one of the most important features. Let's begin by creating a view for the upload form:

```
var AddPhotoView = Backbone.View.extend({
  tagName: "form",
  initialize: function (options) {
    this.photos = options.photos;
  },
  template: _.template($("#addPhotoView").html()),
  events: {
    "click button": "uploadFile"
  },
  render: function () {
    this.el.innerHTML = this.template();
    return this;
  },
  uploadFile: function (evt) {
    evt.preventDefault();
    var photo = new Photo({
      file: $("#imageUpload")[0].files[0],
      caption: $("#imageCaption").val()
    });
    this.photos.create(photo, { wait: true });
    this.el.reset();
  }
});
```

We start with an `initialize` function that assigns a property called `photos` that we get from the `options` object. This `photos` object is actually a collection, so you might wonder why we're not calling it `collection` in the `options` object; as you know, Backbone would handle this assignment automatically for us. The reason we're not doing it that way is so that it's clear that this view isn't for displaying this collection; it needs the collection for another reason (namely, to add a `Photo` model instance). You can write this off as semantics, but I hope the break from a Backbone convention makes someone reading the code pause and look for a reason.

The `template`, `events`, and `render` properties are self-explanatory. The template that we're pulling in is very simple: a little form that takes a file and a caption. This is the code for the template:

```
<script type="text/template" id="addPhotoView">
  <p>Photo: <input type="file" id="imageUpload" /></p>
  <p>Caption: <input type="text" id="imageCaption" /></p>
  <button> Upload </button>
</script>
```

When that button is pressed, the `uploadFile` method is called. In there, we'll cancel the default behavior of submitting the form and use the data to create an instance of the Photo model (coming soon). The `caption` property is obvious, but the `file` property is a little trickier. We start by getting the file input element, and then get the first item in the array property called `files`. This is the data we need to upload the file via AJAX. Then, we save this object by passing it to the collection's `create` method. You might be curious about the `{ wait: true }` part. Hold that thought for a minute, however. It will be explained soon; when it will make sense, I'll explain it.

Finally, we'll clear the form, so they can upload another one if they want to.

Before we can actually get this working, there are a couple of other pieces to build. Most obviously, we need the Photo model and Photos collection. In the last application, our models were pretty simple, but this one is more complex; this is the model class's code:

```
var Photo = Backbone.Model.extend({
  urlRoot: "/photos",
  sync: function (method, model, options) {
    var opts = {
      url: this.url(),
      success: function (data) {
        if (options.success) {
          options.success(data);
        }
      }
    };

    switch (method) {
      case "create":
        opts.type = "POST";
        opts.data = new FormData();
        opts.data.append("file", model.get('file'));
        opts.data.append("caption", model.get('caption'));
        opts.processData = false;
```

Building a Photo-sharing Application

```
                opts.contentType = false;
                break;
            default:
                opts.type = "GET";
        }
        return $.ajax(opts);
    }
});
```

As you know, the `urlRoot` object is the base of the route that this model will GET and POST to on the server, but the big story here is the `sync` method. Normally, all models and collections use the `Backbone.sync` method. This is the method that is called every time we're reading or writing one or more models to or from the server. We can overwrite this at the model level if we need to do something a bit differently, and that's exactly the case here. Backbone doesn't support AJAX file uploads out of the box, so we need to write a `sync` function to do that.

The trick here is that we can't just write a function that does file uploads for creating new photo records. This is because of the fact that this is the method that is used for reading, updating, and deleting this model's instances. As you can see, the `sync` method takes three parameters: the first is the CRUD method that we're about to perform (create, read, update, and delete), the second is the `model` instance, and the third is an `options` object.

Since we'll be using jQuery to do the AJAX call, we only need to set up an `options` object of our own. That's how we start. Of course, it will need a URL, so we call this model class's `url` method. We also need to define a `success` callback. It's important that this callback calls the `success` method of the `options` object; this method will handle some important behind-the-scenes stuff. These properties are important no matter what method we're calling.

Then, we have a `switch` statement; this is for the properties that will differ, depending on the method. In the case that we have `create`, we want to set the type to `POST`. We set the `data` property to a new `FormData` instance; this is how we send the file data. All we do is append the `file` property that we put on the model; we can append the caption as well.

We also need to set `processData` and `contentType` to `false`. This way, we can be sure the file data will get to the server in the way we expect, so we can save it to a file.

We're also setting a default case here, which sets the type to GET. We're not preparing this method for doing updates or deletes, because that's not part of the application we're building. If we ever needed these features, we'd have to expand this.

Chapter 2

Finally, we just need to make the AJAX call by using `$.ajax` and passing it in our `options` object.

We also need a `Photos` collection. For now, we'll keep it simple. We'll create it by using the following code:

```
var Photos = Backbone.Collection.extend({
  model: Photo
});
```

The `sync` method allows us to send our images to the server, but we don't have a route ready to handle the incoming data, so that's our next priority:

```
app.post("/photos", function (req, res) {
  var oldPath = req.files.file.path,
      publicPath = path.join("images", requser.id + "_" +
        (photos.data.length + 1) + ".jpg"),
      newPath = path.join(__dirname, "public", publicPath);

  fs.rename(oldPath, newPath, function (err) {
    if (!err) {
      photos.insert({
        userId: requser.id,
        path: "/" + publicPath,
        caption: req.body.caption,
        username: requser.username
      }, function (photo) {
        res.send(photo);
      });
    } else {
      res.send(err);
    }
  });
});
```

As you saw, we're posting to /photos. Since this function is going to store a photo that needs to be viewable from the browser, we need to put it in the `public` folder. Go ahead and make a folder inside `public` called `images`, which is where we'll put them.

We start with a few paths. First, there's `oldPath`; that's the path to where the file is temporarily stored at the time of the request. Then, there's `publicPath`: this is the path that we'll use in the browser to view the photo; it's just `images` plus the name of the file. We're going to give the image a unique name based on the user's ID and the number of photos we have in the database. Thirdly, there's `newPath`, which is where we're going to store the image relative to the current location.

Building a Photo-sharing Application

To work with files like this in Node.js, we need to use the filesystem module, so add the following line to the top of the file:

```
var fs = require("fs");
```

Then, we can use the `rename` method to move the file. If this goes well, and there's no error, we can store the record for this image in the `photos` database. Notice that instead of a `file` property, we're just storing the `path` property. Once we send this object back to the browser, it will replace the attributes that we had. Once we store the photo, we'll send it back to the browser as confirmation that the deed is done.

Next, move back to the client code in the `app.js` file. We need a route from which to access the upload form. If you look back at our navigation view, you'll see that the route we want to make is `/upload`. You can add the following line to the `routes` object in `AppRouter`:

```
'upload': 'upload',
```

Then, let's create the `upload` function by doing this:

```
upload: function () {
  var apv = new AddPhotoView({ photos: this.userPhotos }),
    photosView = new PhotosView({ collection: this.userPhotos
      });
  this.main.html(this.navView.render().el);
  this.main.append(apv.render().el);
  this.main.append(photosView.render().el);
}
```

We're actually doing a bit more than you bargained for here; there's a second view that we're rendering: a `PhotosView` instance. Before we get to that though, notice that we're using a `userPhotos` property; we have to add that to the router. Add the following line in the `AppRouter` class's `initialize` function:

```
this.userPhotos = options.userPhotos;
```

This gives us access to whatever collection we pass to the router as `userPhotos`. Then, in the `index.ejs` file, where we instantiate the router this line will create that collection:

```
userPhotos: new Photos()
```

Okay, now we create the `PhotosView` class:

```
var PhotosView = Backbone.View.extend({
  tagName: 'ul',
  template: _.template($("#photosView").html()),
  initialize: function () {
    this.collection.on("add", this.addPhoto, this);
  },
```

```
    render: function () {
      this.collection.forEach(this.addPhoto, this);
        return this;
    },
    addPhoto: function (photo) {
      this.$el.append(this.template(photo.toJSON()));
    }
  });
```

This is the `PhotosView` class. Notice that we set the `tagName` property to `ul`; then, inside the `render` function, we just loop over the collection and call the `addPhoto` function, which renders the template and puts the result in the list. This time, instead of using the `template` function for the whole view, we use it to render each model in the collection. Also, notice that in the `initialize` function that we're listening for whenever new photos are added to the collection, we can add them to the list. Now's the time to recall that `{ wait: true }` option that we added when we made the `create` call. When we tell Backbone to wait like this, it won't trigger this `add` event on a model until we've heard back from the server. This is important in this case, because otherwise we won't have the public path for our image. The last piece for this class is the template; of course, the following code goes in the `index.ejs` file:

```
<script type="text/template" id="photosView">
  <a href="/photo/{{id}}"><img src="{{path}}" /></a>
</script>
```

It should all be in place now! You can go to `http://localhost:3000/upload`, choose a file, type a caption, and click on the **Upload** button. The file will be uploaded, and you'll see it appear beneath the form. Congrats! You've just uploaded your first photo. The following screenshot shows how the photo might look like:

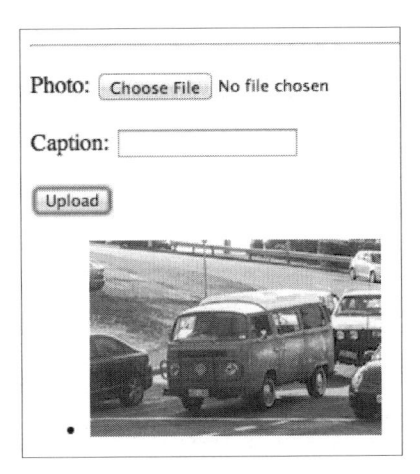

> While building this application, I used photos from `http://unsplash.com`; a great source for free high-resolution photos.

Sending photos from the server to the client

Before we work on another specific page, we need a route from which to get photos from the server. These photos will need to go in a `Photos` collection, but if you think about it for a second, you'll realize that there are several different sets of photos we might get. For example, we could get all the photos from one user, or all the photos from the users that the current user follows. So, hold your breath, here's that route's code:

```
app.get(/\/photos(\/)?([\w\/]+)?/, function (req, res) {
  var getting = req.params[1],
    match;

  if (getting) {
    if (!isNaN(parseInt(getting, 10))) {
      photos.findOne({ id: parseInt(getting, 10) },
        function (photo) { res.json(photo); });
    } else {
      match = getting.match(/user\/(\d+)?/);
      if (match) {
        photos.find({ userId: parseInt(match[1], 10) },
          function (photos) { res.json(photos); });
      } else if (getting === "following") {
        var allPhotos = [];
        req.user.following.forEach(function (f) {
          photos.find({ userId: f }, function (photos) {
            allPhotos = allPhotos.concat(photos);
          });
        });
        res.json(allPhotos);
      } else {
        res.json({});
      }
    }
  } else {
    res.json({});
  }
});
```

Yes, it's a doozy. Let's start with the route; instead of a string, we're using a regular expression that matches the routes we want it to catch. This one catches pretty much anything that begins with `/photos`. We're interested in the following patterns:

- `/photos/11`: Photo with ID 11
- `/photos/following`: Photos of all the users the logged-in user is following
- `/photos/user/2`: Photos of users with ID 2

The capture groups from the route are put into `req.params`, so `req.params[1]` is the second capture group. We're putting that into the `getting` variable, and then we have to inspect if further. Assuming it exists, we check first to see if it's a number (by parsing it and passing it through `isNaN`). If it is a number, which is the easiest case, we find the photo with that ID and send it back.

If it's not a number, we run the `getting` variable against another regular expression to see if it matches `user/ID`. If it does, we'll return all the photos with the matching `userId`.

Finally, if the `getting` variable is the string `following`, we're going to loop over the current user's `following` array and get the photos from each of those users, pushing their photos into the `allPhotos` array, which we'll then return.

At any point, if we run into a pattern we weren't expecting, we'll just return an empty JSON object.

Creating profile pages

Now that we have this route available, we can do a lot more. How about a profile page? If you look back at the navigation view again, you'll see that we created a **My Profile** link, which takes us to `/users/1` (or whatever your ID number is). Of course, this means that we can use it for more than just our own profile page. It will work for any user, if we make the code generic enough.

First, we'll need a way to get the user data from the server (remember, this could be a profile for someone other than the logged-in user). We'll use a model for this by using the following code:

```
var User = Backbone.Model.extend({
  url: function () {
    return '/user-' + this.get('id') + '.json';
  }
});
```

Building a Photo-sharing Application

The URL is different from what we would usually do, but it shows the flexibility of Backbone; we can make the URL look like a path to a JSON file. Of course, this wouldn't be so great if we needed to post to this URL to save a user (especially because a model doesn't usually have an ID until it has been saved). However, since I know we won't need to do that, we can have fun with this one and do it that way. As you might imagine, the server-side code is pretty simpleas you can see in the following code:

```
app.get("/user-:id.json", function (req, res) {
  users.findOne({ id : parseInt(req.params.id, 10) },
    function (user) {
      res.json(safe(user));
    });
});
```

Now that we can get a user, let's add the profile page route to the router by using the following code:

```
'users/:id': 'showUser',
```

Now, add the following method to the router:

```
showUser: function (id) {
  var thiz = this,
      user,
      photos;

  id = parseInt(id, 10);

  function render() {
    var userView = new UserView({
      model: user.toJSON(),
      collection: photos
    });
    thiz.main.html(thiz.navView.render().el);
    thiz.main.append(userView.render().el);
  }

  if (id === USER.id) {
    user = new User(USER);
    photos = this.userPhotos;
    render();
  } else {
    user = new User({ id: id });
    photos = new Photos({ url: "/photos/user/" + id });
    user.fetch().then(function () {
      photos.fetch().then(render);
```

```
      });
    }
  },
```

Again, let's do something that's a little different. Here's the scenario: if users are viewing their own page, there's no reason to pull their user and photo data from the server again; we can use the data we already have in the browser. To see if a user is viewing their own profile, we compare the ID in the route (which we get as a parameter) to the ID on the USER object. If the user is viewing another user's profile, we create a user model and photos collection with just enough data: a model only needs `id`, and a collection only needs `url`. Then, we can have them both fetch the rest of the needed data from the server. In both cases, the `fetch` method returns a jQuery deferred object. If you aren't familiar with deferreds or promises in JavaScript, think of them as a way to wait for data to be ready; we call the deferred's `then` method, passing it a function to call when the data is ready. We'll use promises a lot more in a later chapter.

Wait, can we just hand a URL to a collection object? Not usually. We need to add an `initialize` method to our `Photos` collection class, like so:

```
initialize: function (options) {
  if (options && options.url) {
    this.url = options.url;
  }
}
```

Clever, eh? This way, we can use any URL we want. That's why we created the URL-flexible backend for this class.

In both cases, we then call our internal `render` method. There's something to note about this function. Even though it's inside out router method, it will still be run in the global namespace; this is why we create the `thiz` variable, for use inside the `render` function. Of course, in one case we call it procedurally and in another we call it as a callback, but the same thing will be done; we will render the `UserView` instance. Here's the code for that class:

```
var UserView = Backbone.View.extend({
  template: _.template($("#userView").html()),
  render: function () {
    this.el.innerHTML = this.template(this.model.toJSON());
    var ul = this.$("ul");
    this.collection.forEach(function (photo) {
      ul.append(new PhotoView({
        model: photo
      }).render().el);
```

```
        });
        return this;
    }
});
```

Very simple; it's just a username and a list of your photos. We can even reuse the `PhotoView` class that we made earlier to display individual photos. Notice our use of the `this.$` method; it allows us to search for elements and create a jQuery object for those elements, but it limits the search to elements inside this view instance's `el` property. Finally, here's the template:

```
<script type="text/template" id="userView">
  <h1>{{username}}</h1>
  <ul></ul>
</script>
```

If you try this out, you might notice a problem; when viewing the current user's profile, there won't be any photos. That's because we're using the `userPhotos` property from the router, which is just an empty collection. When we load the page, we should load the user's photos data too. This isn't hard to do. First, back in your `server.js` file, in the `/*` route function, swap out your `res.render` call for the following code:

```
photos.find({ userId: req.user.id }, function (err, photos) {
  res.render("index.ejs", {
    user: JSON.stringify(safe(req.user)),
    userPhotos: JSON.stringify(photos)
  });
});
```

Then, in the `index.ejs` file, use your template delimiters to put that in its place, inside the router instantiation:

```
userPhotos: new Photos(<%- userPhotos %>)
```

Now, you should see your own photos on your profile page, because we're loading photos from the server.

Creating the individual photo page

We've used the `PhotoView` class twice now; it creates a link, as you might recall, to an individual page for each photo. Let's create that page next. This time, we'll start in the router. First, add this route to the `routes` property:

```
'photo/:id': 'showPhoto',
```

Then, here's the `showPhoto` method is partners with:

```
showPhoto: function (id) {
  var thiz = this,
    photo = new Photo({ id : parseInt(id, 10) });

  photo.fetch().then(function () {
    var comments = new Comments({ photo: photo }),
    var photoView = new PhotoPageView({
      model: photo,
      collection: comments
    });

    comments.fetch().then(function () {
      thiz.main.html(thiz.navView.render().el);
      thiz.main.append(photoView.render().el);
    });
  });
},
```

Just as we did with the `showUser` function, we get the photo data by creating a `Photo` instance with `id`, and then calling the `fetch` method. However, we're also creating a `Comments` collection based on this photo. Then, we create a `PhotoPageView` instance, which has both a model (the photo) and a collection (the comments). Once we fetch the comments from the server, we render it. So here's the view:

```
var PhotoPageView = Backbone.View.extend({
  template: _.template($("#photoPageView").html()),
  initialize: function () {
    this.collection.on("add", this.showComment, this);
  },
  events: {
    'click button': 'addComment'
  },
  render: function () {
    this.el.innerHTML = this.template(this.model.toJSON());
    this.collection.forEach(this.showComment.bind(this));
    return this;
  }
});
```

Building a Photo-sharing Application

As you can probably tell, this isn't all of it. In the `initialize` function, we're setting an event to call the `showComment` method whenever a new comment is added to the collection. This is also the method we use inside the `render` method to show each of the already-existing comments. Then, we have an event: a button-click that triggers an `addComment` method. Before we get to these methods, you might want to see the button as well as the rest of the template; here's the template's code, which you should add to the `index.ejs` file:

```
<script type="text/template" id="photoPageView">
  <img src="{{path}}" />
  <p> {{caption}} <small> by {{username}}</small></p>
  <div>
    <textarea id="commentText"></textarea><br />
    <button> Comment </button>
  </div>
  <ul></ul>
</script>
```

So, let's add those methods now, shall we? We'll tackle the longer one first. The following is the code for the `addComment` function:

```
addComment: function () {
  var textarea = this.$("#commentText"),
      text = textarea.val(),
      comment = {
        text: text,
        photoId: this.model.get("id"),
        username: USER.username
      };
  textarea.val("");
  this.collection.create(comment);
},
```

This is pretty similar to the `addPhoto` method in our `AddPhotoView` class. We create an attributes object with the text from the textbox, the ID of the photo we're commenting on, and the username of the commenter. Then, we send them to the server through the collection's `create` method.

When we do this, our `add` event will be triggered, and the `showComment` method will be called. Here's that method:

```
showComment: function (comment) {
  var commentView = new CommentView({ model: comment });
  this.$("ul").append(commentView.render().el);
}
```

Chapter 2

Once again, the magic is elsewhere. You want to see the `CommentView` instance, which is shown in the following code:

```
var CommentView = Backbone.View.extend({
  tagName: "li",
  template: _.template($("#commentView").html()),
  render: function () {
    this.el.innerHTML = this.template(this.model.toJSON());
    return this;
  }
});
```

It's so simple; even its template is simple. Its template's code is given as follows:

```
<script type="text/template" id="commentView">
  <p><strong>{{username}}</strong> said</p>
  <p>{{text}}</p>
</script>
```

Throughout all this, we got so excited that we completely overlooked an important factor: we don't have a `Comment` model or a `Comments` collection yet. Not to worry. We create these by using the following code:

```
var Comment = Backbone.Model.extend();
var Comments = Backbone.Collection.extend({
  model: Comment,
  initialize: function (options) {
    this.photo = options.photo;
  },
  url: function () {
    return this.photo.url() + '/comments';
  }
});
```

Notice the `Comments` collection's `url` function. It takes the `url` of the photo instance that was assigned as a property and appends `/comments` to the end. So, in our `server.js` file, we need to create the GET and POST methods for this route, as shown in the following code:

```
app.get('/photos/:id/comments', function (req, res) {
  comments.find({ photoId: parseInt(req.params.id, 10) },
    function (comments) {
      res.json(comments);
    });
});
```

[61]

Building a Photo-sharing Application

The GET route will return all the photos with the `photoId` property matching the URL parameter. Here's the POST route:

```
app.post('/photos/:id/comments', function (req, res) {
  var comment = {
    text: req.body.text,
    photoId: req.body.photoId,
    username: req.body.username
  };
  comments.insert(comment, function (data) {
    res.json(data);
  });
});
```

This route will take the attributes, create an object out of them, store them in the `comments` database, and return the saved version as JSON.

That's a wrap on the comments feature! You should be able to go to an individual photo page, type a comment in, click on the button, and see your comment appear below. Even better, the comment will still be there when you refresh the page. The following screenshot shows what it may look like:

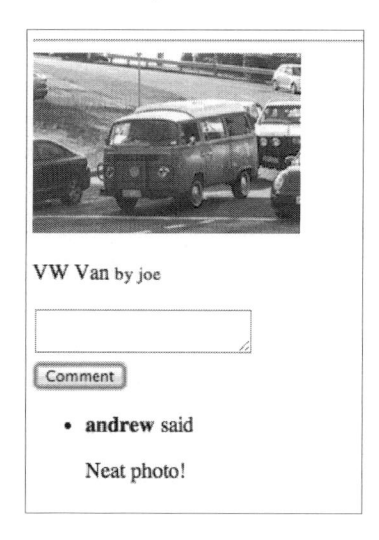

Following users

This brings us to what is easily the most complicated feature of our application: following other users. We want users to be able to choose which users they want to follow, and have those users' photos show up on the home page.

We'll start with the /users route. Add the following line to the router's routes object:

```
'users': 'showUsers',
```

Now, let's create the showUsers function:

```
showUsers: function () {
  var users = new Users(),
      thiz  = this;
  this.main.html(this.navView.render().el);
  users.fetch().then(function () {
    thiz.main.append(new UserListView({
      collection: users
    }).render().el);
  });
},
```

We don't really have a Users collection class yet; that's next. However, you can see that we'll fetch all the users here, and then render a UserListView instance.

The Users collection is very straightforward, as shown in the following code:

```
var Users = Backbone.Collection.extend({
  model: User,
  url: '/users.json'
});
```

Also, we'll need to put the server-side bits in place, as shown in the following code:

```
app.get("/users.json", function (req, res) {
  users.find(function (users) {
    res.json(users.map(safe));
  });
});
```

Now, we can look at the UserListView instance. Actually, it's another one of our wrapper views, only there to pull together a collection of individual model views, as shown in the following code:

```
var UserListView = Backbone.View.extend({
  tagName: "ul",
  render: function () {
    this.collection.forEach(function (model) {
      this.$el.append((new UserListItemView({
        model: model
      })).render().el);
```

Building a Photo-sharing Application

```
    }, this);
    return this;
  }
});
```

As you can see from this code, the one we're really interested in is the `UserListItemView` instance. This is probably the biggest view you'll see today (or at least in this chapter). We'll take it piece by piece, as shown in the following code:

```
var UserListItemView = Backbone.View.extend({
  tagName: "li",
  template: _.template('<a href="/users/{{id}}">{{username}}</a>'),
  events: {
    'click .follow': 'follow',
    'click .unfollow': 'unfollow'
  },
  render: function () {
    this.el.innerHTML = this.template(this.model.toJSON());
    if (USER.username === this.model.get("username")) {
      this.$el.append(" (me)");
    } else {
      this.update();
    }
    return this;
  }
});
```

This is the start. As you can see from the events, we will have follow and unfollow buttons that will trigger respective methods. The `render` function starts by rendering the template, which we'll put inline, because it's small.

More interesting things happen after rendering. First, we check to see if the user we're creating a list item for is the currently logged-in user; if it is, we'll add the text `(me)` to the end of it. Otherwise, we'll call the `update` method.

The `update` method is actually pretty basic. Its goal is to see if the current user is following the user that we're making the list item for. If they're already following that user, we'll put in an **Unfollow** button; otherwise, we'll use the **Follow** button. This method will also be called when one of these buttons is clicked on, so we'll remove buttons when appropriate:

```
update: function () {
  if (USER.following.indexOf(this.model.get("id")) === -1) {
    this.$("#unfollow").remove();
    this.$el.append("<button id='follow'> Follow </button>");
  } else {
```

```
        this.$("#follow").remove();
        this.$el.append("<button id='unfollow'> Unfollow </button>");
    }
}
```

It's pretty simple, actually. If the view's user ID is in the current user's `following` array, we remove an **Unfollow** button and add a **Follow** button. Otherwise, we remove the **Follow** button and add an **Unfollow** button. At this point, we could load the /users page, and we'll have a list of users with follow buttons. However, clicking on them won't do anything. We need to write those `follow` and `unfollow` functions (in the `UserListItemView` class).

These two functions are almost identical, as shown in the following code:

```
    follow: function (evt) {
      var thiz = this,
          f = new Follow({ userId: thiz.model.id });
      f.save().then(function (user) {
        USER.following = user.following;
        thiz.update();
      });
    },
    unfollow: function (evt) {
      var thiz = this,
          f = new Follow({ id: thiz.model.id });
      f.destroy().then(function (user) {
        USER.following = user.following;
        thiz.update();
      });
    },
```

In both cases, we create a new `Follow` model instance. When the goal is to save the `following` array, we set the `userId` property; when the goal is to delete the `following` array, we set the `id` property. In the case of the `follow` function, we save that model; on the server side, this will add the user to the `following` array of the current user. In the case of the `unfollow` function, we delete the model; on the server side, this will remove the user from the `following` array. Again, in both cases, the method that calls to the server will return a deferred object. We'll pass the `then` method, a function that will reset the `following` array on the USER object with the `following` array from the server. In both cases, we'll then call the `update` method to correct the buttons.

Building a Photo-sharing Application

The last step is to create the `Follow` model. Really, we don't need to use a Backbone model here; we just need two AJAX requests. However, we can make hacky use of a model class to do all the hard work for us. The following is the code for the `Follow` model:

```
var Follow = Backbone.Model.extend({
  urlRoot: '/follow'
});
```

That's really it. We can use this class in two ways. If we give a `Follow` instance a `userId` property, we can then call the `save` method to POST to `/follow`. Or, if we create a `Follow` instance with an `id` property, we can call the `destroy` method to send a DELETE request to `/follow/id`.

Things are a little more complicated on the server side. First, let's take a look at the POST route:

```
app.post("/follow", function (req, res) {
  var id = parseInt(req.body.userId, 10);
  if (req.user.following.indexOf(id) === -1) {
    req.user.following.push(id);
    users.update({ id: req.user.id }, req.user, function (err, users)
{
      res.json(safe(users[0]));
    });
  } else {
    res.json(safe(req.user));
  }
});
```

We begin by finding out whether the ID is in the user's `following` list. If it isn't, we'll push it into the array and update the user record in the database. Then, we'll send back the updated user record. Even if the user is already following the chosen user, we'll still send the user data back.

The DELETE route is similar to that POST route:

```
app.delete("/follow/:id", function (req, res) {
  var id = parseInt(req.params.id, 10),
    index = req.user.following.indexOf(id);
  if (index !== -1) {
    req.user.following.splice(index, 1);
    users.update({ id: req.user.id }, req.user, function (err, users)
{
      res.json(safe(users[0]));
    });
```

```
    } else {
      res.json(safe(req.user));
    }
});
```

If the current user is following this user, we'll use the JavaScript `splice` method to remove the item from the array (this method mutates the array, so we don't reassign it to `req.user.following`). Then, we'll update user records in the database and send the updated user back as JSON (we're sending `users[0]` because the `update` function gives an array to the `callback` function, but in our case that array should have only one record).

Now that this is in place, our `/users` route will have working follow/unfollow buttons. We can follow a few other users.

Displaying a followed user's photos

What do we do with followed users? We want to show the photos from the followed users on the home page. First, in the `server.js` file, we need to be able to get all the photos from all the users the current user is following. We're going to write a separate function for this:

```
function followingPhotos(user, callback) {
  var allPhotos = [];
  user.following.forEach(function (f) {
    photos.find({ userId: f }, function (err, photos) {
      allPhotos = allPhotos.concat(photos);
    });
  });
  callback(allPhotos);
}
```

Does it look familiar? It's almost identical to some of the code we had in our photo-fetching route, you know, the one with the regular expression route. Since we've put this code in a function, you can replace the appropriate lines in that function, so they look like the following code:

```
} else if (getting === "following") {
  followingPhotos(req.user, function (allPhotos) {
    res.json(allPhotos);
  });
} else {
```

[67]

The last step on the server side is to send these following photos to the client, where we'll display them on the home page. Let's wrap our previous `res.render` call with the function we just wrote:

```
followingPhotos(req.user, function (followingPhotos) {
  photos.find({ userId: req.user.id }, function (photos) {
    res.render("index.ejs", {
      user: JSON.stringify(safe(req.user)),
      userPhotos: JSON.stringify(photos),
      followingPhotos: JSON.stringify(followingPhotos)
    });
  });
});
```

Now, in the `index.ejs` file, we can add `followingPhotos` to our router options object:

```
followingPhotos: new Photos(<%- followingPhotos %>)
```

We'll have to use the property in our `AppRouter` class, so add the following line to the `initialize` method:

```
this.followingPhotos = options.followingPhotos;
```

The last step is to use this in the router's `index` method; the whole body of that method should now look like the following code:

```
index: function () {
  var photosView = new PhotosView({
    collection: this.followingPhotos
  });
  this.main.html(this.navView.render().el);
  this.main.append(photosView.render().el);
},
```

Now, if you go to the home page, you'll be able to see the photos of the users you are following! Excellent!

Summary

We've covered a lot of ground in the chapter, so let's retrace our steps a bit before moving on.

One of the most important things I want you to take away from this chapter is how data is sent from the server to the client. We've used two different methods here: first, we use a server-side template to put them into the HTML response and send them as part of that. Secondly, we use `fetch` commands from the client and create a completely separate HTTP request for that data. The advantage of the first method is that individual "chunks" of data don't have their own HTTP headers; also, since they're part of the initial request, the user will never wait for data while using the application. The advantage of the second method is that we never load more data than we need to from the server; when we need it, it's easy to request it. This is especially important in an application like this one, where a single user could have hundreds of posted photos over time, and people are likely to follow a lot of users; you wouldn't want to load all the data right from the start. We've mixed it up here so that you can get a feel of how both methods work.

However, you should note that this mixing-it-up actually causes us to load more data than necessary most of the time. This is because we're loading the current user's photos and the photos of the people they follow even when we aren't using that data (for example, on the user's list page). We've actually written all our Backbone code so that we could override the default anchor tag behavior and navigate our entire app with the router's `navigate` method; no page refreshes would be necessary. That might be a good exercise: try implementing functionality that uses Backbone's navigation instead of refreshing the page. If you get stuck, review the code from the last chapter.

Apart from data loading techniques, we saw that the Backbone model and collection classes are actually very flexible and can be used in "nontraditional" ways. I hope you're finding that when you take the magic out of Backbone, and understand exactly what it's doing, you can use it more efficiently. These ideas will be very useful when we build a live data dashboard in the next chapter.

3
Building a Live Data Dashboard

This is going to be a fun chapter. So far, we've created two relatively simple applications. In both cases, we mainly created and read data from the browser. While it's all browser-side stuff, it's pretty static. This time, we're going to do something a lot more interesting; we're going to build a table that keeps a track of events. In an interesting twist, though, we'll build a table that will automatically update based on changes made in other browsers that have our app open.

The following are a couple of chapter spoilers:

- We'll look at better code organization through multiple files
- We'll write code to update and delete model instances
- We'll build an app that polls the server to keep its collection up to date

Once again, we'll start with the project template; however, there are a few modifications we need to make in our last two projects. You may have noticed that our app.js file was getting a bit lengthy; this makes it tough to navigate between our components and to keep our code clean and manageable in general. So in this project, we're going to split our Backbone code into multiple files. We're going to keep our models and collections in models.js, our views in views.js and our router in router.js. You can go ahead and create these files (they'll be empty for now) in the public folder; also, remove app.js. Then, in the index.ejs file, we'll need to replace the script tag for app.js with script tags for those new files, as follows:

```
<script src="/models.js"></script>
<script src="/views.js"></script>
<script src="/router.js"></script>
```

Building a Live Data Dashboard

Planning our application

In the previous chapters, we started writing code immediately. However, in the real world, you're not going to have me to tell you what to write from the beginning. You're going to have to plan your own application. So let's take a moment and do that now.

We want to build an application that will show us a list of past and upcoming events. An event will have a title, a description, and a date on which it occurs. This type of data can be nicely displayed in a table. We'll need to be able to create new events, but we also want to be able to edit and delete the existing events. We also want to periodically poll the server for changes to the set of events so that all the connected clients are up to date.

As this is a pretty basic application, that will be all. Now that we've clarified what it needs to do, we can start thinking in terms of Backbone components. Obviously, we'll need an `Event` model and an `Events` collection. The table will be an `EventsView` instance, and each row will be an `EventView` instance. We'll need a form that is used for creating new events, say the `CreateEventView` class, and another form that is used for editing the existing events, say the `EditEventView` class. We don't need a whole view used for removing events; we just need a button, probably in the `EventView` class.

What about routes? The whole table can be displayed at the home route, which is `/`. The creation form can be at `/create`, and the edit form can be at `/edit/<id>`.

And that's about it! This doesn't really represent the planning process of a real application, but it should make you realize that building applications is about much more than just writing code. There are smart processes you can follow to facilitate the process. If you're relatively new to programming, you should look into topics such as agile development or test-driven development. When you're starting out, these ideas may seem to make your projects take longer than necessary, but believe me, they will make building and maintaining big projects much simpler.

Setting up precompiled templates

Let's start by talking about the templates we use for our view classes. In the previous chapter, we've put our template source text right in the `index.ejs` file, inside script tags. This time we're going to do something different. We're going to precompile our templates. Think about the timeline of a template; it starts as text in a script tag. We've been getting that text and passing it to the `_.template` function that compiles the text into a `template` function, which it returns to us. Then, we pass our data to that function and get the HTML with our data interpolated back. All this must be done before we can display anything for the user.

Chapter 3

What we want to do is cut a few steps out of this process. We want to send the `template` function to the browser, instead of sending the template text and having the browser compile it. To do this, we need to compile the templates as part of our development process.

The easiest way to do this is to use Grunt, a handy build tool. First, we'll need to install it, using the following commands:

```
npm install grunt --save-dev
npm install grunt-contrib-jst --save-dev
```

We won't be learning Grunt in depth here. If you aren't familiar with the library, there are many great resources to learn about it online. Start on the home page http://gruntjs.com/.

We're using npm to install both Grunt and the **JavaScript Templates (JST)** Grunt plugin. JST will do the compiling for us.

Next, we're going to need a `Gruntfile.js` file, which will configure this plugin. Put `Gruntfile.js` in the root of our project directory. In that file, start with the following code:

```
module.exports = function (grunt) {
  grunt.initConfig({});

  grunt.loadNpmTasks('grunt-contrib-jst');
  grunt.registerTask('default', ['jst']);
};
```

You might recollect that, in the previous chapter, we used the `exports` object to export functions from our `signin.js` module. We can also completely overwrite that `exports` object; however, when we do that, we have to use its full name, `module.exports`. To this we assign a function that takes a `grunt` object as a parameter. Inside this function, then, we configure Grunt for our project.

We start by calling the `initConfig` method, which configures all the plugins. After this, we register the plugin with Grunt; and finally, we can register a task. We're creating the default task, which will run when we call `grunt` on the command line. We're simply telling it to run the `jst` task.

Now, let's go back to that `initConfig` method call for a second using the following code:

```
grunt.initConfig({
  jst: {
    templates: {
```

```
        options: {
          templateSettings: {
            interpolate : /\{\{(.+?)\}\}/g
          },
          processName: function (filename) {
            return filename.split('/')[1].split('.')[0];
          }
        },
        files: {
          "public/templates.js": ["templates/*.html"]
        }
      }
    }
});
```

We start with a `jst` property, because that's the name of the task we're configuring. Inside that, we create a target, which is a set of options for our task and the files we want to perform the task on (with those options). We're calling our target `templates`. The first option is the `templateSettings` object, which we've used in both the previous chapters; it allows us to use the curly-brace delimiter syntax. The second option that we're setting is a function that will name the templates. Our templates will be HTML files in the `templates` folder, so by default their names will be their file paths; something like `templates/event.html`. The `processName` function will convert that to just `event`. This name is how we will refer to them from the view code.

In `files`, we choose what files to work on. Here, we're saying that all the template files that match the string, `templates/*.html`, will be compiled into `public/templates.js`.

This might seem like a lot to set up, but now all we need to do is run `grunt` on the command line to get precompiled templates. We'll test this out when we make our views.

Creating the models

Now that we've set up our template-creating process, let's begin with the project code. As earlier, we'll begin with the models. These will go in `models.js`:

```
var Event = Backbone.Model.extend({});
var Events = Backbone.Collection.extend({
  model: Event,
  url: '/events'
});
```

For now, this will do. We'll be coming back later to make some interesting changes.

Chapter 3

In the `server.js` file, we'll make our route functions for the route we just defined in the `Events` class. Before that, though, we'll need our database. We create that as follows:

```
var db = new Bourne("db/events.json");
```

This time, I'm putting the database JSON file in a folder of its own; if you want to do this, make sure you create the `db` folder.

But now, with the database in place, we can create the GET route. This will simply send all the records in our database back to the browser:

```
app.get("/events", function (req, res) {
  db.find(function (err, events) {
    res.json(events);
  });
});
```

The POST route is where the data for new event objects will be sent. We'll collect the properties into an object and insert it; our callback function can just send the updated record back to the browser. Here's what that looks like:

```
app.post("/events", function (req, res) {
  var attrs = {
    title: req.body.title,
    details: req.body.details,
    date: req.body.date,
    createdOn: new Date()
  };

  db.insert(attrs, function (err, event) {
    res.json(event);
  });
});
```

One more server method, and that's for the root route:

```
app.get('/*', function (req, res) {
  db.find(function (err, events) {
    res.render("index.ejs", {
      events: JSON.stringify(events)
    });
  });
});
```

This route is very similar to the get-all routes in both our previous chapters. It will render our `index.ejs` template, sending all our event records to the browser.

Creating controls

Let's begin with some controls. As we had decided, we'll need to be able to open a form to create new events, so let's put a button for this on a control bar at the top of our page.

We can start with the template. If you haven't yet started, create a directory named `templates` at the root of our project. Inside that, create a file named `controls.html`, and put the following code in it:

```
<li><a href="/create"> Create Event </a></li>
```

We're only going to have one control, and it doesn't actually need to be a template, but this gives us the ability to easily extend it later. We can actually test out the precompiling now, by running `grunt` on the command line. When you do that, you should get a message saying that **File "public/templates.js" created**. Great! You can check out the content of that file if you want to:

```
this["JST"] = this["JST"] || {};

this["JST"]["controls"] = function(obj) {
obj || (obj = {});
var __t, __p = '', __e = _.escape;
with (obj) {
__p += '<li><a href="/create"> Create Event </a></li>';

}
return __p
};
```

It's rather messy, but it will do the job for us. The important thing to notice is that we can now reference this template function via `JST.controls`. The last step here is to include this script in our `index.ejs` file, just above our script tag from `views.js`, as follows:

```
<script src="/templates.js"></script>
```

Speaking of `views.js`, we're ready to open that up and get cracking at the view from this template. We'll call it `ControlsView`:

```
var ControlsView = Backbone.View.extend({
  tagName: "ul",
  className: "nav nav-pills",
  template: JST.controls,
  initialize: function (options) {
    this.nav = options.nav;
```

[76]

```
    },
    events: {
      'click a[href="/create"]': 'create'
    },
    render: function () {
      this.el.innerHTML = this.template();
      return this;
    },
    create: function (evt) {
      evt.preventDefault();
      this.nav("create", { trigger: true });
    }
  });
```

As our template is a group of list items (well, a single list item), it makes sense that we use a `<ul>` element for this view. Then, notice that we're getting our template from the `templates.js` file, via `JST.controls`; handy, no? The `render` function is very basic. It just renders our template; we don't even need to pass it any data. It's more interesting that we're listening for the click event on our **Create Event** link. When that happens, we'll prevent the default behavior, which is requesting the `/create` route from the server, and instead we'll send it to our Backbone router.

We did this in *Chapter 1, Building a Simple Blog*, but we did it differently. Back then, we used the actual router object inside our views; we just expected it to be available as a global variable. That was a bad idea. This time, we're improving on that in two ways. First, we're expecting to receive the router as a property in our `options` object when this view is created. You can see in the `initialize` function that we're assigning `this.nav` from `options.nav`. The second improvement is that this isn't actually the whole router object; it's just the router's `navigate` method. This way, we can give select views the power to change routes, and they still can't mess with the rest of the router.

> This is a software design pattern known as dependency injection. Basically, the router's `navigate` method is a dependency that we are injecting into our `ControlsView` class. This allows us to keep unrelated code separate, which can make updating this code in the future a simpler process. For example, if we need to change the way routing is done in our application, we only need to inject a new or an updated dependency into this class, and hopefully not change much at all in this class. Dependency injection is one way to follow the dependency inversion principle, one of the five SOLID design principles. To read more about them, start at the Wikipedia page `https://en.wikipedia.org/wiki/SOLID`.

Lastly, you're probably wondering about the `className` property. As you perhaps suspect, this sets the `class` attribute on our elements. But where are these classes coming from? Well, in this application, we're going to be using Twitter's Bootstrap library, and these classes create a basic navigation/controls bar.

Including Bootstrap

Of course, for this to work, we'll have to add this library to our projects. You can head over to `http://getbootstrap.com` and click on **Download Bootstrap**. There are a bunch of files here, but we don't need them all. In our project's `public` directory, create a folder named `css`, and copy the `bootstrap.min.css` file into that. We'll also need `bootstrap.min.js`, which we'll put in the `public` folder. Bootstrap also comes with the GLYPHICONS fonts (`http://glyphicons.com/`), so you'll have to create a `fonts` folder in the `public` directory, and copy the font files from Bootstrap's `font` directory. With these pieces in place, we can add a link to the `stylesheet` tag in the head of the `index.ejs` file:

```
<link rel="stylesheet" href="/css/bootstrap.min.css" />
```

And then, at the bottom, we link to the JavaScript portion of Bootstrap:

```
<script src="/bootstrap.min.js"></script>
```

> If you aren't familiar with **GLYPHICONS**, it's a collection of symbols that you can use for icons within your web applications. Usually, you have to buy a license, but a few of them are provided with Bootstrap, free for its users.

Starting the router

Now, to render our controls, we need to start building our router. We have created a `router.js` file, so let's open that up, as follows:

```
var AppRouter = Backbone.Router.extend({
  initialize: function (options) {
    this.main = options.main;
    this.events = options.events;
    this.nav = this.navigate.bind(this);
  },
  routes: {
    '': 'index'
  },
```

```
  index: function () {
    var cv = new ControlsView({
      nav: this.nav
    });
    this.main.html(cv.render().el);
  }
});
```

From our `initialize` function, we can see that we expect to get our main element and an `Events` collection as properties of our `options` object. We're also creating a `nav` property; this is the `nav` method that we saw in `ControlsView`. It's important to realize that we can't just send `this.navigate`; we need to make sure that the function is bound to the router object, which we do with its `bind` method. When we bind a function in this way, we're creating a copy of the function whose value of `this` (inside the function copy) is whatever object we pass as a parameter to `bind`; so anywhere we call the function that is stored in `this.nav`, the value of `this` will be consistent. To learn more about `this` in JavaScript, the JavaScript Garden is a great resource and is available at `http://bonsaiden.github.io/JavaScript-Garden/#function.this`.

Our index route is pretty simple right now. We're just rendering our controls. It's a start, however! Now, in `index.ejs`, we can instantiate the router as follows:

```
var r = new AppRouter({
  main: $("#main"),
  events: new Events(<%- events %>)
});
Backbone.history.start({ pushState: true });
```

Now, we can start the server up (`npm start`) and load the page. This should look like what is shown in the following screenshot:

Create Event

As we now have a button, it makes sense to get that button working. Right now, when we click on the button, our route changes to `/create`; but nothing else changes, because we haven't created that route yet. So add this to our router's routes object as follows:

```
'create': 'create'
```

And then add the following function to the router as well:

```
create: function () {
  var cv = new CreateEventView({
    collection: this.events,
    nav: this.nav
  });
  this.main.prepend(cv.render().el);
}
```

We haven't created the CreateEventView view class yet, but you can see that we'll pass it our collection of events and our nav method. We'll render it and append it to the main element.

> You might recall from the previous chapter that we didn't name the collection property collection when we weren't rendering it, so other developers reading our code won't confuse the purpose of giving the view a collection. However, we are naming it collection in this case because the events property is already used by Backbone to assign DOM events.

Building the CreateEventView class

So let's create the CreateEventView view class. Now, let's throw a twist in; since we have Bootstrap on our page, why don't we use its modal component to display our form?

To do this, we'll begin by creating our template. Create templates/createEvent.html and put this in that file:

```
<div class="modal-dialog">
<div class="modal-content">
  <div class="modal-header">
    <button class="close">&times;</button>
    <h4 class="modal-title"> Create New Event </h4>
  </div>
  <div class="modal-body">
    <form>
      <label>Title</label>
      <input type="text" class="form-control" id="title" />
      <label>Details</label>
      <textarea id="details"  class="form-control"></textarea>
      <label>Date</label>
```

```
      <input type="datetime-local" class="form-control" id="date" />
    </form>
  </div>
  <div class="modal-footer">
    <a href="#" class="create btn btn-primary"> Create Event </a>
  </div>
</div>
</div>
```

It's a lot of HTML, but you can see the form in the middle there, right? Actually, the Bootstrap model requires another wrapping `<div>`, but the view class will provide that. Here's the first portion of that view:

```
var CreateEventView = Backbone.View.extend({
  className: "modal fade",
  template: JST.createEvent,
  initialize: function (options) {
    this.nav = options.nav;
  },
  render: function (model) {
    this.el.innerHTML = this.template();
    return this;
  }
});
```

This is what we start with, and it's a very basic view. The most important thing to notice here is the `className` property; these classes style the modal window. However, at this point, if we compile our template and click on our button, our modal window won't appear. What's up with that? If you inspect the page in the developer tools of your browser, you'll see that the view's HTML is added to the page, but it isn't viewable. You can see that in the following screenshot:

```
▼<body>
  ▼<div id="main">
    ▶<div class="modal fade">…</div>
    ▶<ul class="nav nav-pills">…</ul>
  </div>
```

The problem is that we need to use Bootstrap's jQuery modal plugin, which we had loaded earlier (`bootstrap.min.js`). We can use this plugin to show and hide the modal. To show the form, it's as easy as adding the following line of code to our `render` method, right after calling the `template` function:

```
this.$el.modal("show");
```

We get the "jQuer-ified" element and call the `modal` method, passing it the command to show the modal window.

Building a Live Data Dashboard

The next step is to add a few events to this class. There are two buttons to consider: the **Create Event** button (to create new `Event` model) and the **x** button (to close the modal window, not creating a new model):

```
events: {
  "click .close": "close",
  "click .create": "create"
},
```

The `close` method will be very simple. See the following code:

```
close: function (evt) {
  evt.preventDefault();
  this.$el.modal("hide");
},
```

We prevent the default action of the button, and then hide the modal window.

Now, how about writing the `create` method? We write it using the following code:

```
create: function (evt) {
  evt.preventDefault();
  var e = {
    title: this.$("#title").val(),
    details: this.$("#details").val(),
    date: this.$("#date").val()
  };
  this.$el.modal("hide");
  this.collection.create(e, { wait: true });
  return false;
}
```

We collect all the properties for our new event object and use the collection's `create` method to send the data to the server. We're passing the `wait` option because we'll soon have views listening for the creation of new events. This way, the views won't be notified until this event object has been successfully saved on the server.

There's one piece of this puzzle left; when either of the buttons are clicked, the modal is closed, but its DOM elements still exist. To get rid of the elements that make up the view, we need to call the view's `remove` method. This method gets rid of the elements and removes any event handlers connected to those elements. So when exactly should we call this `remove` method? Well, when we hide the modal, it will fade out; we need to remove the view after that. Handily, the jQuery plugin that we're using emits events at different points. We can listen for the `hidden.bs.modal` event, which will fire once the modal's fade-out sequence has completed.

So, in the view's `initialize` method, we'll listen for that event using the following code:

```
this.$el.on("hidden.bs.modal", this.hide.bind(this));
```

When it fires, we'll call the `hide` method on our view. That method looks like this:

```
hide: function () {
  this.remove();
  this.nav('/');
},
```

We call the view's `remove` function to get rid of the DOM and events; then, we use the `nav` method to send our users back to the home page.

Now, let's pause for a moment and think about how the user might go through our application. They can start on the home page and click on the **Create Event** button, which will take them to the /create route. However, it doesn't reload the page; it just fades in the modal. When they close the modal window (either by submitting the form or closing the form), they'll be taken back to the home route; the form will fade out and the control bar will still be there. However, it's also possible that the user will go directly to /create. They'll get the form, which will work fine; however, when they close the modal, they'll be taken back to the home route, but the page will be blank. This is because we're not triggering the router's `index` method when we move back to that route (no {trigger: true}). Why not trigger that method?

We're not triggering it because there's a better way here; even if the user goes directly to /create, we want to render the controls (and the table that will eventually be there). This means that, in the `create` router method, we need to check to see whether `index` has been called yet. In our case, we'll do that simply by checking for the existence of the navigation. In the `create` method, add this just before appending the `CreateEventView` instance:

```
if ($("ul.nav").length === 0) {
  this.index();
}
```

Now, if a user goes directly to the /create route, the router's `index` method will be called if it hasn't been rendered.

Creating the events table

At this point, we're successfully creating new event records and storing them in our database. The next step is to display the table of events. We'll start with the `EventsView` class.

Actually, we'll start with template for this view. In `templates/events.html`, we'll create the `thead` and `tbody` elements as follows:

```
<thead>
  <tr>
    <th data-field="id">ID</th>
    <th data-field="title">Title</th>
    <th data-field="details">Details</th>
    <th data-field="date">Date</th>
    <th data-field="createdOn">Created On</th>
    <th> Actions </th>
  </tr>
</thead>
<tbody></tbody>
```

As you can see, our table will show the five fields that our events have. We also have a sixth column for actions: the edit and delete actions. We have a data attribute on each one of the table heading elements, with names that match the property names of the `Event` records. We'll use these later for sorting. You can go ahead and run `grunt` on the command line to compile this template function.

Now, how about `EventsView`? We can compile this using the following code:

```
var EventsView = Backbone.View.extend({
  tagName: "table",
  className: "table",
  template: JST.events,
  initialize: function (options) {
    this.nav = options.nav;
  },
  render: function () {
    this.el.innerHTML = this.template();
    this.renderRows();
    return this;
  },
  renderRows: function () {
    this.collection.forEach(this.addRow, this);
  },
  addRow: function (event) {
```

```
      this.$("tbody").append(new EventView({
        model: event,
        nav: this.nav
      }).render().el);
    }
  });
```

We start by making the element for this view a table; we're also adding the class `table` to get Bootstrap's table styling. In the `initialize` method, we can see that we're taking the `nav` method in the `options` object so that we can change routes. In `render`, we're rendering the template and then calling `renderRows`. The `renderRows` method loops over every item in our `Events` collection and calls `addRow`. You might wonder why we don't put the single line of code in this method right in the `render` method; it's because we'll need it in its own method later. That `addRow` method will take a single event object as a property and render an `EventView` instance, placing it in that `tbody` element that we put in the template. We'll be coming back to this view to add and adjust things, but let's go over to the `EventView` class now.

As we did earlier, we'll start with the template. The following code snippet should be the content of `templates/event.html`:

```
<td>{{id}}</td>
<td>{{title}}</td>
<td>{{details}}</td>
<td>{{date}}</td>
<td>{{createdOn}}</td>
<td>
  <button class="edit btn btn-inverse">
    <span class="glyphicon glyphicon-edit glyphicon-white"></span>
  </button>
  <button class="delete btn btn-danger">
    <span class="glyphicon glyphicon-trash"></span>
  </button>
</td>
```

The first portion of the template is simple. We're just placing the properties of the `Event` object in the `<td>` elements. In the last `<td>` element, we've got two buttons; we're using Bootstrap's button and Glyphicon classes to get the right styling. These will be the edit and delete buttons.

The following code snippet is the start of the `EventView` class:

```
var EventView = Backbone.View.extend({
  tagName: "tr",
  template: JST.event,
```

Building a Live Data Dashboard

```
    initialize: function (options) {
      this.nav = options.nav;
    }
  });
```

It is similar to the other views that we've seen so far. The `render` method, however, will be slightly more involved. Before that, we need to add another third-party library: Moment (http://momentjs.com/). This library is a great tool to use for quickly formatting dates. Download the script from the website and add it to the `index.ejs` file, anywhere above the `views.js` file as follows:

```
<script src="/moment.min.js"></script>
```

With that in place, we can add a `render` method to the `EventView` class as follows:

```
render: function () {
  var attrs = this.model.toJSON(),
      date = moment(attrs.date),
      diff = date.unix() - moment().unix();

  attrs.date = date.calendar();
  attrs.createdOn = moment(attrs.createdOn).fromNow();
  this.el.innerHTML = this.template(attrs);

  if (diff < 0) {
    this.el.className = "error";
  } else if (diff < 172800) { // next 2 days
    this.el.className = "warning";
  } else if (diff < 604800) { // next 7 days
    this.el.className = "info";
  }

  return this;
},
```

This is easily the most complex `render` method that we've seen yet. We start with a few variables. We get the attributes of our model first. Then, we create a `moment` object and pass it the `date` property of our model. A `moment` object wraps a date and gives us access to several helpful date-related methods. Finally, we use Moment's `unix` method (which returns the time in seconds since the Unix Epoch) to get the difference between the time this event takes place and right now.

Next, we use that `date` object we just created to overwrite the default date value in the attribute object to be something more readable. We're using Moment's `calendar` method to give us a date string such as `Monday at 6:30 PM` (or `10/30/2014` for dates further away). Then, we replace the `createdOn` property with a different date string. With the Moment's `fromNow` method, we get a string such as `6 hours ago`. Then, we pass our updated attributes object to the `this.template` function for rendering.

After rendering, we make one final adjustment. Bootstrap has a few handy classes used for coloring table rows, so we'll color a row differently depending on the time of the event. If the value of `diff` is less than 0 (which means the event began some time before this table was rendered), we'll add the `danger` class, resulting in a red row. If the event occurs within the next two days (`diff < 172800`), we'll go with `warning` (a yellow row). If the event is in the next week (`diff < 604800`), the `success` class gives us a green row.

Let's head back to the router to put the `EventsView` and `EventView` classes to work. Here's the new `index` method:

```
index: function () {
  var cv = new ControlsView({
    nav: this.nav
  }),
  av = new EventsView({
    collection: this.events,
    nav: this.nav
  });
  this.main.html(cv.render().el);
  this.main.append(av.render().el);
},
```

With this in place, we can reload the home page and see the table. If you add a few events, you should see something like what is shown in the following screenshot:

ID	Title	Details	Date	Created On	Actions
	Create Event				
1	Backbone Conference	You'll want to be there!	Monday at 12:00 PM	8 minutes ago	
2	Top Secret Meeting	[CLASSIFIED]	Tomorrow at 6:00 PM	7 minutes ago	
3	Meet John and Sue	Coffee, at the usual place.	Last Wednesday at 3:00 PM	6 minutes ago	
4	Birthday Party	It's Emily's 25th!	12/28/2013	4 minutes ago	

Building a Live Data Dashboard

Things are looking pretty good at this point, you'll have to agree. However, there's still a lot to do before we finish this application. Let's begin by getting that delete button to actually delete a record.

Deleting a record

As the button is already in place, we just have to wire it up. In `EventView`, let's add the event listener as follows:

```
events: {
  "click .delete" : "destroy"
},
```

You know what's next. We need to create the `destroy` method in the `EventView` class. It can be done as follows:

```
destroy: function (evt) {
  evt.preventDefault();
  this.model.destroy();
  this.remove();
},
remove: function () {
  this.$el.fadeOut(Backbone.View.prototype.remove.bind(this));
  return false;
}
```

The `destroy` method will call the model's `destroy` method and then call this view's `remove` method. Normally, that would be all, but we want to add a touch more. We want to fade the table row out and then remove the DOM elements. So, we're overwriting the default Backbone View `remove` method. We'll use jQuery to fade the element out. The `fadeOut` method that jQuery has takes a callback, a function that will be called after the fadeout is complete. We can get the usual Backbone View `remove` method from the `Backbone.View.prototype` object. Of course, we have to call it on the right view instance by binding the method to the current view, `this`.

We haven't called a Backbone model's `destroy` method before, as we're doing here in the view's `destroy` method. This method sends a DELETE request to the server, to the route `/events/<id>`. We'll need to create a method for this in our `server.js` file as follows:

```
app.delete("/events/:id", function (req, res) {
  db.delete({ id: parseInt(req.params.id, 10) }, function () {
    res.json({});
  });
});
```

Chapter 3

It's pretty basic; our database has a `delete` method, so we call that, passing it a query object with the `id` we get from the route. What we return is irrelevant, so we'll return an empty object.

With that code in place, you can now click on the delete button in any of our events' table rows, and that row will fade away. Refresh the page, and you'll see that it's gone for good.

Editing event records

The next step is to allow users to edit their event records. Wiring up our edit button will be simple. First, we listen for the click in the `events` object of `EventView`, like this:

```
"click .edit": "edit"
```

And secondly, we navigate to the edit route for that event:

```
edit: function (evt) {
  evt.preventDefault();
  this.nav("/edit/" + this.model.get("id"), { trigger: true });
}
```

We want our edit routes to act just like our create route does. If the user clicks on an edit button, a modal will fade in and allow editing of the event records. But they should also be able to go directly to the edit route and the table will load under the modal. This means that our router's `edit` method should be very similar to its `create` method.

First, we'll add the route to the router's `route` object as follows:

```
'edit/:id': 'edit'
```

Then, the `edit` method itself using the following code:

```
edit: function (id) {
  var ev = new EditEventView({
    model: this.events.get(parseInt(id, 10)),
    nav: this.nav
  });

  if ($("ul.nav").length === 0) {
    this.index();
  }

  this.main.prepend(ev.render().el);
}
```

[89]

Building a Live Data Dashboard

We haven't created `EditEventView` yet, but if you look back at the `create` method, you'll see how similar these both are. That calls for a little refactoring as we have done in the following code snippet:

```
create: function () {
  var cv = new CreateEventView({
    collection: this.events,
    nav: this.nav
  });
  this.modal(cv);
},
edit: function (id) {
  var ev = new EditEventView({
    model: this.events.get(parseInt(id, 10)),
    nav: this.nav
  });
  this.modal(ev);
},
modal: function (view) {
  if ($("ul.nav").length === 0) {
    this.index();
  }
  this.main.prepend(view.render().el);
}
```

We've pulled the common code out into a `modal` method. Then, in both `create` and `edit`, we pass the view we want to render to that method.

Next, we need to create the `EditEventView` class. If you pause for a moment and think about this, you'll realize that since we want it to act like the `CreateEventView` class, it'd be great if we could somehow reuse as much of the code for that view as possible. Really, the main difference between the `create` and `edit` views is that, in the `edit` view, the current values of the record will already be in the form input elements. We'll also want the form heading and button text to be appropriately changed.

We can start with the `createEvent.html` file under `templates`. We'll prepare it to take the values we need to pass to it as follows:

```
<div class="modal-dialog">
<div class="modal-content">
  <div class="modal-header">
    <button class="close">&times;</button>
    <h4 class="modal-title"> {{ heading }} </h4>
  </div>
  <div class="modal-body">
```

```
      <form>
        <label>Title</label>
        <input type="text" class="form-control" id="title"
value="{{title}}" />
        <label>Details</label>
        <textarea id="details"  class="form-control">{{details}}</textarea>
        <label>Date</label>
        <input type="datetime-local" class="form-control" id="date"
value="{{date}}" />
      </form>
    </div>
    <div class="modal-footer">
      <a href="#" class="modify btn btn-primary"> {{btnText}} </a>
    </div>
  </div>
</div>
```

Notice that we're not just expecting values in the form input elements, we're also expecting a heading and text for the button. And, as this template will be used by both `CreateEventView` and `EditEventView`, let's rename it to `templates/modifyEvent.html`.

Don't forget to recompile the template (`grunt`, on the command line).

Since almost all the behavior we want for the `EditEventView` class is the same as we created for the `CreateEventView` class, let's extract as much as possible out into a `ModifyEventView` class. The following code is what we have come up with:

```
var ModifyEventView = Backbone.View.extend({
  className: "modal fade",
  template: JST.modifyEvent,
  events: {
    "click .close": "close",
    "click .modify": "modify"
  },
  initialize: function (options) {
    this.nav = options.nav;
    this.$el.on("hidden.bs.modal", this.hide.bind(this));
  },
  hide: function () {
    this.remove();
    this.nav('/');
  },
```

Building a Live Data Dashboard

```
    close: function (evt) {
      evt.preventDefault();
      this.$el.modal("hide");
    },
    render: function (model) {
      var data = this.model.toJSON();
      data.heading = this.heading;
      data.btnText = this.btnText;
      this.el.innerHTML = this.template(data);
      this.$el.modal("show");
      return this;
    },
    modify: function (evt) {
      evt.preventDefault();
      var a = {
        title: this.$("#title").val(),
        details: this.$("#details").val(),
        date: this.$("#date").val()
      };
      this.$el.modal("hide");
      this.save(a);
      return false;
    }
  });
```

There are a few key differences between this class and the `CreateEventView` class. First, notice that in the `render` method, we're adding `heading` and `btnText` to the data that we put into the template. We'll get to where these come from in a minute. The other thing is that, in the `modify` method, we're calling `this.save` instead of `this.collection.create`. This is one of the big differences between creating a record and updating a record; the way we save them. So we'll need to create a `save` method for each, saying how exactly to do the saving.

Now if this view class acts as a parent class, or a superclass, what about the child views? Well, the `EditEventView` is very simple as follows:

```
  var EditEventView = ModifyEventView.extend({
    heading: "Edit Event",
    btnText: "Update",
    save: function (e) {
      this.model.save(e);
    }
  });
```

First, notice how we're creating this view: `ModifyEventView.extend`. Backbone's class-creating functionality allows us to extend our own views in the same way that we extend `Backbone.View`. Of course, we get access to all the methods and properties of `ModifyEventView`, plus whatever we add. This is where we add the `heading` and `btnText`, which our `render` method uses. This is also where the `save` method comes in. In this view, we're just using the model's `save` method to send the updated attributes back to the server. We'll create a server method for this in a second. But first, we need to update our `CreateEventView` to use `ModifyEventView` using the following code:

```
var CreateEventView = ModifyEventView.extend({
  heading: "Create New Event",
  btnText: "Create",
  initialize: function (options) {
    ModifyEventView.prototype.initialize.call(this, options);
    this.model = new Event();
  },
  save: function (e) {
    this.collection.create(e, { wait: true });
  }
});
```

Besides the `heading`, `btnText`, and `save` parts that we're familiar with, we're also overwriting the `initialize` method. We do call the parent class' `initialize` method in there, but there's something more. If you think about our template for a second, you'll see why. Our template expects to receive attributes to fill in the form inputs with, but the `CreateEventView` class doesn't have a model to give it; its job is to create a model! So what we're going to do is create a disposable `Event` object with blank attributes, so that no values are actually filled in, but we won't get any errors from the template function.

However, you probably realize that a blank `Event` object won't actually have any attributes. What we need to do is add default values so that the `Event` objects will have empty properties to pass to the template. In the `models.js` file, insert the following code:

```
var Event = Backbone.Model.extend({
  defaults: {
    title: "",
    details: "",
    date: ""
  }
});
```

This is our updated model class. Very simple, but it solves our view problems.

Building a Live Data Dashboard

Don't forget, we're calling `this.model.save` in our `EditEventView` class. This will send the updated attributes to the server via a PUT request to `/events/<id>`. In `server.js`, here's how we process those PUT requests:

```
app.put("/events/:id", function (req, res) {
  var e = {
    title: req.body.title,
    details: req.body.details,
    date: req.body.date
  };

  db.update({ id: parseInt(req.params.id, 10) }, e,
    function (err, e) {
      res.json(e);
    });
});
```

We'll round up the attributes into an object and pass it to our database's `update` method. To find the right record to update, we'll pass a query object with the record's ID. Then, we will return the updated record to the browser as JSON to complete the transaction.

Making it live

At this point, we have a pretty decent application. We can create events that show up in our table. We can update and remove these events as well. However, if multiple people are using the same table of events, we might want to regularly poll the server for changes to the dataset. This way, someone could leave the page open, like a dashboard of sorts, and it would always be up to date.

This feature sounds like it might be tricky to implement, but it's actually much easier than you think. The first step is to go to the `model.js` file, and extend our `Events` collection by adding these methods to it:

```
initialize: function (models, options) {
  this.wait = (options && options.wait) || 10000;
},
refresh: function () {
  this.fetch();
  setTimeout(this.refresh.bind(this), this.wait);
}
```

The `refresh` method is the important one here. Mainly, we're calling the collection's `fetch` method. This will get the set of models from the server and set them as the model for collection. However, it does it in a smart way. If there are any new models, it will fire an `add` event; if there are any updated models, it will fire a `change` event; and, if any models were removed, it will fire a `remove` event. And it will leave any untouched models alone. Then, we set a timeout, to call this method again after a certain number of seconds.

We've also added an `initialize` method to allow the option of how many seconds to wait between fetches. If the `options` object has a `wait` property, we'll use that. Otherwise, it's 10 seconds.

Now, in the `initialize` method for the `EventsView` class, we just have to call the collection's `refresh` method like this:

```
this.collection.refresh();
```

Getting the updates is that simple. Now, we need to listen for the events and do the right thing.

Any new records added to the collection from the update will fire an `add` event on the collection. Thus, in `EventsView`, we should listen for that. We also need to add this to its `initialize` method. So, here's the whole `initialize` method, with both of these updates:

```
initialize: function (options) {
  this.nav = options.nav;
  this.listenTo(this.collection, 'add', this.addRow);
  this.collection.refresh();
},
```

Previously, we used the `on` method to listen to events. However, `listenTo` is an alternative form. It does pretty much the same thing, but it allows the listener—the view, in this case—to keep a track of the events it is listening for. This way, if we ever delete the view object, the `remove` method can detach those events and conserve browser memory. Here, we're telling our view to listen for an `add` event on the collection; when this occurs, we call `addRow`. As we know, this will add an `EventView` class to our table.

That takes care of additions via AJAX updates. The `remove` and `change` events will be called on the event model. This means that we listen for the changes in our `EventView`. In its `initialize` method, we'll listen for the events. Here's the whole new `EventView` `initialize` method:

```
initialize: function (options) {
  this.nav = options.nav;
```

Building a Live Data Dashboard

```
    this.listenTo(this.model, "remove", this.remove);
    this.listenTo(this.model, "change", this.render);
},
```

We've already created the `render` and `remove` methods, so this is all that we need.

And that's all! Now, you can open `http://localhost:3000` in multiple browser windows. Go ahead and add an event in one browser window; you should see it show up in the other, in less than 10 seconds. You can edit or remove an event, and you'll see the change in the other window. Pretty cool, eh? And it only required a minimal amount of code.

Sorting events

There's one more feature we're going to add to our application. We have a table of events, so why not add the ability to sort the rows by whichever field we click on?

First, we need to sort the models in the collection. You already know that when we make a collection object, we pass it an array of model objects. We can have the collection sort these upon creation, by adding a comparator to the `Events` class. In `models.js`, add the following line to the `Events` collection class:

```
comparator: 'date',
```

Adding this line will sort the models in the collection by the `date` field. This will sort the models initially added to the collection, and any models subsequently added. However, it will not re-sort the models after one of them has been changed. This is important because we want our table rows to reorder if necessary when we edit an event record. We can implement that rather easily. However, when we edit a model, it will emit a `change` event, which bubbles up to the collection. We can listen for this in the `Events` collection's `initialize` method as follows:

```
this.listenTo(this, 'change', this.sort);
```

It's as simple as listening for the `change` event on the collection itself; when that occurs, we manually call the `sort` method on the collection.

However, there's something more to do in the collection. The default `sort` method will only sort in one direction. We want to be able to click on a heading a second time and get a reverse sort. So, we'll have to write a `reverse` method ourselves. Insert the following code in the `Events` collection:

```
reverse: function (options) {
  this.sort({ silent: true });
  this.models = this.models.reverse();
  this.trigger('sort', this, options);
}
```

Chapter 3

First, we call `sort`; we pass it the `silent` option so that the `sort` event will not be fired. Then, we get the internal `models` property; this is the array that holds the model instances in our collection. We call the native array method `reverse` to reverse the order of the models in the array. We reassign this reversed array back to the `models` property. Finally, we trigger the `sort` event; this is the event that would usually be triggered by the `sort` method, but we silenced that one so that we could reverse the array. We pass the collection object and any options passed to `reverse` as parameters of the `sort` event.

If our collection is sorted, when we loop over it in the `EventsView` class to add the record to a table, they will be added in the right order. But we want to be able to click on the table headings and sort the rows by the clicked heading. So the next step is to listen for the click event in our `EventsView` class. Add the following code to that class:

```
events: {
  'click th[data-field]': 'sort'
},
```

Here, we listen for a click on any of the table headings that have the `data-field` attributes that we put into the template. So, let's write this `sort` method in `EventsView` as follows:

```
sort: function (evt) {
  var target = evt.currentTarget,
      c = this.collection;

  c.comparator = target.getAttribute("data-field");

  if (target.getAttribute("data-direction") === "asc") {
    c.reverse();
    this.fixSortIcons(target, "desc");
  } else {
    c.sort();
    this.fixSortIcons(target, "asc");
  }
}
```

We start by getting the element that was clicked (the `target`); we also make a shorter variable for the collection, just because we use it a lot in this method. Next, we set the new comparator on the collection. Then, we need to figure out which direction we're trying to sort in. We do this by another attribute on our table headings `data-direction`. If the attribute is `asc`, we'll do the reverse sort. Otherwise, if it's `desc`, we'll do a regular sort.

Building a Live Data Dashboard

But where does this attribute come from? We didn't put it in the template. Well, notice the `fixSortIcon` method we're calling. This method does two things. First, as we expect, it will set the `data-direction` attribute on the element. But we're also setting an icon; an arrow that will indicate the direction of the sort. Here's that method:

```
fixSortIcons: function (target, dir) {
  var icon = 'glyphicon glyphicon-arrow-' + (dir === 'asc' ? 'down' : 'up');
  this.$("th i").remove();
  target.setAttribute("data-direction", dir);
  $("<i>").addClass(icon).appendTo(target);
},
```

This method takes two parameters: the target element (the table heading that the user clicked on) and the direction (`asc` or `desc`). First, we get the name for the Glyphicons arrow icons: up for `desc`, down for `asc`. To show this icon, we're going to need an `<i>` element. But, for anything other than the first sort, there's going to be an `<i>` element from the previous sort. The next step is to remove those. Then, we set the attribute on the target element. The last step is to create the `<i>` element, add the appropriate class, and append it to the target element.

So now, when we click on a header, the collection will sort by that property. But, how do we actually reorder the table rows? As you know, when the collection is sorted, a `sort` event will be emitted. Let's capture that in the `EventsView` `initialize` method like this:

```
this.listenTo(this.collection, 'sort', this.renderRows);
```

As we saw earlier, the `renderRows` function will add a row for each record in the collection. We already have rows in the table, so we have to figure out what to do with those. The easiest thing to do would be to simply empty the `<tbody>` element and make a bunch of new `EventView` instances. However, this isn't great for memory management. We should properly remove the views with their `remove` method, to unhook event listeners, and then we could create new `EventViews` class. We're going to take an alternate approach; however, we're going to reorder the views that we've already created. This means that we need to keep references to the `EventView` instances. In the `EventsView` `initialize` method, let's create a `children` property to keep track of these views. This can be done with the following little code snippet:

```
this.children = {};
```

Then, we need to change the `addRow` method so that it makes use of this property. It should now look like this:

```
addRow: function (event) {
  if (!this.children[event.id]) {
    this.children[event.id] = new EventView({
      model: event,
      nav: this.nav
    }).render();
  }

  this.$("tbody").append(this.children[event.id].el);
},
```

Now, this method will first check to see whether there's a property in our `children` object with the ID of this event. If not, we'll create a new `EventView` object, render it, and store it in the `children` object. Whether it's freshly created or not, we'll append it to `<tbody>`. The beauty of this is that even if it's already in `<tbody>`, this will move it to the end. After running through the collection, the table rows will be properly sorted.

That's everything in place! Now, head over to the browser and give the sorting feature a once around. The following screenshot shows the things in action:

ID	Title	Details	Date ↓	Created On	Actions
2	Top Secret Meeting	[CLASSIFIED]	Last Saturday at 6:00 PM	4 days ago	
1	Backbone Conference	You'll want to be there!	Wednesday at 12:00 PM	4 days ago	
4	Birthday Party	It's Emily's 25th!	Saturday at 8:00 PM	4 days ago	

And now, sorting by the ID column can be seen in the following screenshot:

ID ↓	Title	Details	Date	Created On	Actions
1	Backbone Conference	You'll want to be there!	Wednesday at 12:00 PM	4 days ago	
2	Top Secret Meeting	[CLASSIFIED]	Last Saturday at 6:00 PM	4 days ago	
4	Birthday Party	It's Emily's 25th!	Saturday at 8:00 PM	4 days ago	

Summary

We've covered a lot in this chapter. Previously, we'd only created and read models on the server. Now, we know how to update and delete models on the server as well. This is bread-and-butter stuff for Backbone applications. Many of the apps you build will use all the four CRUD operations: creating, reading, updating, and deleting.

Another important thing to take away is the way we updated the collection by fetching from the server. You won't do it this way in every application—regularly polling the server—but the events that we listened for will be the same in every case. In fact, there's a common Backbone convention here; listen for the `change` event on a model and rerender the view that shows that model. Usually, you'll only need to call the `render` method to do that. As the main element of the view is already in the DOM, there's no need to reappend it; it will update when `render` is called.

Also, a notable thing in this chapter is the way we created a `view` class and then extended it with two child view classes. Don't forget that your models, collections, and views have the `extend` method, just like their Backbone parents. You can use this to your advantage when you find yourself creating two or more extremely similar components.

Finally, remember that discarding views is about more than just deleting its DOM elements. It's important to do it properly, by calling the view's `remove` method. However, as we saw, it's more than just that. When listening for events in the view's `initialize` method, it's better to use `this.listenTo` than `this.model.on` or `this.collection.on`. This way, the view can unhook these events when we remove it.

After creating this `events` dashboard, you might look at it and think that it makes a neat calendar. However, we can do much better for a calendar. We'll build that in the next chapter.

4
Building a Calendar

We're going to build a calendar in this chapter. You might think that's what we built in the last chapter, but this one is going to be different; it will be like a very boiled-down version of Google Calendar. We'll be able to view a month or a day at a time, and plan events that span a certain number of hours.

In this chapter, we will discuss the following ideas:

- Better application component organization, with only one global variable for the whole application
- Putting model functionality inside model methods
- Using disposable models to encapsulate important information that we don't need to store on the server
- Displaying a single model instance in multiple views

You can begin with the project template, as we have done before. However, we'll be using precompiled templates as we did in the previous chapter, and we'll also be separating our code into `models.js`, `views.js`, and `router.js`. You may choose to copy the previous project and clear out the custom code instead, so that you'll have the `Gruntfile.js` file that we created last time.

Planning our application

Once again, we'll begin by planning our application. Our primary model will be the `Event` model. It has the same name as the model we created in the last chapter, but it's a bit different. This one will have a title, date, and start time and end time. We'll allow multiple events in one day, but events cannot overlap (because we can't be at two events at one time). Then, we'll also create a `Calendar` collection class to hold our events.

Building a Calendar

Our application will have two screens. The first will be a month view, in a standard, tabular, wall-calendar style. Then, a click on one of the days in that view will switch us to a day view, which will give the hour-by-hour breakdown of events for that day. This will also be the screen from which we can create new events.

Creating the model and collection

Let's start with the `Event` model class, which will go in the `models.js` file of the `public` folder. Separating our code into multiple files is a good first step for organization, but we can go one step further. Previously, each of our classes has been referenced by its own global variable. You probably know that this isn't a really wise technique. If we're using other libraries, frameworks, or plugins, we don't want two components to use the same variable name and mess up the works. In this application, we're going to put all our classes safely inside a single global object. So, we start the `models.js` file with the following code:

```
window.App = window.App || {};
App.Models = {};
```

The first line may seem a bit tricky; why not just use `var App = {};`? Well, the technique I've used here allows us to not worry about the order our files are loaded in the browser. This line first checks to see whether `window.App` exists. If it does, it assigns it to itself (basically, it does nothing). If it doesn't exist, we can be sure that this is the first of our files to load, and so we create it as a blank object. This technique will work as long as we begin all our custom JavaScript files in this application in that way.

The next line creates a `Models` property. Our model and collection classes will be properties of this object.

Now, we're ready to create our `Event` model class, like this:

```
App.Models.Event = Backbone.Model.extend({});
```

We're going to start with a basic model, but we'll be coming back to add a lot of functionality to it. As I mentioned earlier, putting model functionality inside model methods is one of the most important action points discussed in this chapter.

We also have our collection class, which is this code:

```
App.Models.Calendar = Backbone.Collection.extend({
  model: App.Models.Event,
  url: "/events",
});
```

There's nothing new or unique here. Notice that we do need to refer to our model class by its full name as a property, because it's not a global variable anymore.

There's actually one more model that we need to create; however, this model isn't one that we're going to store instances of on the server, or allow our users to know about; it's just a class that we're going to use internally, to make some of our view code simpler. Remember, we're making a calendar; this means that we're going to need a lot of information about each month that we display: the name of the month, the number of days, and the day of the week that the month starts on, just to name a few things. So, we're going to create a `Month` model class, and use this to keep track of all of this data. The following is the code for the `Month` model class:

```javascript
App.Models.Month = Backbone.Model.extend({
  defaults: {
    year : moment().year(),
    month: moment().month()
  },
  initialize: function (options) {
    var m = this.moment();
    this.set('name', m.format('MMMM'));
    this.set('days', m.daysInMonth());
    this.set('weeks', Math.ceil((this.get('days') + m.day()) /
      7));
  },
  moment: function () {
    return moment([this.get('year'), this.get('month')]);
  }
});
```

> I want to make it clear that we don't need to use a `Backbone` model class here. A simple JavaScript constructor function, with a few methods on the prototype, would be sufficient. However, since we're working with Backbone, we'll create a model class so we can see how to use a model that has a disposable data wrapper of sorts.

We've included the `defaults` property, not so much because we expect to need `defaults`, but as a simple way of documenting what properties we expect the `options` object we pass to the `Month` constructor to have. When we create a `Month` instance, we need to give it a year and a month, both as numbers. As you might expect, we're using the Moment library heavily in this application, because we're going to do a lot of the date math. Remember that the Moment library uses zero-indexed values for month numbers, so, January is 0, and December is 11.

Building a Calendar

In the `initialize` method, we start by calling the `moment` method, which you can see at the bottom of the class. This method simply returns a new `moment` object. The `moment` constructor can take an array with time values (year, month, date, hour, and so on). We only need `year` and `month`, so we're passing it only these two values. The rest of the values will default to their earliest possible values, so this `moment` object will be for midnight on the first day of our month. That's perfect.

So, back in the `initialize` method, we call the `moment` method. Then, we set a few other properties that our `Month` object will need: the string name of the month, the number of days in the month, and the number of weeks in the month. The last property will be important when we render the month table; we'll need to know how many table rows we need. We can find the number of weeks for the month by adding the number of days in the month to the day value from the `moment` object. This will be a numerical value for the day of the week that the first day of the month falls on. Handily, this is also the number of days from the previous month that we need to pad the beginning of the month with. We then divide this number by 7, and round up.

With these classes in place, we're ready to start the router, so open the `router.js` file from the `public` directory. As in the `models.js` file, we'll start with the following line:

```
window.App = window.App || {};
```

Then, we'll write the router class, which will initially render the page for the user:

```
App.Router = Backbone.Router.extend({
  initialize: function (options) {
    this.main = options.main;
    this.calendar = options.calendar;
    App.Router.navigate = this.navigate.bind(this);
  },
  routes: {
    '': 'month',
    ':year/:month': 'month'
  },
  month: function (year, month) {
    var c = this.clean(year, month);

    this.main.html(new App.Views.Month({
      collection: this.calendar,
      model: new App.Models.Month({ year: c[0], month: c[1] })
    }).render().el);
  }
});
```

As in our previous applications, our router constructor expects to receive a main element that our views will render in, and a collection object that we call `calendar`. We make these local in our `initialize` method. We also make a bound copy of the router's `navigate` method so that our views can change routes. This time, we do this by making it a class property of the `Router` class.

Next, we have our routes. Things are a bit different this time, in that both routes will call the same method: `month`. The second one makes sense; any route of the pattern `/year/month` will show that month. However, we want the root route to show the current month; that's why it calls the same method.

Then, the `month` method takes the year and month parameters and passes them to a `clean` function to make sure they are usable. This will return an array with year and month values that we can use. What about the root route, which doesn't have those parameters? The clean method will take care of that. After that, we can put a new `App.Views.Month` view into our main element. This view will take two properties: the `calendar` collection and a `Month` model. We create a `Month` instance, passing it the year and month from the cleaned array.

The `clean` method is pretty simple:

```
clean: function (year, month, day) {
  var now = moment();
  year  = parseInt(year, 10)                || now.year();
  month = (parseInt(month, 10) - 1) % 12    || now.month();
  day   = parseInt(day, 10)                 || now.day();
  return [year, month, day];
}
```

The function takes three parameters: `year`, `month`, and `day`. These will be strings, because that's how they come from the route. Each one will be parsed as an integer, but it is possible that one of these won't parse to a number. If that's the case, we'll get the current year, month, or day from a `moment` object. Then, we'll return an array with the numbers we need. These built-in defaults mean that the root route will get the current year and month. It also has an interesting side effect; the route `/what/4` will show April of the current year.

So, with the router in place, we can go over to the `index.ejs` file in the `views` folder. You'll want to start by making sure all our scripts are in place. Don't forget to get the Moment library, as we did in the previous chapter, and add `models.js`, `views.js`, and `router.js`. Finally, let's instantiate the router, as shown in the following code:

```
<script>
  var r = new App.Router({
    main: $("#main"),
```

```
    calendar: new App.Models.Calendar([])
  });

  Backbone.history.start({ pushState: true });
</script>
```

Notice that when we create our Calendar, we put in an empty array. Normally, this is where we would get models from the server, but we're going to do it a bit differently this time. Let's hardcode some sample data right here. This way, we can focus on the frontend code for now. We'll get the backend stuff soon enough. So, inside that array, add some models, as shown in the following lines of code:

```
{ "title": "event one", "date": "2014-01-06", "startTime":
  "10:00", "endTime": "12:00", "id": 1 },
{ "title": "event two", "date": "2014-01-08", "startTime":
  "00:00", "endTime": "24:00", "id": 2 },
{ "title": "event three", "date": "2014-01-09", "startTime":
  "18:00", "endTime": "21:00", "id": 3 }
```

You'll probably want to change the dates to be current when you're reading this. This is because the calendar will default to showing the current month, so you'll be able to see these events.

There's one more thing to do in the `index.ejs` file; we can't really get a nice-looking calendar without doing a bit of styling, so we're going to do just that—add the following line in the head of the file:

```
<link rel="stylesheet" href="/style.css" />
```

We'll add this style sheet file later. Now, we're ready to create our views.

Creating the month view

The month view will display the month as a table, just like a wall calendar. Events will show within the cell of the appropriate day. This will require several nested views, so let's begin with the `Month` view. Here's how we start:

```
App.Views.Month = Backbone.View.extend({
  template: JST.month,
  render: function () {
    this.el.innerHTML = this.template(this.model.toJSON());
    var weeks = this.model.get('weeks');

    for (var i = 0; i < weeks; i++) {
      this.$("tbody").append(new App.Views.WeekRow({
```

```
        week : i,
        model : this.model,
        collection: this.collection
      }).render().el);
    }
    return this;
  }
});
```

We'll give this class a `JST.month` template and a `render` method. Before we discuss the `render` method, let's take a look at the template file.

> Notice how we're not naming our views `MonthView` and `WeekRowView`, as we had before. Instead, they're just `Month` and `WeekRow`. We're doing this because we'll have to refer to them as `App.Views.Month` or `App.Views.MonthTable` anyway, so there's no need to say `View` twice.

As you can tell, the following code will go in the `month.html` file, in the `template` folder:

```
<h1>
  <span class="prev"> &larr; Previous Month </span>
  {{name}} {{year}}
  <span class="next"> Next Month &rarr; </span>
</h1>
<table class='month'>
  <thead>
    <tr>
      <th>Sunday</th>
      <th>Monday</th>
      <th>Tuesday</th>
      <th>Wednesday</th>
      <th>Thursday</th>
      <th>Friday</th>
      <th>Saturday</th>
    </tr>
  </thead>
  <tbody>
  </tbody>
</table>
```

There's a heading at the top, which will have the name and year for the month we are displaying. There will also be buttons to move to the next and previous months. Underneath that, there will be a `<table>` element, which will display the month. Don't forget to run `grunt` to compile the template.

Building a Calendar

Now, look back at the `render` method. We start by rendering our template, passing to it the data from the `Month` model. Then, we get the `weeks` property of the `month` model; this tells us how many rows our table needs (one row per week). Finally, we loop that many times, appending a new `WeekRow` view to the `<tbody>` element each time. A `WeekRow` instance takes three properties: the number of the week (0 for the first, 1 for the second, and so on), the `month` model, and the `calendar` collection.

The last step for this view is to make our next month and previous month buttons work. Add the following events property to the `Month` view:

```
events: {
  'click .prev': 'prev',
  'click .next': 'next'
},
```

These event listeners need the `prev` and `next` methods to work, so let's add those methods to this class too:

```
prev: function () {
  var route = this.model.moment()
    .subtract(1, 'month').format('YYYY/MM');
  App.Router.navigate(route, { trigger: true });
},
next: function () {
  var route = this.model.moment()
    .add(1, 'month').format('YYYY/MM');
  App.Router.navigate(route, { trigger: true });
}
```

When the `<span>` elements are clicked on, we'll call the `next` or `prev` methods, respectively. Both methods get the next or previous month by adding or subtracting one month to the `moment` instance of the `month` model. Then, we format it as necessary and trigger the route change.

Building the week row

The `WeekRow` view, which we're about to create, is more complex than what we've done so far. Before we look at the code, think for a minute about a week row in the table. There are three cases. The first week of a month will probably need a few blank cells before the first day, the middle weeks will have seven days, and the last week will have only the days that are left. This will require a little extra code in the `render` method. Here's the class:

```
App.Views.WeekRow = Backbone.View.extend({
  tagName: 'tr',
  initialize: function (options) {
```

```
      if (options) {
        this.week = options.week;
      }
    },
    render: function () {
      var month = this.model;

      if (this.week === 0) {
        var firstDay = month.moment().day();
        for (var i = 0; i < firstDay; i++) {
          this.$el.append("<td>");
        }
      }

      month.weekDates(this.week).forEach(function (date) {
        date = month.moment().date(date);
        this.$el.append(new App.Views.DayCell({
          model: date,
          collection: this.collection.onDate(date)
        }).render().el);
      }, this);

      return this;
    }
  });
```

The element of each `WeekRow` view is `<tr>`. In the `initialize` method, we get the `week` option; as you know, the `model` and `collection` properties come automatically. In the `render` method, we start by creating a `month` variable, just as a shortcut to this model. Next, we look for our first special case: the first week. If we're creating the row for the first week, we first need to find what day of the week the month starts on. We can do this with `month.moment().day()`. The `day` method returns the zero-based index of the day of the week. This is exactly what we need, because if the month starts on a Sunday, we'll get a 0, which is the number of blank cells we'll need, and so on.

So, the `firstDay` variable is the number of blank cells we need. We then loop, appending as many empty `<td>` elements as we need.

Building a Calendar

The next step is to add the right number of `DayCell` views to the `WeekRow` view. This sounds simple; but it's actually a little tricky, for two reasons. First, because the first week probably won't have seven days, we'll have to figure out how many it should have. The second reason is that we'll need to do a bit of math to get the date number for that cell. To make the view code simpler here, we will create a method in our `App.Models.Month` class. The `weekDates` method will take a week number and return an array with the dates for that week. In the `models.js` file in the `Month` class, add the following method:

```
weekDates: function (num) {
  var days  = 7,
      dates = [],
      start = this.moment().day();

  if (num === 0) {
    days -= start;
    start = 0;
  }

  var date = num*7 + 1 - start,
      end  = date + days;

  for (; date < end; date++) {
    if (date > this.get('days')) continue;
    dates.push(date);
  }
  return dates;
},
```

We start by creating a few variables; the number of days in a week, an array of dates to return at the end, and the day of the week that this month starts on. Then, if we're working on the first week here, we subtract `start` from `day`, because the first week doesn't have seven days in it. Then, we set `start` to `0`, for later use.

Next, we do a bit of math to get `date`, the first date for this week. We multiply the week number by 7, and then add 1, so it isn't zero-indexed. Finally, we subtract `start` to correct for a week that doesn't start on Sunday. Lastly, we create the `end` variable, which we'll use to stop the loop.

Then, we loop from `date` to `end` and push the incrementing `date` into the `dates` array. It's important that we compare `date` to the number of days this month should have and not push it into the array if `date` is greater than this value.

Finally, we return the `dates` array.

Now, if you look back at the `WeekRow` view's `render` method, things should make more sense. We get the array of dates for that week and loop over it with the native `forEach` method. For each `date` variable, we create an actual `moment` object. We get the month's `moment` object and mutate it by calling the `date` method, which sets the date (day of the month) on the object. We then pass that `date` variable and part of the calendar collection to a new `DayCell` view, which we render and append to the element.

Notice that I said "part of the calendar collection"; we're calling the `onDate` method, which returns a new `Calendar` collection instance with only the events on the date we pass to the method. This `onDate` method goes in the `models.js` file in the `Calendar` collection. However, before we get there, we need to create another method; this is a method of the `Event` class:

```
start: function () {
  return moment(this.get('date') + " " + this.get('startTime'));
},
```

The `Event` class's `start` method returns the new `moment` instance for the start time of the event. As you can see, we get this by concatenating the date and start time of the event, and then passing the resulting string to the `moment` function.

We'll use this method in the `onDate` method, as follows:

```
onDate: function (date) {
  return new App.Models.Calendar(this.filter(function (model) {
    return model.start().isSame(date, 'day');
  }));
}
```

This calls the collection's `filter` method, and it only returns models whose dates are the same as the one passed into the `onDate` method. Then, the array that `filter` returns is passed to a new `Calendar` instance.

> Note that we don't need the start time of the event for this purpose, just the date on which the event occurs on is enough. However, we'll be using the `start` method in other places.

Building a Calendar

Building the day cells

Things are coming together nicely! We're now ready for that `DayCell` view class that we're using within our `WeekRow` views. Let's start with the template in the `dayCell.html` file, in the `templates` folder. The following is the code for this template:

```
<span class="date">{{num}}</span>
<ul>
  <% titles.forEach(function (title) { %>
    <li>{{ title }}</li>
  <% }); %>
</ul>
```

We're doing something new in this template. We've got a bit of logic. Previously, we only used the double curly braces to delimit values to interpolate. However, we can use the `<%` and `%>` delimiters to run any JavaScript file we want. Of course, it isn't smart to do this for a lot of code, but we're just using it to loop over an array. Since every cell represents a day on the calendar, each could have several events. We'll pass this template an array of the titles for those events. Then, inside the template, we will loop over the titles and add a list item for each one.

How about the view class? It is shown in the following code:

```
App.Views.DayCell = Backbone.View.extend({
  tagName: 'td',
  template: JST.dayCell,
  events: {
    'click': 'switchToDayView'
  },
  render: function () {
    this.el.innerHTML = this.template({
      num: this.model.date(),
      titles: this.collection.pluck('title')
    });
    return this;
  },
  switchToDayView: function () {
    App.Router.navigate(this.model.format('YYYY/MM/DD'), {
      trigger: true
    });
  }
});
```

Every instance will be a `<td>` element. When rendering, we'll pass the date number, which we get from the moment instance we passed in as the model. We'll also use the collection's `pluck` method to get a single property from every instance in the collection; here, we're plucking the `title` property from each `Event` instance.

Also, notice the `events` object. We're listening for a click on the root element. When that happens, we'll use `App.Router.navigate` to get to the individual day view. We get the route by formatting the `moment` instance.

Believe it or not, we now have enough in place to actually see something in the browser. Compile your templates, start up your server, and load up `http://localhost:3000/` in the browser. You should see something like the following screenshot:

← Previous Month		January 2014			Next Month →	
Sunday	Monday	Tuesday	Wednesday	Thursday	Friday	Saturday
			1	2	3	4
5	6 • event one	7	8 • event two	9 • event three	10	11
12	13	14	15	16	17	18
19	20	21	22	23	24	25
26	27	28	29	30	31	

It's all right, but not that pretty. We can fix that, however. Remember the link to the `style.css` file that we put in the `index.ejs` file? Create that file in the `public` directory now.

We'll start with the following code:

```
body {
  font-family: sans-serif;
  margin: 0;
}
```

This will set the font and margin for the whole page. Then, we move on to view-specific styling:

```
.prev, .next {
  font-size: 60%;
}
```

Building a Calendar

```
h1 {
  text-align: center;
  margin: 0;
}
```

This is for the `Month` view's header. It will shrink the next and previous buttons just a bit, and center the header on the screen.

To give our table a border, we'll add the following code:

```
table {
  border-collapse: collapse;
}

td {
  border: 1px solid #ccc;
}
```

These are for any table; so this styling will be used on the individual day page, where we will have another table. However, we need to do a few things specifically for the month table, as shown here:

```
table.month {
  table-layout: fixed;
  width: 1000px;
  height: 600px;
  margin: auto;
}
```

You'll recall that we added the `month` class to our month's `<table>` element. We're taking advantage of that here. If you aren't familiar with the `table-layout` attribute, it basically makes sure that all of our columns are of the same width.

Next, we want to style the individual cells. This is how that's done:

```
table.month td {
  position: relative;
  vertical-align: top;
}
table.month td .date {
  font-weight: bold;
  position: absolute;
  font-size: 100px;
  bottom: -23px;
```

```
right: -4px;
color: #ececec;
z-index: -1;
}
```

We have to position the <td> elements relatively so that we can position the <span> elements with the date class absolutely inside them, for effect. This is an old trick that will let us position the <span> elements absolutely in their parent (a <td> element), instead of in the whole page. The rest of this is just for looks.

The user will click on these <td> elements to take them to the individual day pages, so let's give the user a little feedback when they hover over a cell, shall we?

```
table.month td:hover {
  cursor: pointer;
}
table.month td:hover .date {
  color: #ccc;
}
```

The last order of business is the unordered list of event titles that each cell will have. Here's the styling for them:

```
td ul {
  list-style-type: none;
  padding: 0;
  margin: 0;
  font-size: 80%;
  height: 100%;
  overflow: scroll;
}

td li {
  padding: 3px 10px;
  margin: 2px 0;
  background: rgba(223, 240, 216, 0.5);
  border: 1px solid rgb(223, 240, 216);
}
```

Notice that the <ul> element has overflow: scroll. This way, if a single day has many events, it won't make extra table rows at all; it will just make the rows scroll.

Building a Calendar

With all this styling in place, you can refresh the page and see what is shown in the following screenshot:

Much better, don't you think?

Creating the individual day screen

Right now, when we click on a cell in our table, our route will change, but nothing will change on the screen. This isn't because we aren't triggering a change with our route-swap; we are. We just haven't created that method in our router yet. So, that's our next stop.

In the `router.js` file, add the following line to the `Router` class's `routes` property:

```
':year/:month/:day': 'day'
```

Then, we need the `day` method that we're calling there:

```
day: function (year, month, day) {
  var date = moment(this.clean(year, month, day));
  this.main.html(new App.Views.Day({
    date: date,
    collection: this.calendar
  }).render().el);
},
```

[116]

This method renders the `App.Views.Day` view, the top-level view for the individual pages. It takes a Moment object for the date we're displaying and the collection of events. We get a `moment` object for the date by passing the clean-up properties to the `moment` method.

> You might expect us to limit this collection to only events for the specific date the user is looking at with our `onDate` method. However, we're passing in the whole collection, because this is the `Calendar` instance to which we want to add new event instances. This is because our month view uses the `this.calendar` collection, and we want to make sure any event we add in a day view will show up in the month view immediately, with no page refresh required.

The `App.Views.Day` view is a wrapper view. It holds three main views:

- `DayTable`: This provides the hour-by-hour breakdown of the day
- `Details`: This provides a closer look at whichever event the user is currently hovering over
- `CreateEvent`: This provides a form used to create a new event

We'll use CSS to split the screen in two vertically. On the left, we'll have the `DayTable` view; on the right, we'll have the `Details` view and the `CreateEvent` view. The job of the `Day` view class is to put these three views in place.

We'll start with the template, by adding the following code in the `day.html` file, in the `templates` folder:

```
<h1> {{ date }} </h1>
<p class='back'>&larr; Back to Month View </p>
<div class="splitView">
</div>
```

We'll show the date at the top of the page, with a link to go back to the month view. Then, we have a `<div>` element with the `splitView` class.

We interrupt this code to give you the following CSS code for that `splitView` class. Put this code in the `style.css` file:

```
.splitView > * {
  width: 45%;
  margin: 2%;
  float: left;
}
```

Building a Calendar

Now, let's start the `Day` view class:

```
App.Views.Day = Backbone.View.extend({
  template: JST.day,
  initialize: function (options) {
    this.date = options.date;
  },
  events: {
    'click .back' : 'backToMonth'
  },
  render: function () {
    this.el.innerHTML = this.template({
      date: this.date.format("MMMM D, YYYY")
    });
    this.$('.splitView').append(new App.Views.DayTable({
      date: this.date,
      collection: this.collection
    }).render().el);
    return this;
  },
  backToMonth: function () {
    App.Router.navigate(this.date.format('/YYYY/MM'), {
      trigger: true
    });
  }
});
```

There's more, but we'll start with this. We set the template. In the `initialize` method, we get the `date` property. Then, we wire up an event. When the back button is clicked on, we'll call the `backToMonth` method, which will change the route back to the month screen in the same way we switched to the day screen.

Then, inside the `render` method, we put together part of the solution. We get the `<div class='splitView'>` element and append a new `DayTable` view instance. This view takes the date for this page and the collection of events.

This `DayTable` view is probably the most unique view that we'll have created up to this point in the book. As you expect, it will be an HTML table, with each row representing an hour of the day. The left column will be the time, and the right column will show the title of the event, if one is occurring during that hour. The tricky part is that most events will probably span more than one hour, so we'll have to figure out where to start and stop events.

First, how about the template for this view? Store the following code in the dayTable.html file in the templates folder:

```
<thead>
  <tr>
    <th> Time </th>
    <th> Event </th>
  </tr>
</thead>
<tbody>
</tbody>
```

As with our other table-based views, the template is the core of a table. You can see the two columns: time and events.

We'll take this view class in parts. The DayTable view's code is as follows:

```
App.Views.DayTable = Backbone.View.extend({
  tagName: 'table',
  className: 'day',
  template: JST.dayTable,
  events: {
    'mouseover tr.highlight td.event': 'hover',
    'mouseout  tr.highlight td.event': 'hover'
  },
  initialize: function (options) {
    this.date = options.date;
    this.listenTo(this.collection, 'add', this.addEvent)
    this.listenTo(this.collection, 'destroy', this.destroyEvent)
    this.hours = {};
  }
});
```

The element for this view will be a table with the day class. We're listening for two events on this view; any table row that has an event will have the highlight class, and every table cell in the second column will have the event class. When the user moves over or out of one of the cells with an event title in it, we'll call the hover method to highlight that event.

In the initialize method, we'll get the date option, and then listen to our collection for models being added or destroyed. It's important we know when this happens, so we can add or remove them from the table. We'll write the addEvent and destroyEvent methods to do this.

Building a Calendar

Finally, we're creating an `hours` object, which we'll use to keep track of the `Hour` views, each of which will be a row in our table. We used this technique in the previous chapter, so we could easily sort the rows in our table. This time, we're doing it because when we want to add or remove an event from the day, we don't actually want to add or remove the `Hour` view; we just want to add or remove the event title from that view. You'll see how this works soon.

With these pieces in place, we can move on to the `render` method:

```
render: function () {
  this.el.innerHTML = this.template();

  for (var i = 0; i < 24; i++) {
    var time = moment(i, "H").format('h:mm A');
    this.hours[time] = new App.Views.Hour({ time: time });
    this.$('tbody').append(this.hours[time].render().el);
  }
  this.collection.onDate(this.date).forEach(this.addEvent, this);
  return this;
},
```

This should make a lot of sense. We render our template first. Then, we loop 24 times; each time, we create an `App.Views.Hour` view instance, store it in the `this.hours` property for later use, and then append it to the `<tbody>` element. We can get the time text by creating a `moment` object with our incrementing variable; since just `i` isn't an understood date format, we need to pass `"H"` as a second parameter, so it knows that this is just the hour. Then, we format it as a nice time string. We use this time string as the property name when storing the view instance in `this.hours`. At this point (if we had an `Hour` view class), we would have a complete table, with a row for each hour of the day. However, all rows would be empty; we haven't rendered any events yet. That's why we next filter `collection` for this day's events, and loop over them, calling the `addEvent` method for each one.

The tricky part, as I mentioned earlier, is that one `Event` model instance will probably need to span several `Hour` view instances. To write the `addEvent` method, we're first going to add an `hours` method to the `Event` model class.

Add the following code to the `App.Models.Event` class in the `models.js` file:

```
hours: function () {
  var hours = [],
      start = this.start(),
      end   = this.end();
```

```
  while (start.isBefore(end)) {
    hours.push(start.format('h:mm A'));
    start.add(1, 'hour');
  }
  return hours;
}
```

We start by creating the currently empty `hours` array, which we'll eventually return. Then, we get the model's `start` and `end` time. We've already created the `start` method, but we need to create the `end` method. It's a little more complex than the `start` method. Add the following code to the same class that we're working on:

```
end: function () {
  var endTime = moment(this.get('date') + " " +
    this.get('endTime'));
  if (this.get('endTime') === '00:00') {
    endTime.add(1, 'day');
  }
  return endTime;
},
```

As in the `start` method, we create the `moment` object by concatenating `date` and `endTime`. However, there's one special case; if the event ends at midnight, it is technically ending on the next day. However, our `moment` object will be pointing to midnight of the event date, which is the first hour of the day. So, if the end time is midnight, we'll add one day to the `moment` object. Then, we return.

Let's get back to the `hours` method. After getting the `start` and `end` times, we can loop when the `start` time is before the `end` time. We'll push a time string into the `hours` array; notice that we're formatting it as we did in the table. Then, we add an hour to the `start` object. Eventually, `start` will be the same as `end`, and the loop will stop. Then, we'll return that `hours` array.

With this method, if we have an event that goes on from 1:00 P.M. to 4:00 P.M., we'll get the following array:

`['1:00 PM', '2:00 PM', '3:00 PM']`

You may think that we want 4:00 P.M. in there as well, but we don't. This is because each `Hour` view instance represents a full hour; so, the hour with the label `1:00 PM` refers to the hour from 1:00 P.M. to 2:00 P.M.

Building a Calendar

With this method in place, we can go back to `App.Views.DayTable` and write the `addEvent` method. Remember that we're calling this method for each event that we need to display in the table. The following is the code for the `addEvent` method:

```
addEvent: function (evt) {
  evt.hours().forEach(function (hour) {
    this.hours[hour].displayEvent(evt);
  }, this);
},
destroyEvent: function (evt) {
  evt.hours().forEach(function (hour) {
    this.hours[hour].removeEvent();
  }, this);
},
```

The `addEvent` and `destroyEvent` methods are very similar, so we're looking at them together. In both cases, we get the array of hours for the given event, and then loop over it with the native array's `forEach` method. For each hour, we get the view from `this.hours`. In the `addEvent` method, we call the view's `displayEvent` method, passing the event along to that method. In the `destroyEvent` method, we just call the view's `removeEvent` method; there is no need to pass the event along.

Before we get to the `Hour` view class, let's write the last method of this class: `hover`. This method is called whenever we move the mouse over or out of one of the event titles in our table. Here's the code for the `hover` method:

```
hover: function (e) {
  var id = parseInt(e.currentTarget.getAttribute('data-id'), 10),
    evt = this.collection.get(id);

  evt.hours().forEach(function (hour) {
    this.hours[hour].hover();
  }, this);

  this.collection.trigger("hover", evt);
}
```

Since this method is triggered by a DOM event, we'll get a DOM event object as our parameter (actually, since we're using jQuery, it will be a jQuery-wrapped DOM event object). The first order of business in this method is to figure out what `Event` model instance the row we're hovering over is a part of. We can do that by getting the ID of the `Event` instance. The `currentTarget` property of that DOM event object will be the element that caused the event to be triggered; later, when we render it, we'll give it the `data-id` property that we get here. Since we're listening for mouse events on the `<td class='event'>` element, that's what the `currentTarget` property will be.

Once we know what the ID is, we can call the collection's `get` method to find the model with that ID. Once we get that event model, we can get the hours for that event with `hours`. We then loop over those hours to find the `Hour` view instances that are displaying this event, and call their `hover` methods. Finally, we'll trigger a `hover` event on our collection, passing the event model as a parameter. This is something new; so far, we've only listened for built-in events (such as `add` and `destroy`) on our models and collections. However, we can also use the `trigger` method to create our own events. We can call our events whatever we want; we're calling this one `hover`. Elsewhere, we will listen for this event and perform an action when it happens.

You might think that we should be listening for these mouse events in the `Hour` view, since that's the view that will be affected. However, that won't work in this case, because we need to change multiple `Hour` views when a single one is hovered over.

We're finally ready to create the `Hour` view. Its template is very simple. Put the following lines in the `hour.html` file of the `templates` folder:

```
<td class='time'> {{ time }}</td>
<td class='event'></td>
```

The template only expects the time; we'll fill in the event name (if one is required) from the JavaScript file.

Now, in our `views.js` file, add the following code:

```
App.Views.Hour = Backbone.View.extend({
  tagName: 'tr',
  template: JST.hour,
  initialize: function (options) {
    this.time = options.time;
  },
  render: function () {
    this.el.innerHTML = this.template({ time: this.time });
    return this;
  },
  displayEvent: function (model) {
    this.$el.addClass("highlight");
    this.$('.event').attr('data-id', model.get('id'));
    this.$(".event").text(model.get('title'));
  },
  removeEvent: function () {
    this.$el.removeClass('highlight');
    this.$('.event').removeAttr('data-id');
    this.$('.event').text('');
  },
```

Building a Calendar

```
    hover: function () {
      this.$el.toggleClass('hover');
    }
  });
```

As we know, this view will be a `<tr>` element. In the `initialize` method, we get the `time` property. The `render` method is extra simple in this case, because a lot of the action takes place in the `displayEvent` and `removeEvent` methods. As we saw, the `addEvent` method in the `App.Views.DayTable` view class will call this `displayEvent` method, passing it the `event` model that occurs at that hour. In the `displayEvent` method, we'll add the `highlight` class to that hour, add the `data-id` attribute, and put the title text into the `<td>` element with the `event` class. When removing an event, we do the opposite; remove the `highlight` class and the `data-id` attribute, and set the text to nothing.

Finally, there's the `hover` method. This simply toggles the `hover` class on the `<tr>` element. Now, before checking this out in the browser, let's add a little bit of styling, add this to the `style.css` file:

```
table.day tr.highlight td.event {
  background: rgb(217, 237, 247);
  color: rgb(53, 103, 132);
}
table.day tr.highlight.hover td.event {
  background: rgb(252, 248, 227);
  color: rgb(53, 103, 132);
}
table.day td {
  padding: 4px 0;
  width: 100px;
  text-align: center;
}
table.day td.event {
  width: 500px;
}
```

Chapter 4

It's nothing much; it just adds some color and spacing to the table. With all this in place, we can now load up our day view. You should see something like what is shown in the following screenshot:

> **January 6, 2014**
>
> ← Back to Month View
>
> | Time | Event |
> |---|---|
> | 12:00 AM | |
> | 1:00 AM | |
> | 2:00 AM | |
> | 3:00 AM | |
> | 4:00 AM | |
> | 5:00 AM | |
> | 6:00 AM | |
> | 7:00 AM | |
> | 8:00 AM | |
> | 9:00 AM | |
> | 10:00 AM | event one |
> | 11:00 AM | event one |
> | 12:00 PM | |
> | 1:00 PM | |
> | 2:00 PM | |
> | 3:00 PM | |

Not a bad look, eh? If you hover over either of the colored cells, you should see both of them switch to the yellow background.

That's the left half of our split view. Now, it's time to create the right-hand side. You'll recall that the right-hand side will have the `details` view and the creation form. Let's begin with the `details` view.

Once again, we'll start with the template: `details.html` in the `templates` folder. Its code is as follows:

```
<h2>{{ title }}</h2>
<% if (start) { %>
<p> {{ start }} - {{ end }} ({{ duration }}) <p>
<p><button> Delete Event </button>
<% } %>
```

Building a Calendar

We're again using a bit of logic in the template. If the `start` value is not just an empty string, we'll render the two paragraphs. We'll show the `start` and `end` times for the event, as well as the duration. Finally, we'll have a **Delete Event** button, which will allow us to delete events.

The reason we're using this bit of logic is because when the page is first loaded, the user won't be hovering over any event. In that case, we'll show a default instruction.

Back in the `views.js` file, we'll create the following view class:

```
App.Views.Details = Backbone.View.extend({
  template: JST.details,
  events: {
    'click button': 'delete'
  },
  initialize: function () {
    this.data = {
      title: "Hover over an event to see details",
      start: '',
      end: '',
      duration: ''
    };
    this.render();
  },
  render: function () {
    this.el.innerHTML = this.template(this.data);
    return this;
  },
  changeModel: function (model) {
    this.model = model;
    var s = this.model.start(),
        e = this.model.end();
    this.data = {
      title: model.get('title'),
      start: s.format('h:mm A'),
      end: e.format('h:mm A'),
      duration: e.diff(s, 'hour') + ' hours'
    }
    return this.render();
  },
  delete: function () {
    this.model.destroy();
  }
});
```

We'll do something a bit different in the `initialize` method this time. First, we'll create some default filler data, called `this.data`, for the view, which will be displayed before the user first hovers over an hour. Then, we'll call the `render` method right away in the `initialize` method. This isn't a pattern you see very often, but there's really no reason not to do it. In the `render` method, we take that data and render the template. The important method in this class is the `changeModel` method. It takes a model as a property and recreates the `data` property from that. We put the `start` and `end` times in variables, so we don't have to call those methods twice. Then, we re-render the view, by calling the `render` method again.

You might wonder why we assign `this.model` in the `changeModel` method. This is because we'll need it in the `delete` method. We need to get a reference to the currently displayed model, so we can destroy it when the delete button is clicked on (you can see that we're connecting to the `delete` method in the `events` property). Of course, for the destruction of the model to work, we'll need to write a server method; we'll get to that.

But first, we want to render this view. To do this, go back to the `render` method in the `App.Views.Day` view class. So far, this method only creates a `DayTable` view (the left-hand side of the screen). Add the following code to that method:

```
var div = this.$('div').append('<div>')

this.details = new App.Views.Details();
div.append(this.details.el);
```

First, we create a `<div>` element on the right-hand side of the split view. Then, we create a `Details` view instance and append it to that `div` element. Notice that, since we call the `render` method internally, we don't have to call it here. Also, we keep a reference to the `Details` view instance as `this.details`. This is because we need it in the `showDetails` method, which we'll add as a new method in the `Day` view class. The `showDetails` method's code is as follows:

```
showDetails: function (model) {
  this.details.changeModel(model);
}
```

This just calls the `changeModel` method on the `Details` view. But where does this method get called? Remember that `hover` event that we triggered ourselves, when the user moves over a row? Go back up the `initialize` method of the `Day` view class, because we're going to listen for that event there with this single line of code:

```
this.listenTo(this.collection, 'hover', this.showDetails);
```

Building a Calendar

Great! With all this in place, you can test it out by hovering over an event; the `details` view should look something like what is shown in the following screenshot:

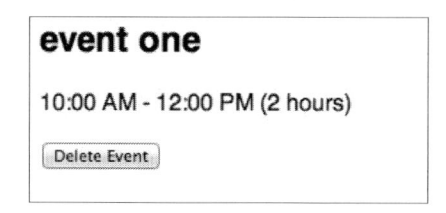

event one

10:00 AM - 12:00 PM (2 hours)

[Delete Event]

We only have one view left: the `CreateEvent` view. We'll start with the `createEvent.html` template. Here's its code:

```
<p><input type="text" id="eventTitle" /></p>
<p><input type="time" id="eventStartTime" /></p>
<p><input type="time" id="eventEndTime" /></p>
<p><button> Create Event </button></p>
<p class="error"></p>
```

As you can see, it's the insides of a form; the view element will be the `<form>` element itself.

Here's the beginning of the class:

```
App.Views.CreateEvent = Backbone.View.extend({
  tagName: 'form',
  template: JST.createEvent,
  initialize: function (options) {
    this.date = options.date;
  },
  events: {
    'click button': 'createEvent'
  },
  render: function () {
    this.el.innerHTML = this.template();
    return this;
  }
});
```

You understand all this by now; even the `render` function is simple. In the `initialize` function, we're taking a `date` option, because we'll need to know on what date we're creating an event on. Where the fun starts is in the `createEvent` method. You can see that we're listening for a click on the button in our form and calling the `createEvent` method when it happens.

Chapter 4

Here's that method:

```
createEvent: function (evt) {
  evt.preventDefault();

  var model = new App.Models.Event({
    collection: this.collection.onDate(this.date),
    title: this.$("#eventTitle").val(),
    date: this.date,
    startTime: this.$("#eventStartTime").val(),
    endTime: this.$("#eventEndTime").val()
  });

  if (model.isValid()) {
    this.collection.create(model, { wait: true });
    this.el.reset();
    this.$(".error").text('');
  } else {
    this.$(".error").text(model.validationError);
  }

  return false;
}
```

It's a biggie, I know. We start by preventing the default form submission. Then, we use the data from the form and `date` from the constructor to create a new model instance. When creating a model like this, it isn't saved to the server right away. We either have to call the `save` method on the model or pass it to a collection's `create` method.

You're probably wondering why we're making the `collection` object an attribute of this model instance. This is actually a bit of a hack. The first part of the explanation comes from the second part of the method. You can see that we're calling the model's `isValid` method. Backbone has the ability to do validation on our models. If our attributes don't conform to given patterns, we can prevent them from saving. We're doing it very explicitly here, by calling this method. If the model is valid, we'll save the model to the server by passing it to the collection's `create` method (we pass {wait: true} because our `DayTable` view is listening for additions to the collection, so it can add them to the table; this way, it won't be added until we're sure it has been saved). Then, we clear out the form elements, and remove any error from the error paragraph. That error would occur if the model didn't validate. Instead of saving, we would have displayed the model's `validationError` property in that paragraph.

Right now, we're calling the model's `isValid` method, but we haven't created any validation rules yet. Backbone's validation feature is barebones. In our Event model class, we'll create a method named `validate`. Whenever we try to save a model, this method will be called. As a parameter, the `validate` method will receive an object containing the attributes of the model. Inside the method, we write whatever code we want. If everything checks out, we don't return anything. However, if there's a problem, we can return an error message (it can be a simple string or something more complex). The error message will then be assigned to `model.validationError`.

So, let's write the validation method:

```
validate: function (attrs) {
  if (attrs.collection) {
    var takenHours = _.flatten(attrs.collection.invoke('hours'));

    var hours = this.hours().map(function (x) {
      return takenHours.indexOf(x);
    }).filter(function (x) {
      return x > -1;
    }).length;

    this.unset('collection');

    if (hours > 0) {
      return "You already have an event at that time.";
    }
  }
}
```

This is the second part of the explanation for why we included the `collection` object in our model's attributes. What we need to validate is the `start` and `end` times. If the event we're trying to create overlaps with other events that are already in the calendar, we can't allow the new event to be created. However, from within the model's `validate` method, there's no way to access the collection. So, we pass it as an attribute of the model we're validating, using the `onDate` method to limit it to events on this date. Sure, it's a hack; but it works.

We start by making sure that our attributes include a `collection` attribute. If we have it, the first job is to figure out what hours of the day are already taken. We can find the hours for each event individually by calling the `hours` method we created. We can use the collection's `invoke` method to call that method on all its models; it will return an array of results. Since each result is an array, we have an array of arrays. Then, we can use Underscore's `flatten` method to turn that into a one-dimensional array. The result is an array with all the hours that are already taken.

Next, we do a bit of functional-style programming. We start by calling `this.hours` to get the array of hours during which this event occurs. Then, we map that to the value of `takenHours.indexOf(x)`. This will loop over the hours of this event and get their index in the `takenHours` array. The important bit here is that if an hour isn't in `takenHours`, it will return `-1`. Next, we use the array's `filter` to filter it, only keeping the values that are greater than `-1`. Finally, we get the `length` value of the resulting array. Following this logic, the `hours` variable will be the number of values that overlap between the `takenHours` and `this.hours` arrays.

Then, we'll remove the `collection` property with the `unset` method because we no longer need it.

Finally, if the overlapping hours count is greater than 0, we'll return an error; you already have an event at that time. With this method in place, you can look back at the `createEvent` method and understand exactly what we're doing.

The last step for the `CreateEvent` class is to put it on the screen. Go back to the `render` method of the `App.Views.Day` class and add the following code:

```
div.append(new App.Views.CreateEvent({
  date: this.date.format('YYYY-MM-DD'),
  collection: this.collection
}).render().el);
```

We're putting it in the `div` element that we created to the right-hand side of the split view. As required, we give it the `date` string and the `collection` object, and then render it. Now, our page should look like what is shown in the following screenshot:

Writing the server code

The server code is very simple for this application. First, we need to render the `index.ejs` template with the event models in the database. So, make sure our GET request catch-all looks like the following code:

```
app.get('/*', function (req, res) {
  db.find(function (err, events) {
    res.render("index.ejs", { events: JSON.stringify(events) });
  });
});
```

Now, in the `index.ejs` file of the `views` folder, in the router creation code, remove the dummy records that we put in and replace it with the template data, like this:

```
calendar: new App.Models.Calendar(<%- events %>)
```

Back in the `server.js` file, we need the route that the POST request is sent to when we're creating a new `Event` model. Its code is as follows:

```
app.post('/events', function (req, res) {
  var b = req.body;
  db.insert({
    title: b.title,
    date: b.date,
    startTime: b.startTime,
    endTime: b.endTime
  }, function (err, evt) {
    res.json(evt);
  -});
});
```

We get the request body, and then create our record from its properties. Once we have saved the record, we'll send it back to the server.

Finally, we'll need the route that is called when we destroy a model. This is a DELETE request, and this is what it looks like:

```
app.delete('/events/:id', function (req, res) {
  var id = parseInt(req.params.id, 10);

  db.delete({ id: id }, function () {
    res.json({});
  });
});
```

We get the ID of the record, find the related row, and return an empty response. That's it for the server. With this code in place, you're ready to give it a try. Go to an individual day page and add a few events. You should get something like what is shown in the following screenshot:

You can see all the components in play here; the table of hours, the hover effect, and the details view. You can even see the error message when we try to create an event that overlaps with another.

There's one last step; a nicety, really. If you go back to the month view, you will notice that the events in each day cell don't appear in order of time. Instead, they appear in the order we created them. It would be nice if they appeared in order of occurrence, and this is very simple to do. In the App.Models.Calendar class (in the models.js file), we can write a comparator method to keep things in order:

```
comparator: function (a, b) {
  return a.start().isAfter(b.start());
},
```

We can simply return the result of the moment object's isAfter method to see which should come first; Backbone takes care of the rest.

Summary

We've done a lot of new and interesting things in this chapter. The most difficult part was getting the hover effect. It required us to find all the views that represented a single model instance. Most of the time, in a Backbone application, you'll have a single view representing a model instance at a time. However, as you've seen here, while this is the norm, it certainly isn't the only way possible.

The other neat use of Backbone was the `Month` class that we created. We're really just using it as a handy wrapper; there's no reason we couldn't have written a simple function that returned an object literal. However, the way we've done it shows off the flexibility of Backbone.

The last, but arguably most important, idea from this chapter is the idea of moving appropriate logic into the model class, instead of putting it in the view class. Good examples of this are the `App.Models.Calendar` class's `onDate` method or the `App.Models.Event` class's `hours` method. This is one of the big ideas of the Model-View-Controller pattern. Of course, Backbone isn't strictly MVC, but a lot of the principles still apply. As much as you can, make your model classes fat and your views and routers thin. This doesn't mean putting view or routing logic in the model. It means that any logic that isn't specifically about views or routing should probably be in a model class. For more on this topic, there's a lot of great MVC material online; you could start with `http://dev.tutsplus.com/tutorials/mvc-for-noobs--net-10488`. In the next chapter, we'll take things to a whole new level when we create a real-time, two-way chat application.

5
Building a Chat Application

So far, all the applications that we've built have used plain old Backbone. This isn't to say that we haven't used helper libraries, but that we haven't yet used any libraries that extend Backbone itself. However, such libraries do exist; the Backbone GitHub wiki has a whole list of them (https://github.com/jashkenas/backbone/wiki/Extensions%2C-Plugins%2C-Resources). In this chapter, we'll use one of these libraries to make building this application a little simpler.

We'll be focusing on the following ideas:

- Using a third-party library to make large applications easier to handle
- Doing real-time communication between the server and the client

Outlining the application

Before we get started, let's define exactly what it is we're going to build. It will be an online chat application; a user will go to the website, choose a screen name, choose a room, and chat with other members in the room. There won't be real user accounts; you join by simply giving a name, kind of like a simpler version of IRC. If someone else is using that name, you'll have to choose another. Users will also be able to create new rooms.

We will be using a few new tools in this chapter: Socket.IO and Marionette. **Socket.IO** (http://socket.io) is a real-time communication library that allows the client to talk to the server quickly and easily. Think of it as a publish and subscribe system (like Backbone's `trigger` and `listenTo` methods) between the client and the server; you can read more about that design pattern on Wikipedia (https://en.wikipedia.org/wiki/Publish_and_subscribe). We'll use this to make the live aspect of our chat application a lot easier to write.

Building a Chat Application

Marionette (http://marionettejs.com), however, is a little more interesting. It bills itself as a composite application library for Backbone.js that aims to simplify the construction of large scale JavaScript applications. Here's the idea; as you may have noticed from all the previous chapters, a lot of the code that we write in Backbone applications is repeated in each application. For example, we have views for both models and collections. Often, the collection view will loop over the models in the collection and render a model view for each of them, putting them in a container element. As this is a common pattern, Marionette wraps all this up for us and allows us to write just a few lines to do it all. However, Marionette also offers other tools that make managing large applications a little easier. We'll look at a bunch of these in this chapter.

Setting up the application

We have to begin this application with a bit of server-side code. We will use Express as our primary server; however, we also want to use Socket.IO, so we have to set it up. Copy the template to start the new project. Then, in the project directory, go ahead and install all our packages and then Socket.IO with npm as follows:

```
npm install
npm install socket.io --save
```

Now, to get Express and Socket.IO to play together nicely, we need to do things a bit differently in our `server.js` file. First, we require the `http` library of Node.js and `socket.io`. Here's how:

```
var http = require('http');
var socketio = require('socket.io');
```

Then, we have to wrap our Express application (the `app` object) in a Node.js server object as follows:

```
var server = http.createServer(app);
```

Now we have a server. The final step to getting things working with Socket.IO is to create a Socket.IO instance that listens to our server. We do that this way:

```
var io = socketio.listen(server);
```

Currently in the `server.js` file, you'll have the code that calls the `app.listen` function. However, as we're now wrapping our Express app in a Node.js server object, we need to call `listen` on that. So remove the `app.listen` call, and replace it with the following code:

```
server.listen(3000);
```

At this point, you should be able to boot up the server (`npm start`) and go to `http://localhost:3000` and get our blank page.

Preparing our template

The next step takes us into the `views/index.ejs` file. Marionette, of course, is a client library, but Socket.IO has a client component too; so we'll need to add script tags for both of them. Put these just below the tag for `backbone.js`:

```
<script src="/backbone.marionette.js"></script>
<script src="/socket.io/socket.io.js"></script>
```

Socket.IO on the backend will send the right file to that route, even though we never put `socket.io.js` in place. However, we do need to download Marionette. If you head over to the Marionette downloads page (`http://marionettejs.com/#download`), you'll see there are a few versions available. The Marionette library uses two main components: `Backbone.Wreqr` and `Backbone.BabySitter` (both have been built by the same good folks who made Marionette). You can download Wreqr, BabySitter, and Marionette separately, or you can get them bundled together. Make sure you download the bundled version and place it in the `public` directory.

Also, we will split our application into many smaller pieces and place them in their own files, similar to how we've done in the previous two chapters. For each file we make, you would want to add a script tag for it to the `views/index.ejs` file. In this case, the order will matter, and we'll see why that is and how to order them correctly.

A word about Socket.IO

Socket.IO makes it really easy to send data back and forth between the server and the client. As we've seen, this is one of the most important parts of Backbone; sending our models to and from the server. It would be relatively easier to replace the `Backbone.sync` function (as we did in *Chapter 2, Building a Photo-sharing Application*) with an implementation that uses Socket.IO. For example, we might do something like what is shown in the following code:

```
var SOCKET = io.connect('http://localhost:3000');

Backbone.sync = function (method, model, options) {
  var success = function (data) {
    if (options.success) options.success(data, null, null);
    model.trigger('sync', model, data, options);
  };
```

Building a Chat Application

```
    var data;
    if (method === 'create' || method === 'update') {
      data = model.toJSON();
    } else {
      data = { id: model.get('id') };
    }
    socket.emit(method, data, success);
};
```

If you haven't used Socket.IO before, this code won't make much sense just yet; but look at this again towards the end of the chapter and it should be clear. While we could write a Backbone application using Socket.IO this way, that's not the way we're going to be doing it here. To the get the live aspect of our chat application, we can't use the regular Backbone methods that talk to the server, such as `save` and `create`; we'll need to take things into our own hands. Part of the beauty of Backbone is that this will work out fine; if we decide to use Backbone to build an application that doesn't really fall within its *normal* usage, there's no extra friction from Backbone. However, you should know that you can use Socket.IO to do the syncing of a normal Backbone application.

Creating modules

Almost all of our code in this chapter will be put into modules, which Marionette will provide for us. But we need to start with some application preparation code. Previously, we've seen how we can put all the components of our application in a single global variable. Marionette takes this a step further by giving us an `Application` class; it's more than just an object onto which we can hang our own classes. As you'll see, it provides a lot of other interesting features.

So we start in the usual `app.js` file. Here's the code that we'll put in that file for starters:

```
_.templateSettings = {
  interpolate: /\{\{(.+?)\}\}/g
};

var App = new Backbone.Marionette.Application();
App.on('initialize:after', function () {
  Backbone.history.start({ pushState: true });
});
```

We're already familiar with template settings for Underscore, so the other lines are what you should focus on. The first line is how we create our single global variable for our application. All the special classes and components that Marionette gives us are available through the `Backbone.Marionette` namespace, and here, we will create an instance of the `Backbone.Marionette.Application`.

The way a Marionette application object works is that we'll eventually start up the application with `App.start()`. When we do that, any initializers we have added (with the `App.addInitializer` method) to the application will be run. We haven't added any initializers yet, but we will later.

In the final part of that code, we're listening for the `initialize:after` event. Marionette fires many different events at many points in the life of an application, and this is one of them. As you probably suspect, this event is fired after all the initializers we set up have been run. Once the application is initialized, we can start the router by starting Backbone's history mechanism, as we've done before.

Now that we have a basic application object, we can create modules. In general, in any programming language or library, modules are a way of grouping related code into one piece; the internals are kept hidden, and only the pieces we choose can be accessed from outside the module. This is exactly how Marionette uses them.

Our first module will be very simple; it's the Socket module. The file will be `public/socket.js`. The following is the code for this file:

```
App.module('Socket', function (Socket) {
  Socket.io = io.connect('http://localhost:3000');
});
```

This is the Marionette way of creating a module. We call the `App.module` method; it takes two parameters. The first is the name of the module. The module will be made available as a property of our `App` object by this name. As we call it `Socket` here, we'll be able to access this module in other places through `App.Socket`.

The second parameter is a function; of course, in this function we create the module. You might expect that whatever object we return from this function becomes our module, but that's not actually how it works. Instead, the `App.module` function will pass a parameter to our function; we will call it `Socket` as well. This is the object that will become our property. Anything we make a property of that object will be accessible from the `App` object. So in all our other modules, we can call the `App.Socket.io` property. However, what exactly is this property that we've just created?

The script that we added to the `index.ejs` file will give us a global `io` object that we can work with. We create our connection by calling the `connect` method and passing it the URL to which we want to connect. Since we're running our local server on port 3000, this is the path we connect to; if you were to use this in a public application, you'll want to put the public URL for your application in there. So this is our connection object, and as we just saw, we'll be able to access it from other modules.

Creating users

Next, we'll create users. Unlike some of our previous applications, these aren't user accounts that users can log into. Instead, a user is just someone who is currently using our chat application; all they need to provide is a screen name. So a collection of users is really just a list of currently used screen names.

So, create a `public/user.js` file and start with the following code:

```
App.module('User', function (User) {
  var UserModel = Backbone.Model.extend({});

  User.Collection = Backbone.Collection.extend({
    model: UserModel,
    initialize: function () {
      var thiz = this;
      App.Socket.io.on('user:join', function (user) {
        thiz.add(user);
      });

      App.Socket.io.on('user:leave', function (user) {
        thiz.findWhere(user).destroy();
      });
    }
  });
});
```

Here's how we start. First, we create a basic `UserModel` class (we can't just call it `User` because that would overwrite our module variable). Then, we create a collection class. As we've done before, we give it the model class. Things begin to get interesting in the collection's `initialize` function. Remember, we're not using the normal channels for communicating with the server here, so, we need to set up a way to discover when other users join or leave the site. We'll use Socket.IO on the server to emit a `user:join` event whenever a user joins the site; the event will send the new user's data to the client, which is an object with a name property, such as `{ name: 'Andrew' }`. We can listen for this event with `App.Socket.io.on`; this method takes the name of the event we're listening for and a function that will be run each time the event occurs. As you can see, each time a user joins, we'll add that user to the collection.

We also need to know when a user leaves. We'll listen for the `user:leave` event; when this happens, we'll use the collection's `findWhere` method to find that `UserModel` instance, and then destroy it, removing it from the collection. A Backbone collection's `findWhere` method will return the first model that matches the attributes hash we pass to it. Since we'll make sure that each name is unique on the server side, we can be sure we're destroying the right user.

One last thing to point out is that we will keep the `UserModel` class local to the module, but we will make the `Collection` class public by putting it on the `User` object. This is because we will never need to use the model class directly (only through the collection), so we can keep it hidden. There's no need to give the code outside this module access to more functionality from within this module than we need to.

Now that we've created our model and collection classes, let's make views for them. These views go in the `User` module too. The views look like this:

```
var ItemView = Backbone.Marionette.ItemView.extend({
  tagName: 'li',
  template: '#user'
});

User.CollectionView = Backbone.Marionette.CollectionView.extend({
  tagName: 'ul',
  itemView: ItemView
});
```

Here, we're using two of the handy view classes that Marionette gives us: `Backbone.Marionette.ItemView` and `Backbone.Marionette.CollectionView`. We commonly create views specifically to render individual models or collections, and these classes wrap up that common code for us. First, we create an `ItemView` class. The only properties we need to give it are `tagName` and `template`. These are both properties that we usually use; however, you'll notice something different about the `template` attribute. Instead of getting the template text via jQuery and using Underscore to convert it to a template function, all we have to do is set the template to a selector string. Here, we will set it to #user. Of course, we'll put this template in the `index.ejs` file, with the following lines of code:

```
<script type='text/template' id='user'>
  {{ name }}x
</script>
```

A simple template for sure. However, it shows how the extensions that Marionette provides can make complex applications simpler.

Building a Chat Application

The `User.CollectionView` is even simpler. We don't have to give it a `tagName`, but we can, and as our `ItemView` instances are list items, it makes sense to make the elements of `CollectionView` a list. Then, we only have to say what `itemView` is. In our case, this is the `ItemView` class we just created. The way a `Marionette.CollectionView` works is that it will loop over the collection, create an `itemView` for each item, and append it to the collection's element.

So that's our first module. We'll be creating several more modules in this application, but the `User` module is a good example of a typical Marionette module.

We've created three files here (`app.js`, `socket.js`, and `users.js`), so let's add them to the `index.ejs` file. Make sure that `app.js` comes first. We will add the three files using the following code:

```
<script src="/app.js"></script>
<script src="/socket.js"></script>
<script src='/users.js'></script>
```

Building the layout

The next step is the layout. This isn't something we've done in the previous applications, but it is something that Marionette gives us. This functionality allows us to organize and manipulate the many views we'll have on screen at once. In a large application, this can get tricky, and Marionette has two classes that make this simpler: `Region` and `Layout`. A region is basically an area of the screen, an object we can use to easily show and hide views or layouts. A layout is basically a group of regions.

We're going to create a `Layout` module for our layout classes. The following is the whole of our `public/layout.js` file:

```
App.module('Layout', function (Layout, App) {
  Layout.Layout = Backbone.Marionette.Layout.extend({
    template: '#appLayout',
    regions: {
      users: '#users',
      rooms: '#rooms',
      conversation: '#conversation',
      controls: '#controls'
    }
  });

  Layout.MainRegion = Backbone.Marionette.Region.extend({
    el: '#main'
  });
});
```

The first class is the layout for our application. Think of it as a view class but with no model or collection to display. Instead, it gives us access to several regions. Just like with the `ItemView`, the `template` property is a selector for the template. The template is as follows:

```
<script type='text/template' id='appLayout'>
  <div id='users'></div>
  <div id='conversation'></div>
  <div id='rooms'></div>
  <div id='controls'></div>
</script>
```

As you can see, we have four main areas, and these are the regions. We have a list of users, a list of rooms, the actual chat conversation, and a controls area where the user will log in and type in their message. In our `Layout` class, we have a `regions` property, which defines what the regions of our layout are. Each one is a selector, pointing to each of the four `<div>` elements in our template. When we create an instance of this `Layout` class, we'll be able to control the content of each of these regions individually.

After that comes the `MainRegion` class, which is a `Marionette Region`. This time, instead of setting a `tagName`, we will set the `el` property. When we do this, the class will use an existing DOM element instead of creating a new one. This is simply a region within which we will render our layout. In fact, this is our next step; to make our `App` object aware of this main region. In `app.js`, we need to add a call to the `addInitialize` method we discussed earlier. This can be done as follows:

```
App.addInitializer(function () {
  App.addRegions({
    main: App.Layout.MainRegion
  });
});
```

Our `App` object has an `addRegions` method that takes an object as a parameter. The property names are the names of the regions, and the value is the region class we're using. Here, we will create a single region, `main`, with our `MainRegion` class. Notice how, since we assigned `main` as a property of `Layout` in `layout.js`, we can access it via `App.Layout.MainRegion`.

Starting the router

Without a doubt, the most complex part of this chapter's application is the router, and with more advanced applications, this will often be the case. Due to this, Marionette's recommended pattern is to split the functionality of the Backbone router into two parts. The first part is still called the router; its job is to decide what should be done based on the current route. Then, there's the controller that actually performs the action decided upon by the router. Marionette has the `Marionette.AppRouter` class for the routing functionality. Interestingly, Marionette provides no framework for the controller. All that's required is a basic object with the right methods. We will create a constructor function and place all our methods on the prototype. So, let's create `router.js` within `public` and get started.

As Marionette recommends shifting most of the traditional Backbone router's work to the controller, the router itself is very minimal. Here's how it starts:

```
App.module('Router', function (Router) {
  var Router = Backbone.Marionette.AppRouter.extend({
    initialize: function () {
      App.layout = new App.Layout.Layout();
      App.main.show(App.layout);
    },
    appRoutes: {
      '': 'index'
    }
  });
});
```

We wrap this in a `Router` module. Then, we use Marionette's `AppRouter` class; as in many other Backbone classes, we create an `initialize` function that will run when we create our router instance. This is where we render our layout. We create a new instance of our `Layout` class and pass it to the `main` region's `show` method. As you'll see in the controller, this is the Marionette way of rendering layouts and views. we never call the `render` method ourselves. Instead, we pass a layout or view instance to a region's `show` method.

Also, notice that we're making our layout instance a property on our `App` module: `App.layout`. This is how we'll access our four regions from within the controller using `App.layout.users` or `App.layout.controls`. As these are regions, they will have the `show` method, to which we can pass the views we want to render.

Finally, instead of a `routes` property, our `AppRouter` will have an `appRoutes` property. This works just like the `routes` method of a normal router, except that the methods we call will be in the controller instead of on the router itself. We will start with a simple `index` route.

Now, let's start with the controller. This also goes inside the `Router` module that we've created. The controller can be started like this:

```
function Controller () {
  this.users = new App.User.Collection();
}
Controller.prototype.index = function () {
  App.layout.users.show(new App.User.CollectionView({
    collection: this.users
  }));
};
```

There's a lot more to come, but this is what we can do right now with the code we've already written. In the constructor function, we'll create a `users` property. This is the collection that will manage our list of users. As our router will be looking for a method called `index`, we'll add that to `prototype` of our `Controller` function. This method simply creates an `App.User.CollectionView` instance and renders it in the `users` region of our layout.

Before we load up our page, we need to instantiate the router. At the bottom of the `Router` module, add the following code:

```
App.addInitializer(function () {
  var r = new Router({
    controller: new Controller()
  });
});
```

Here, we instantiate our router, passing it a new `Controller` object as a property in an options object. The router will use this object as the controller for our application.

The last step to having some code we can actually run is to add a few lines to the `index.ejs` file. This can be done as follows:

```
<script src='/layout.js'></script>
<script src='/router.js'></script>
<script>
  App.start();
</script>
```

We add our layout and router modules, and then, right at the bottom, we start the application. Remember that, even when we add other script tags later on, it is important that the `router.js` script should be the last one loaded because it references almost all the other files.

Building a Chat Application

Now, you can run `npm start` to boot the server up and load `http://localhost:3000` in a browser. At this point, you won't see anything at all on the page; however, open the developer tools and you'll see that things are starting to take shape. We can see this in the following screenshot:

```
▼<body>
  ▼<div id="main">
    ▼<div>
      ▼<div id="users">
          <ul></ul>
        </div>
        <div id="conversation"></div>
        <div id="rooms"></div>
        <div id="controls"></div>
      </div>
    </div>
```

You can see that our layout has been rendered and that the `<ul>` element of our `User.CollectionView` instance is present. Even though we aren't rendering any content, this is an important step. We've written a lot of code that might seem disparate and unconnected, but it has all come together to create the humble beginnings of our application. Now that we have the infrastructure working, we can start to think about specific features.

Letting users join the fun

Our first serious feature will be allowing users to choose a screen name and join the chat rooms. We'll need a view with a form where a user can submit their name. However, as part of this, we'll need a way to ask the server if this name has been taken yet.

For all this, we go back to the `User` module, and add a method to the `User.CollectionView`, using the following code:

```
addUser: function (name, callback, context) {
  App.Socket.io.emit('join', name, function (joined) {
    if (joined) App.name = name;
    callback.call(context joined);
  });
}
```

This method takes the `name` that the user wants to use as well as a `callback` function. Inside the method, we use another Socket.IO method: `emit`. This is the flip side of the `App.Socket.io.on` method we saw earlier in this class's `initialize` method. The `on` method listens for events while `emit` actually makes the occurrence of the event. The `emit` method takes at least one parameter; the name of the event that we're triggering. We can then pass as many subsequent parameters as we like; these are pieces of data that we can associate with the event. If the server is listening for this event, it will receive these parameters. We pass the user's name and a function. The name makes sense; if the server is going to tell us whether this name is already in use, we need to send it the name. However, the function is a little different. We receive the function on the server side, but when we call the function (from the server, remember!) it will be executed here in the browser. This is not only incredibly cool, it's also very useful. On the server, we'll pass that function a Boolean value; `true` if the user can use this name and has been added to the list of current users or `false` if the name is already in use.

If the user has successfully joined the chat rooms, we'll set their screen name as a property of our `App` object, so we can access it from other places. Then, we'll call the `callback` function that was passed to the `addUser` method, passing it the `joined` value. The `context` parameter is actually just a nice touch. I'm not a fan of having to put the value of `this` in a variable every time I enter a callback function, so when I have the option, I'll create functions that take a context as a final parameter. This way, I can use `this` as I want inside the function.

With that in place, let's move over to `server.js`. We haven't written any Socket.IO-specific code yet, but we're going to start that now. Start by adding this to `server.js`:

```
var users = {};
io.sockets.on('connection', function (socket) {
});
```

We start with a `users` object; it's empty right now, but as users join, it will be used. As we aren't creating actual user accounts, there's no need for this record to be persistent; a regular object will do.

Earlier, we created the `io` object. This object has a `sockets` object on which we have the `on` method, which we can use to listen for connections being opened from browsers. As you can see here, we're listening for the `connection` event. The callback function here will be run when a new connection is made. The new socket (the connection to the browser) is a parameter of the function.

Building a Chat Application

Inside this callback, we'll start by listening for the `join` event that the `User.CollectionView` class' `addUser` method was emitting. Add this inside that callback function:

```
socket.on('join', function (name, response) {
  if (userExists(name)) {
    response(false);
  } else {
    response(true);
    users[socket.id] = { name: name };
    io.sockets.emit('user:join', { name: name });
  }
});
```

Remember that when we emitted the `join` event, we sent the name and a function along with it. You can see these here on the server as the parameters of the function that will be called when this event occurs. In this function, we check to see whether the user exists using a `userExists` function, which we haven't written yet. If the user already exists, we'll call that `response` function (that is executed on the client, remember?) and pass `false` (because the user can't join under that name). However, if the user doesn't currently exist, we'll respond with `true`. Then, we'll add the user to the `users` object. We can use the unique `socket.id` as a key. Finally, we'll emit the `user:join` event, passing a basic user object as the data associated with that event. All the currently connected clients (including the client that sent the join event) will receive this event. Remember that in our `User.Collection` class' `initialize` method, we're listening for this event. This is how the client can learn about new users joining the chat room.

You might wonder why we can't just look at the users in the collection to see whether a name is in use, instead of asking the server whenever a new user tries to join. After all, if the collection is a list of currently connected users, it should know whether the name is already in use. The problem with this is that in some scenarios, which we haven't yet come to, the user will try to join before the server has had the chance to send the current list of users to the collection.

This is something we have to add. When a new socket is connected, we need to send it the list of the currently connected users. This can be done as follows:

```
Object.keys(users).forEach(function (id) {
  socket.emit('user:join', users[id]);
});
```

The `Object.keys` method takes an object and returns an array of its keys. We can loop over all the users in our `users` object and emit the `user:join` event for each one. There's an important difference between this event and the `user:join` event we emitted previously. In the `join` event listener, we use `io.sockets.emit`, which emits the event to all sockets. Here, we use `socket.emit`. This way, only that socket will receive these events.

With this code in place, we're ready to write the view that allows our users to join the chat rooms. We'll put this code in our `User` module:

```
User.LogInView = Backbone.Marionette.ItemView.extend({
  tagName: 'form',
  template: '#form',
  model: new Backbone.Model({
    placeholder: 'name',
    button: 'Join'
  }),
  events: {
    'click button': 'addUser'
  },
  ui: {
    'input': 'input'
  },
  addUser: function (e) {
    e.preventDefault();
    var name = this.ui.input.val();
    this.collection.addUser(name, function (joined) {
      if (joined) {
        this.trigger('user-added');
      } else {
        this.ui.input.val('');
      }
    }, this);
    return false;
  }
});
```

Building a Chat Application

Here, we create a `Marionette.ItemView` class, so we don't have to write the `render` method ourselves. Instead of passing in a `model`, when creating an instance of this class, we're putting it right here in the class definition (this is possible in a regular Backbone view too; it's not special to Marionette). We're doing this because of the template. Normally, our views that display forms don't have models, but this one does because we want to use this template for multiple views. We will use a template with the ID `form`. The template is as follows:

```
<script type='text/template' id='form'>
  <input type='text' placeholder='{{placeholder}}' />
  <button> {{button}} </button>
</script>
```

This is very basic. It has only an input element and a button. The placeholder text and the button text need to come from a model, so that's why we add a basic Backbone model with the right attributes to this class definition.

The `events` property is not new or special. When we click on the button, we'll call the `addUser` method (of this class). The `ui` property, on the other hand, is special to Marionette views; we often need to reference specific elements of the view from within view methods, and the `ui` property is a shortcut to access them. The keys are the names by which we'll refer to the element, and the value is a selector for the element. In this case, we find the input element and call it `input`. You can see this in use in the `addUser` method. Instead of searching for the input element with `this.$("input")`, we can just reference `this.ui.input`; it's even a jQuery object.

In `addUser`, we start by preventing the default submission of the form. Then, we get whatever name the user typed into the textbox, and send it to the collection's `addUser` method. In our callback function, if the user has successfully joined the chat rooms, we'll trigger the `user-added` event on this view. This is the Backbone equivalent of emitting an event with Socket.IO (this isn't Marionette-specific; you can trigger and listen for events in plain Backbone applications as well). Later, we'll listen for this event. If the user did not join successfully, we'll clear the input element so that they can try a new name.

Now, go back to the `Controller.prototype.index` method in the `router.js` file. We need to render a `LogInView` instance, like this:

```
var loginView = new App.User.LogInView({
  collection: this.users
});
App.layout.controls.show(loginView);
```

Notice that this is where the collection in the `addUser` method comes from. With this code in place, things are starting to get interesting. If you open `http://localhost:3000`, you'll see a textbox and button. Type in a name and click on **Join**; and the name will appear above in the list. Now, the magic begins. Open the site in another browser tab. You'll see the first name already in the list. Go ahead and add another one; it will appear in the list. Now, go back to the first window. You'll see that it also received the second name. Isn't that amazing! This works for two reasons. First, Socket.IO makes sure every new user is added to the user collection of every connected browser. Then, Marionette's `CollectionView` will immediately render new models added to the collection, which is why it appears in the list without us doing any manual rendering or watching the collection for changes.

There's a little problem, though. If you close the second window and go back to the first one, you'll find that both names are still in the list. We need to remove a name from the collection when a user closes the site.

This is done in `server.js`. When a socket disconnects from the server, we get a disconnect event; so let's listen for that (within the `connection` event callback). We can do that as follows:

```
socket.on('disconnect', function () {
  if (users[socket.id]) {
    io.sockets.emit('user:leave', users[socket.id]);
    delete users[socket.id];
  }
});
```

When this socket disconnects, we check the user's object to see whether there's an entry for this Socket ID. Remember, if the user never tried to join the chat rooms (maybe they loaded the page and then closed it), they won't have an entry; that's why we check. If they do, we'll emit a `user:leave` event to all sockets, and then delete that entry from our users hash.

Now, we know that our user collection is listening for the `user:leave` event, and when it occurs, the user will be removed from the collection. Accordingly, Marionette will update the `User.CollectionView`. Now, if you do our quick-and-dirty test in the browser again, you'll see that when you close the second browser window, the second name disappears from the first window. Clever, no?

Building a Chat Application

Before leaving the user module behind, let's add one more feature. Later, we'll be writing some CSS for our application; so let's highlight the user's own name in the list. In the `ItemView` class in the `User` module, let's add a method called `onRender`. This method will be called after the view has been rendered. Here's how that looks:

```
onRender: function () {
  if (this.model.get('name') === App.name) {
    this.el.className = "highlight";
  }
}
```

It's quick and simple. If the model we're rendering this view for has the same name as the user in this browser, add the class `highlight` to the element.

Joining a room

Once a user has selected their screen name, the next step is selecting a room. This is a bit more complex than choosing a name because they can either choose from a list of existing rooms, or they can start a new room by typing in a new name. If the user types in the name of an existing room, they'll go to the existing rooms because we obviously can't have multiple rooms with the same name. The tricky part in all this is that while we're calling them rooms, they're actually more like tags. The only place they exist is as a property on the chat messages; they aren't stored on their own. When a user creates a new room, there's no actual record of the room until they write the first message in that room. If they create a room and then close the page, the room doesn't exist. All this will make it a bit trickier to keep track of the rooms, but we love a good challenge, right?

Open a new file, `rooms.js`, in `public`. Just like our `user.js` file, this will have a model, collection, model view, collection view, and form view. The following code shows how we start with this file:

```
App.module('Room', function (Room) {
  var RoomModel = Backbone.Model.extend({
    url: function () {
      return '/room/' + this.get('name');
    }
  });
});
```

We call the module Room, and we start with RoomModel. This model has a single method; it returns the URL for the room. The plan is to eventually allow users to go straight to the room of their choice by having it in the URL. This makes specific rooms easy to bookmark. Of course, they'll still have to enter their screen name before they can actually see the room, but it will omit the "choose a room" step from the process. We'll use this method to get the route to a given room model. Next, we write the collection, which looks like this:

```
Room.Collection = Backbone.Collection.extend({
  model: RoomModel,
  initialize: function () {
    App.Socket.io.on('room:new', this.getRoom.bind(this));
  },
  getRoom: function(room) {
    return this.findWhere({ name: room }) || this.add({ name: room });
  }
});
```

Just like in our User.Collection class, the initialize method here listens for an event. In this case, it's the room:new event. When that happens, we'll call this class's getRoom method. This method probably doesn't look like what you'd expect. Its purpose, in this context is to add the room to the collection if it isn't already there. You might expect it to look something like the following code:

```
addRoom: function (room) {
  if (!this.findWhere({ name: room }).length) {
    this.add({ name: room });
  }
}
```

However, later on we'll also need a method that takes a room name, and either returns the existing room by that name or creates a new room with that name, and this is exactly what the getRoom method does. As it turns out, the logic in getRoom is exactly the same as this example addRoom method. If the room doesn't exist, add it. So our getRoom method is a two-for-one deal.

Let's move over to server.js for a moment. When a new socket connects, we need to send the list of existing rooms to this room collection. Inside the function that is run when a new socket connects, add this code:

```
db.find(function (err, records) {
  var rooms = {};
  records.forEach(function (record) { rooms[record.room] = 0; });
  Object.keys(rooms).forEach(function (room) {
    socket.emit('room:new', room);
  })
});
```

Building a Chat Application

What we're doing in the preceding code is finding all the records in our database; these records are the chat messages. What we need to do is convert this array of messages into a list of the rooms that they are in. Although we don't have any messages yet, each one will have a `room` property. We loop over each model and add a property to a disposable `rooms` object. As an object can't have multiple properties with the same name, the result will be an object whose keys are a unique list of the existing rooms. Then, we can use `Object.keys` to get an array of just those keys; finally, we'll loop over that array and emit the `room:new` event for each room. As we've just seen, the `Room.Collection` instance will catch these on the browser's end and fill the list.

Now that we have our model and collection, we can make their respective views as follows:

```
var RoomView = Backbone.Marionette.ItemView.extend({
  tagName: 'li',
  template: '#room',
  events: {
    'click a': 'chooseRoom'
  },
  chooseRoom: function (e) {
    e.preventDefault();
    Backbone.history.navigate(this.model.url(), { trigger: true });
  }
});

Room.CollectionView = Backbone.Marionette.CollectionView.extend({
  tagName: 'ul',
  itemView: RoomView
});
```

The `RoomView` class is the item view in this case. It will be a list item element; the template has the ID `room`. Here's that template:

```
<script type='text/template' id='room'>
  <a href='/room/{{ name }}'>{{ name }}</a>
</script>
```

As you can see, the list of rooms will be links; then in the view, we'll listen for a click on one of these anchor elements. When that happens, we'll prevent the default reloading of the page, and use Backbone to navigate to the room's URL. This time, instead of pulling a method from the router, we're using the `Backbone.history.navigate` method. Of all the ways of changing the route that we've looked at, this is clearly the best one (of course, it's good to know about the others).

The `Room.CollectionView` class is very basic. We just make the wrapping element a list and point to the item view.

This is all we need to display the list of existing rooms. However, if a user wants to create a new room, we need a view for that. So, here's that view:

```
Room.CreateRoomView = Backbone.Marionette.ItemView.extend({
  tagName: 'form',
  template: '#form',
  model: new Backbone.Model({
    placeholder: 'room name',
    button: 'Join'
  }),
  events: {
    'click button': 'createRoom'
  },
  ui: {
    'input': 'input'
  },
  createRoom: function (e) {
    e.preventDefault();
    var name = this.ui.input.val().toLowerCase()
        .replace('/ /g, '_').replace(/\W/g, ''),
      room = this.collection.getRoom(name);
    Backbone.history.navigate(room.url(), { trigger: true });
    return false;
  }
});
```

The `Room.CreateRoomView` class will use the same form template that we used in `Login View`, so the whole class will look pretty similar. We're adding the model here, so we can set the template's placeholder text and button text. When the button is clicked, we'll call the `createRoom` method. This method will prevent the default form submission and then get the text from the input element. As our room names will be used in URLs, we need to clean the name up a bit by first replacing all spaces with underscores and then removing all other non-word characters. Then, we pass the room name to the collection's `getRoom` function. As we know, this will return a room (either a newly created one or an existing one with that name). Then, we'll navigate to that room's URL.

Now that we have these classes, we can use them. First, in `index.ejs`, add the `Room` module:

```
<script src='/rooms.js'></script>
```

Building a Chat Application

Then, in the `Controller` function in `router.js`, add the following line of code. It will be the collection object that our application uses to keep track of the rooms:

```
this.rooms = new App.Room.Collection();
```

Now, go to our controller's `index` function; we've already written part of it, but here's the whole new and improved version:

```
Controller.prototype.index = function () {
  App.layout.users.show(new App.User.CollectionView({
    collection: this.users
  }));
  App.layout.rooms.show(new App.Room.CollectionView({
    collection: this.rooms
  }));

  var loginView = new App.User.LogInView({
    collection: this.users
  });
  App.layout.controls.show(loginView);
  loginView.on('user-added', function () {
    App.layout.controls.show(new App.Room.CreateRoomView({
      collection: this.rooms
    }));
  }, this);
};
```

As earlier, we render the list of users and the login form. However, we're also rendering our new rooms collection in the appropriate collection view in the `rooms` region of the layout. Then, we listen for the `user-added` event on the login form. Remember, that event will be emitted when a user successfully joins the site. When that happens, we'll render a different view in the `controls` region; the view to create a new room. We can't forget to give that view the collection, to which it can add the new room. The Backbone on method takes a context variable as a third parameter, so we can use `this` inside the callback.

Now, if you test our application, you'll see that after you put in a screen name, the form will change and ask for a room name, as shown in the following screenshots:

Of course, there's no list of room names to choose from as we haven't stored any messages yet, but if you look at the DOM, you'll see the empty `<ul>` element waiting. Type in a room name and click on the button, and two things should happen. First, the room name should appear on screen in a list. Second, the URL will change to the room route.

This URL change means we need to add a route to our `Router` class. In the `appRoutes` property, add this line of code:

```
'room/:room': 'room'
```

This means that we need to create a `room` method on our controller prototype. Before we write the method, think of this; if choosing a room sends our user to the room route, it's also possible that the user could directly to the route. If they do this, the room will be selected, but the user will not have chosen a screen name. This means that this method will have to check for the presence of a screen name, and if a screen name hasn't been given, we'll have to get one before showing the room.

First, as it is possible that this route will be loaded directly (and not via Backbone through the room link), we'll need to render the user list and the room list. Since we'll do this first in all the routes we will end up creating, let's move that into a helper function:

```
Controller.prototype.showUsersAndRooms = function () {
  App.layout.users.show(new App.User.CollectionView({
    collection: this.users
  }));
  App.layout.rooms.show(new App.Room.CollectionView({
    collection: this.rooms
  }));
};
```

The `showUsersAndRooms` method on the controller prototype renders those views in the right regions.

Let's write one more helper function. As we figured out, if the user hasn't selected a screen name yet, we'll need to display the same view we're showing in the `index` route: `logInView`. So let's write a `showLogin` function:

```
Controller.prototype.showLogin = function () {
  var loginView = new App.User.LogInView({
    collection: this.users
  });
  App.layout.controls.show(loginView);
  return loginView;
};
```

We'll create `loginView`, display it in the `controls` region, and then return the view. We return it because the route function that calls this helper function will probably want to listen for that `user-added` event. With these two helper functions in place, we can really clean up the `index` function as follows:

```
Controller.prototype.index = function () {
  this.showUsersAndRooms();
  this.showLogin().on('user-added', function () {
    App.layout.controls.show(new App.Room.CreateRoomView({
      collection: this.rooms
    }));
  }, this);
};
```

However, the reason for creating these helper functions is that they'll also be useful in the room route function we need to create:

```
Controller.prototype.room = function (room) {
  this.showUsersAndRooms();
  App.room = this.rooms.getRoom(room);
  if (!App.name) {
    this.showLogin().on('user-added', function () {
      // render chat room conversation
    });
  } else {
    // render chat room conversation
  }
};
```

We first render the users and rooms lists. Then, we set a property on our global `App` object for the room that the user chooses to view. Then, we check to see whether `App.name` is set. If the user has come from the `index` route (or has switched rooms by clicking on a link from the list), `App.name` will be set. If it isn't set, we'll show the login form. If the name is set, or after the name is set (determined by the `user-added` event we're listening for), we'll need to render the chat room conversation. To do this, we need to create the `Chat` module.

Building the chat module

To create the `Chat` module, we'll create the `chat.js` file within `public`. Once again, we'll start with the model and collection classes:

```
App.module('Chat', function (Chat) {
  var Message = Backbone.Model.extend({});
```

```
  Chat.Collection = Backbone.Collection.extend({
    model: Message,
    initialize: function (models, options) {
      var thiz = this;
      App.Socket.io.emit('room:join', options.room, this.add.
bind(this));

      App.Socket.io.on('message:new', function (data) {
        if (data.room === options.room) {
          thiz.add(data);
        }
      });
    }
  });
});
```

The `Message` model is very simple, but the `Chat.Collection` class is a little more interesting. First, notice that this function takes two parameters: `models` and `options`. We never actually expect to receive any models, but it is a Backbone convention for a collection to receive these two parameters. So, we'll follow this convention. We expect that option's object to have the name of the room that these messages are in. Once we have that name, we can emit the `room:join` event with two parameters: the name of the room and a callback function. The function is this collection's `add` method. We expect the server to call the callback function with a list of all the messages currently in the room. Then, for all messages created after the collection is created, the server will emit a `message:new` event. We'll pick up on this `message:new` event here, and if the room on the new message is in the same room as the room this `Chat.Collection` instance is for, we'll add it to the collection.

Also, we'll add item and collection views as we've done before. Here's how that works:

```
  var MessageView = Backbone.Marionette.ItemView.extend({
    tagName: 'li',
    template: '#message'
  });

  Chat.CollectionView = Backbone.Marionette.CollectionView.extend({
    tagName: 'ul',
    itemView: MessageView,
    onRender: function () {
      setTimeout(this.render.bind(this), 60000);
    }
  });
```

Building a Chat Application

The `MessageView` is simple: a list item element that will render the message template. Here's that template:

```
<script type='text/template' id='message'>
  <strong> {{ user }} </strong>:
  {{ text }}
  <span> {{ moment(date).fromNow() }} </span>
</script>
```

Every message will have a user name, the text of the message, and the date and time when the message was created. Notice that we're not displaying the date value as it is. Instead, we use the Moment library to convert that date to a string such as `10 minutes ago`. As we've done in previous applications, we can go ahead and download Moment (http://momentjs.com) and add the appropriate script tag to `index.ejs`.

The `CollectionView` makes use of the `onRender` function in an interesting way. After the view renders, this function will set a timeout, to recall the `render` method again in 60 seconds. This is done so that the *time ago* timestamp will update on our message views.

The last view for this module is the `Chat.CreateMessageView` view:

```
Chat.CreateMessageView = Backbone.Marionette.ItemView.extend({
  tagName: 'form',
  template: '#form',
  model: new Backbone.Model({
    placeholder: 'message',
    button: 'Post'
  }),
  events: {
    'click button': 'addMessage'
  },
  ui: {
    'input': 'input'
  },
  addMessage: function (e) {
    e.preventDefault();
    App.Socket.io.emit('message:new', {
      user: App.name,
      text: this.ui.input.val(),
      room: App.room.get('name'),
      date: new Date()
    });
    this.ui.input.val('').focus();
```

```
      return false;
    }
  });
```

This is very similar to our other two form views. We have the model for setting the placeholder and button text. Then, when we click on the button, we run the `addMessage` method. This method will prevent the form from getting submitted, and then emit a `message:new` event to the server. As data, we get the user's name, the text in the input element, the name of the room that the user is currently in, and the current date and time. All this data is sent to the server. Then, we clear the input element, and focus it for the next message.

Now that we're done with `chat.js`, add it to the `index.ejs` file.

So what happens on the server? Well, that's where we listen for the the `message:new` event:

```
socket.on('message:new', function (data) {
  db.insert(data, function (msg) {
    io.sockets.emit('message:new', msg);

    db.find({ room:data.room }, function (msgs) {
      if (msgs.length === 1) {
        io.sockets.emit('room:new', data.room);
      }
    });
  });
});
```

When that happens, we'll insert the data into the database. Once it has been successfully saved, we'll emit the `message:new` event to all connected clients. Those viewing the room this message was in will see it almost immediately. We also search the database for records in the same room. If a user has started a new chat room, there will be only one message with that room name (the one we just saved). However, this also means that all the other clients don't yet have this room in their `Room.Collection` object. So, we'll send them all a `room:new` event with the room's name.

Back to the controller

With the `Chat` module created, we can turn back to the controller, where we want to render the chat for the chosen room. Let's create a helper function for this:

```
Controller.prototype.showChat = function () {
  App.layout.controls.show(new App.Chat.CreateMessageView());
  App.layout.conversation.show(new App.Chat.CollectionView({
```

Building a Chat Application

```
    collection: new App.Chat.Collection([], {
      room: App.room.get('name')
    })
  }));
};
```

In the `controls` region, we put `Chat.CreateMessageView`. Then, in the `conversation` region, we render a `Chat.CollectionView` instance. Now, in our `Controller.prototype.room` method, we can call this `showChat` method:

```
Controller.prototype.room = function (room) {
  this.showUsersAndRooms();
  App.room = this.rooms.getRoom(room);
  if (!App.name) {
    this.showLogin().on('user-added', this.showChat.bind(this));
  } else {
    this.showChat();
  }
};
```

Now, this route is complete. Once we have a name, we'll show the chat messages.

Adding some other routes

Right now, we have two routes. However, we want to add a few more. Next, we'll add a `/user/:name` route, so that the user can skip the logging-in step. For example, I could go directly to `http://localhost:3000/user/Andrew`, and I wouldn't have to log in; I could just choose a room. While this may not be practical or realistic, I think it's a fun touch that is very simple to add.

In the router class, add the following route:

```
'user/:user': 'user'
```

Now, let's write this method in the controller as follows:

```
Controller.prototype.user = function (user) {
  this.showUsersAndRooms();

  this.users.addUser(user, function (joined) {
    if (joined) {
      App.layout.controls.show(new App.Room.CreateRoomView({
        collection: this.rooms
      }));
    } else {
```

```
        Backbone.history.navigate('', { trigger: true });
      }
    }, this);
};
```

First, we'll call our `showUsersAndRooms` helper method to display the lists of users and rooms. Then, we'll call the user collection's `addUser` method. Remember that this method will decide whether the user can use the screen name they chose. Since the screen name is part of the URL, we get it as a parameter to the function. In the callback function, if the user has successfully joined, we'll display `CreateRoomView` where they can start a new room (alternatively, they can click on a room in the rooms list). Otherwise, we'll redirect them to the root route where they can choose an unused screen name.

So, we've made it possible for someone coming to our application to choose either their screen name or a room right from the URL. Why don't we take it one step further and allow users to do both? We can make it work in both ways:

```
/room/Pets/name/Andrew
/name/Andrew/room/Pets
```

In the router, add the following lines of code to the `appRoutes` property:

```
'room/:room/user/:user': 'room_user',
'user/:user/room/:room': 'user_room'
```

We'll start with the `room_user` method:

```
Controller.prototype.room_user = function (room, user) {
    this.showUsersAndRooms();
    App.room = this.rooms.getRoom(room);

    this.users.addUser(user, function (joined) {
      if (joined) {
        this.showChat(room);
      } else {
        Backbone.history.navigate(App.room.url(), { trigger: true });
      }
    }, this);
};
```

We start by calling `showUsersAndRooms` again. Then, we get the room model through the name given to us in the URL. Lastly, we try to log the user in. If they join successfully, we'll show the chat room they chose. If they need to pick another screen name, we'll redirect them to the URL for that room.

With this in place, the `user_room` method simply switches the order of the parameters:

```
Controller.prototype.user_room = function (user, room) {
  this.room_user(room, user);
};
```

With that, we have all the functionality we need in place! Our application is just about finished. All it needs now is a coat of paint.

Writing CSS

Since styling isn't the main purpose of this book, we've left this for the end; if you aren't interested, jump to the chapter summary.

While our application is functioning very well right now, it's certainly not easy on the eyes. Let's fix that. First, we'll link to a stylesheet from the `<head>` element in the `index.ejs` file as follows:

```
<link rel="stylesheet" href="/style.css" />
```

Now, create that file in `style.css` within `public`. We'll start with some generic styling:

```
body {
  font-family: sans-serif;
  padding: 0;
  margin: 0;
}

ul {
  margin: 0;
  padding: 0;
  list-style-type: none;
}
```

It's really just a mini reset; we use several `<ul>` elements in this application, so this will be important.

The next few lines of code are mainly for styling the list of users:

```
#users, #rooms {
  float: left;
  width: 13%;
  margin: 1%;
  font-size: 80%;
}
```

[164]

```css
#users li {
  padding: 5px;
  border-bottom: 1px solid #ccc;
}
.highlight {
  font-weight: bold;
  background: #ececec;
}
```

The users and room lists will be the sidebars on the left and right, respectively. We'll set their width and margin, shrink the font size a bit, and then float them to the left. We then do some basic styling for the user list items. You'll recall that we added the `highlight` class to the user view for the logged-in user; we're defining that class here.

Next, we style the list of rooms with these lines:

```css
#rooms li {
  padding: 0;
  border-bottom: 1px solid #ccc;
}
#rooms li a {
  text-decoration: none;
  color: #000;
  display: block;
  padding: 5px;
}
#rooms li a:hover {
  background: #ececec;
}
```

Then, we provide some styling for the user list; it's a bit more complex as the list items have anchor elements inside them. Of course, we add some basic hover styling.

Next, we style the conversation itself:

```css
#conversation {
  float: left;
  width:68%;
  margin: 1%;
  margin-bottom: 60px;
}

#conversation li {
  padding: 10px;
  border-bottom: 1px solid #ececec;
```

```
}
#conversation li span {
  color: #ccc;
  font-size: 75%;
  float: right;
}
```

The `conversation` region goes in the middle, between the two sidebars, so it is important that it be floated to the left-hand side as well. The `<span>` element we style is where the date and time of the message will be displayed, so we shrink the text a bit, and move it to the right.

Finally, we style the controls:

```
#controls {
  background: #ececec;
  padding: 10px;
  position: fixed;
  bottom: 0;
  width: 100%;
}

#controls input {
  border: 1px solid #ccc;
  padding: 5px;
  width: 300px;
}

#controls button {
  border: 1px solid #ccc;
  background: #efefef;
  padding: 5px 15px;
}
```

The last portion of the CSS styles is the `control` region. This is where all the forms will be displayed. We're doing something a bit different here. We're using a position that is fixed to attach it to the bottom of the screen. Now, the conversation can get as long as it wants, but the message form will always be visible.

Now, the code is complete. The following is a screenshot of the final application in use:

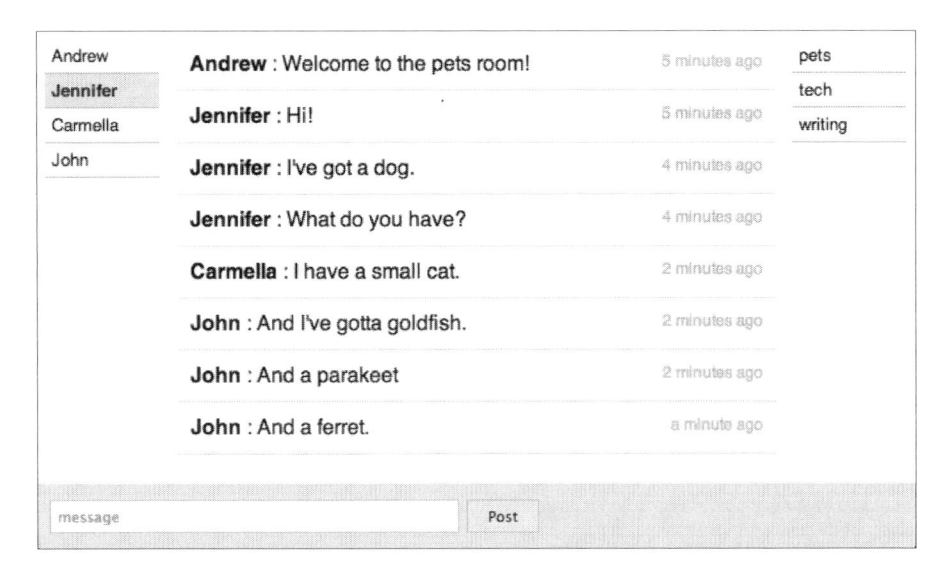

Summary

I hope you found this chapter interesting. The biggest idea we've looked at here is using Marionette instead of plain Backbone to build our application. As you've seen, when using a framework designed for large applications, there's a lot more of what you might call scaffolding code. Basing everything on an application object, using modules, splitting routers and controllers, it all makes for a lot more moving parts. Here's the thing; the application we've built here really can't be called large, so you might think it doesn't really make that much sense to use Marionette. However, if you've worked on any large projects, you know that the more code that's involved, the more you'll appreciate the constructs that a framework like Marionette gives you. That extra level of boundaries is certainly not required, but I think you'll find that it can be extremely helpful and that it keeps a huge project manageable as it grows and changes.

The other big idea in this chapter was Socket.IO. In this application, we completely ignored the built-in syncing channels that Backbone gives us, but as I mentioned earlier, that's not the only way it can be done. Now would be a good time to go back and look at the implementation of `Backbone.sync` using Socket.IO, and maybe even build a small application to test it. The bigger thing to take away from the way in which we used Socket.IO is that Backbone is just another tool, and there's no one right way to use it. Don't ignore the conventions and suggestions of the Backbone community, but don't be afraid to bend it to your will and see what happens. We'll do more of this in the next chapter when we create a podcast subscription application.

6
Building a Podcast Application

In this chapter, there will be an interesting twist. All the applications we have built so far have been pretty heavy on the client code, but rather light on the server. The truth is, the web applications you're going to build aren't always going to be this way. Often, you'll have to perform a lot of heavy lifting on the backend as well as on the frontend; and the application we're going to build here will be this way.

So, in this chapter, we'll focus on the following ideas:

- Building an application that is both server- and client-intensive
- Duplicating some of Marionette's functionality, without using Marionette
- Parsing and simplifying a data file before storing it

What are we building?

In this chapter, we'll be building a podcast-listening application. As you probably know, a podcast feed is very similar to a regular blog's RSS feed. The primary difference is what the fields are; so, even though we're building a basic podcast **catcher**, a lot of it could go towards building a regular RSS reader. So, here's what we will have: people can make accounts for our application, and then subscribe to podcast feeds. We'll load in all existing episodes, and users can listen to them and see the show notes and links right in our app. Each time a user opens the application, each of the podcasts they subscribe to will be checked for new episodes. They'll be able to listen to episodes, or just mark them as listened to.

Building a Podcast Application

Here's a look at the completed project:

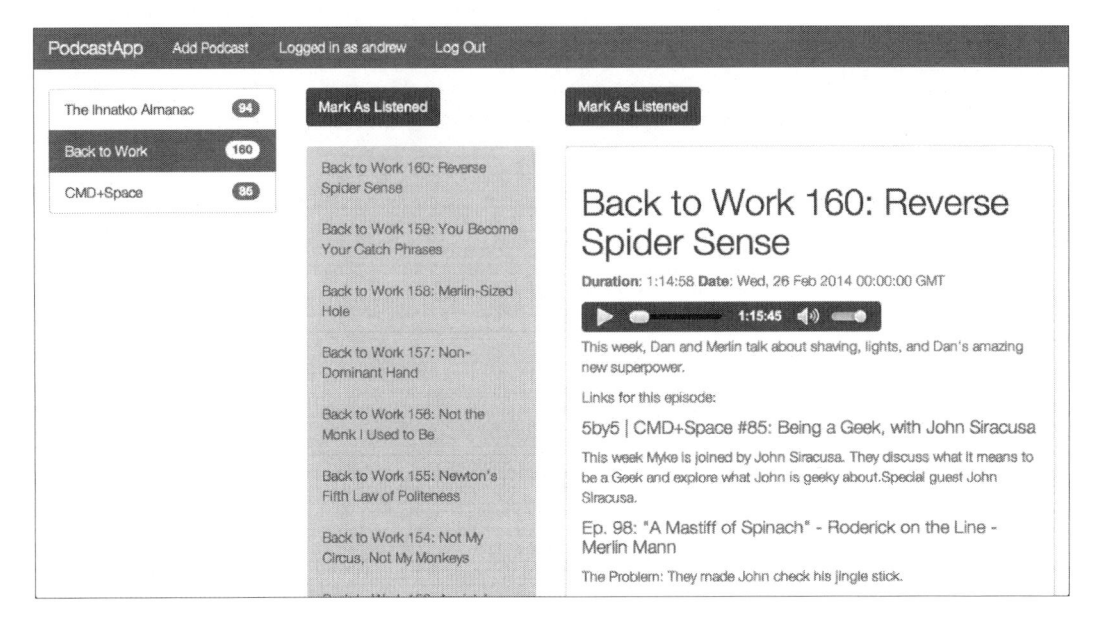

It doesn't sound or look like a lot, maybe, but there's a lot to do, so let's get started.

Building user accounts

We'll start with user accounts. You'll remember that in *Chapter 2*, *Building a Photo-sharing Application*, when we built the photo sharing application, we created a `signin.js` file; we'll want to use that here. We can set this up by following these steps:

1. Copy the template directory to create a new project, and then copy the `signin.js` file into the new directory. You'll want to add the following line to the top of the `server.js` file:

    ```
    var signin   = require("./signin");
    ```

2. Now, as you might recall, this requires a few more Node.js packages. Go ahead and install `passport`, `passport-local`, and `bcrypt` by using the following command in the terminal:

    ```
    npm install bcrypt passport passport-local --save
    ```

3. The bcrypt and passport-local packages are used in the sigin.js file, but we require passport in the server.js file; we'll also create the users database, as you can see here:

```
var passport = require("passport");
var users    = new Bourne("users.json");
```

4. Then, we need to make sure our express application is configured for this. Here's the complete configure block that we saw in our photo sharing application:

```
app.configure(function () {
  app.use(express.urlencoded());
  app.use(express.json());
  app.use(express.multipart());
  app.use(express.cookieParser());
  app.use(express.session({ secret: 'podcast-app' }));
  app.use(passport.initialize());
  app.use(passport.session());
  app.use(express.static('public'));
});
```

5. Next, we configure passport to use the methods that we have in our signin.js file:

```
passport.use(signin.strategy(users));
passport.serializeUser(signin.serialize);
passport.deserializeUser(signin.deserialize(users));
```

6. We need to create the routes for logging in, logging out, and making user accounts. If the user is getting the /login route, we'll render the login.ejs (coming soon) file. Once they enter a username and password, the results will be saved to the /login route with the help of the POST request, where authentication will occur. Then, to log out at /logout, we'll call the logout method that passport has added to the request object, and redirect back to the root. So, here are the routes:

```
app.get("/login", function (req, res) {
  res.render("login.ejs");
});

app.post('/login', passport.authenticate('local', {
  successRedirect: '/',
  failureRedirect: '/login'
}));
```

Building a Podcast Application

```
app.get("/logout", function (req, res) {
  req.logout();
  res.redirect('/');
});
```

7. The last route related to user accounts is the `/create` route; this is the route that will be used to create new accounts. It's a lot of code, but it's pretty basic. We create an attributes object with the username and hashed password. Then, we check to see if the user exists. If they do, we go back to the root route. Otherwise, we'll create the user account and redirect to the root route, the difference being that we are now logged in. The following is the code for the `/create` route:

```
app.post('/create', function (req, res, next) {
  var userAttrs = {
    username: req.body.username,
    passwordHash: signin.hashPassword(req.body.password)
  };
  users.findOne({ username: userAttrs.username },
    function (existingUser) {
      if (!existingUser) {
        users.insert(userAttrs, function (err, user) {
          req.login(user, function (err) {
            res.redirect("/");
          });
        });
      } else {
        res.redirect("/");
      }
    });
});
```

8. The final flare for this portion is the `login.ejs` file, in the `views` directory. As you'll see, from all the extra classes and wrapping elements, we will use Twitter Bootstrap again. However, this time, we'll not use the default version. You can go to Bootswatch (http://bootswatch.com) to find other themes based on Bootstrap; all the same classes, but different styling. This way, you can choose any theme from Bootswatch that you'd like and get a different skin to your application, but you don't need to change the HTML code at all. I'm going to choose the Simplex theme (http://bootswatch.com/simplex), but you can choose a different one if you prefer. Download the CSS file and add it to the `public` directory. As you can see from the following template, we'll also have our own style sheet, `style.css` of the `public` directory, for a few customizations. We'll add to this file later.

Here's what should go inside the `login.ejs` file:

```html
<!DOCTYPE html>
<html>
<head>
  <title></title>
    <link rel="stylesheet"  href="/bootstrap.min.css" />
    <link rel="stylesheet"  href="/style.css" />
</head>
<body>
<div class='container'>
<div class='row'>
  <h1> Sign In </h1>
  <form method="post" action="/login">
    <div class='form-group'>
      <label>Username</label>
      <input name='username' type='text' class='form-
        control' />
    </div>
    <div class='form-group'>
      <label>Password</label>
      <input name='password' type='password' class='form-
        control' />
    </div>
    <button class='btn btn-primary'> Login </button>
  </form>

  <h1> Create Account </h1>
  <form method="post" action="/create">
    <div class='form-group'>
      <label>Username</label>
      <input name='username' type='text' class='form-
        control' />
    </div>
    <div class='form-group'>
      <label>Password</label>
      <input name='password' type='password' class='form-
        control' />
    </div>
    <button class='btn btn-primary'> Create </button>
  </form>
</div>
</div>
</body>
</html>
```

9. The next step is the root/catch-all route. If a user is logged in, we'll render the `index.ejs` file; otherwise, we'll have to redirect to `/login`. This is a good first version of the root route; if the `req.user` value is not set, we'll redirect to the login page. Otherwise, we'll render the index template. Here's the code for this route:

```
app.get('/*', function (req, res) {
  if (!req.user) {
    res.redirect("/login");
    return;
  }
  res.render('index.ejs', {
    username: req.user.username
  });
});
```

Subscribing to and storing podcasts

This application is a little different from our previous applications in terms of the data that we need to store. Before, we've always stored only data that we get from the user. This time, a user is only going to give us a URL—the path to a podcast feed—and we have to get all the data from that. Then, later, we need to check that same source for updates. This requires a lot more work on our part.

You might be thinking about how we're going to get this podcast data. Of course, there are only two places from which we can pull in this data: the client and the server. Both are possible; however, things will go a lot more smoothly if we choose to get this data on the server side. Here's why: to prepare the data on the client side would require us to first get the feed (which is a little more than simple, because it's a cross-domain request); then, we have to parse that to get the podcast and episode data we need, before sending the data back to the server for storage. This could take a rather long time, especially if the podcast has many episodes. If the user closes the application during this process, all or part of the data will be lost, and things could get messy. It's much better to do all that work on the server side, where the processing can continue even if the user closes their browser tab. So, we will focus on data processing next.

Now, there's going to be a fair bit of code involved in getting the podcast data, so we're going to create a custom Node.js module especially to work with podcasts. So, create a `podcasts.js` file in the project directory, and let's get started.

Chapter 6

First off, there are two other Node.js packages that we are going to use in this module:

- **xml2js** (https://www.npmjs.org/package/xml2js) will allow us to convert the podcast feed XML into JSON; it really won't be pretty JSON, but it will be usable.
- **q** (https://www.npmjs.org/package/q) is an asynchronous promises library.

So, install these two packages by executing this command:

```
npm install q xml2js --save
```

> If you haven't worked with promises before, you can think about them like this: often in JavaScript, you'll pass a callback to a function call so that the function can be run after some data is ready; a **promise** is an object that encapsulates that expected data. You can pass that promise object around and add multiple callbacks to it, all of which will be run when the data is ready. You can even add callbacks after the data is ready (of course, those will be run right away). For a really good introduction and explanation of promises, I recommend you check out the great article *JavaScript Promises ... In Wicked Detail* by Matt Greer (http://mattgreer.org/articles/promises-in-wicked-detail/). It will explain their benefits and how to use them.

In the `podcasts.js` file, we'll require the following libraries:

```
var http         = require('http');
var Bourne       = require('bourne');
var Q            = require('q');
var parseString  = require('xml2js').parseString;
var pcdb = new Bourne('podcasts.json');
var epdb = new Bourne('episodes.json');
```

We require the native-to-Node.js `http` library so that we can make a request for the podcast feed file. Also, we will create two Bourne databases here: one for podcasts, and the other for episodes. We won't even need to access these databases from the `server.js` file.

The following is the first method we'll write for getting the actual feed file:

```
function get (url) {
  var deferred = Q.defer();
  var req = http.get(url, function (res) {
    var xml = '';
```

```
    res.on('data', function (chunk) {
      xml += chunk;
    });
    res.on('end', function () {
      deferred.resolve(xml);
    });
  });
  return deferred.promise;
};
```

The method takes a URL and passes it to the `http.get` method. The callback we give to that method gets a response object. We can listen for the `data` event on that object and concatenate the data into a string, which we'll name `xml`. Then, when the request is finished (signaled by the `end` event), we use the XML string to resolve the `deferred` object we create at the top of the method. At the end of the method, we return the `promise` object for our `deferred` object. Now, we can use this method as shown in the following code:

```
get('http://podcast.com/feed.xml').then(function (xml) {
  // use the xml
});
```

The `promise` object we return has a `then` method. The value that we pass to the `deferred` object's `resolve` method will be passed as a parameter to the function we pass to the `then` method when the request is complete. So this is how we get the XML data for a podcast. Now, we need to convert it to JSON and get the values that we want. The `parse` function looks like this:

```
function parse(xml) {
  var deferred = Q.defer();
  parseString(xml, function (err, result) {
    var rss = result.rss.channel[0];
    var episodes = rss.item.map(function (item) {
      return {
        title:       item.title[0],
        duration:    item['itunes:duration'][0],
        audio:       item.enclosure[0].$.url,
        link:        item.link[0],
        description: item['content:encoded'][0],
        pubDate:     item.pubDate[0],
        listened:    false
      };
    });
```

```
      var info = {
        title: rss.title[0],
        link:  rss.link[0],
        image: rss['itunes:image'][0].$.href,
        lastUpdated: +new Date()
      };

      deferred.resolve({ info: info, episodes: episodes });
    });
    return deferred.promise;
  }
```

The parse function takes the XML input. We pass the XML input to the parseString function from xml2js to convert it to JSON. Then, we can start pulling the data we want out of the result. Unfortunately, xml2js doesn't give us a very clean JSON structure to work with; almost every value is an array, but most only have a single value in them. That's why we get the first element of an array in every case. Where the element has attributes instead of child elements, xml2js uses a property named $. Once we get the general information about the podcast and the data for each episode, we put them into an object that goes to resolving another promise.

With these two methods in place, we can now create a Podcast constructor function as a handy wrapper that is used to manage an individual podcast. This constructor function will need to work in two ways to be most useful in our server.js file. If we pass it a URL, it will assume we're creating a new podcast record, and will get and store the data. However, if we pass it a number, if will assume that the number is the ID of an already-stored podcast, and get that out of the database. Since storing and fetching this data will be asynchronous operations, we'll use promises to wait for the right time to act.

So, the Podcast constructor is a rather large function; we'll take it piece by piece. We will start with the following code:

```
  function Podcast(feed, userId) {
    var self        = this;
    var info        = Q.defer();
    var episodes    = Q.defer();
    this.info       = info.promise;
    this.episodes   = episodes.promise;
    this.ready      = Q.all([this.info, this.episodes]);
  }
```

Building a Podcast Application

The `feed` parameter will be either the URL or the ID, as we discussed earlier. The `userId` parameter will be the ID of the user who is subscribing to this podcast. Then, we'll create two deferred objects called `info` and `episodes`. We assign their promises as properties of the object we will create with this function so that we can use them when they are ready. We'll also create a `ready` property; this is another promise object that will resolve when all the promises we pass it in an array are resolved. This makes for a nice convenient way to do something when both the `info` and `episodes` promises are ready. You can see this in the following code, which is the next part of the `Podcast` function:

```
if (typeof feed === 'string') {
  get(feed).then(parse).then(function (data) {
    data.info.userId = userId;
    data.info.feed = feed;

    pcdb.insert(data.info, function (err, data) {
      info.resolve(data);
    });

    self.info.then(function (record) {
      data.episodes.forEach(function (e) {
        e.podcastId = record.id;
      });

      epdb.insertAll(data.episodes, function (err, records) {
        episodes.resolve(records);
      });
    });
  });
}
```

If the type of the parameter `feed` is a string, we know that we're creating a new podcast record. We'll get and parse the feed, using the methods we created earlier. Then, we add the feed URL and the `userId` parameter to the `info` property of the data we get back. This `info` property is now ready to be stored in the database. We'll store it in `pcdb`, the podcasts' database. In the callback for that, we'll resolve the `info` deferred object, because the `info` property has now been stored (this means our podcast record has an ID in our database).

One of the beautiful things about promises is that we can have multiple `then` calls to them. So, even though we created the `this.info` promise to be used outside the podcast object, we can wait for its resolution inside as well. That's the next step. When the `info` promise resolves, we need to store the episodes. You can see why it's important to wait until the podcast record is stored; we need to add the podcast's ID as the `podcastID` property to each episode object.

Once we have done that, we can insert all the records into the `episodes` database, and then use them to resolve the `episodes` promise.

Here's what we do if the `feed` parameter isn't a string:

```
  else {
    pcdb.findOne({ id: feed }, function (err, record) {
      info.resolve(record);
    });

    epdb.find({ podcastId: feed }, function (err, records) {
      episodes.resolve(records);
    });
  }
```

If the `feed` parameter is not a string, then we have created this podcast record previously, and we need to find it. We start by finding the podcast by that ID, and resolve the `info` promise. Then, we find all the episodes with that `podcastID` property and use them to resolve the `episodes` promise. Believe it or not, that's all we need to do for our `Podcast` constructor.

Next, we'll need to be able to check the feed for new episodes. So for this, we'll need an `update` method. This method is a little long and involved, and it actually doesn't do anything too complex. Here's the outer shell:

```
  Podcast.prototype.update = function () {
    var deferred = Q.defer();
    this.ready.spread(function (info, oldEpisodes) {
      function resolve () {
        epdb.find({ podcastId: info.id }, function (err, records) {
          deferred.resolve(records);
        });
      }

      var now = +new Date();
      if (now - info.lastUpdated > 86400000) {
        // update the podcast
      } else {
        resolve();
      }
    });
    return deferred.promise;
  };
```

Building a Podcast Application

We wait for our `this.ready` promise to be resolved; as you'll recall, this means that we're waiting for both `info` and `episodes` to be resolved. This promise has a `spread` method, which will spread the resolved values for these promises out so that each one is received as an individual parameter. As you can see, these are the `info` and `oldEpisodes` parameters. Then, we create the `resolve` function, which we'll use in several places inside this method. This function will simply find all the episodes for this podcast and resolve the deferred with them. So, the promise for the `update` method will return all the episodes for this podcast, not just the new ones.

Now, we'll call this `update` method every time a user loads the applications. However, most podcasts update about once a week, so there's no need to check for new episodes every time they load the page. So, we'll check once a day. When we subscribe to a podcast, we set the `lastUpdated` property to the current date and time as a Unix timestamp, using the unary plus operator (the single plus sign at the beginning, which is a shortcut for converting a `Date` object to a timestamp. Here, we get the current timestamp subtract to get the difference. If there is a difference of more than 86,400,000 (that's the number of milliseconds in a day), it means that we haven't updated this podcast in the last day, so we'll proceed with the update. Otherwise, we'll call resolve, which will just use the current episodes.

So, what if we want to do the update? The following code goes in place of the `// update the podcast` comment:

```
get(info.feed).then(parse).then(function (data) {
  if (data.episodes.length > oldEpisodes.length) {
    var oldTitles = oldEpisodes.map(function (e) {
      return e.title;
    }),
    newEpisodes = data.episodes.filter(function (e) {
      return oldTitles.indexOf(e.title) === -1;
    });

    epdb.insertAll(newEpisodes, resolve);
  } else {
    resolve();
  }
  pcdb.update({ id: info.id }, { lastUpdated: now });
});
```

As you can see, we begin by getting and parsing the XML feed. Then, we check to see whether the list of retrieved episodes is greater than the list of current episodes. If it is so, we know we have new episodes to store. The next part is to figure out what episodes these are. We start by getting just the titles from the currently stored episodes, and put that in `oldTitles`. The next step is to find all the episodes with titles that aren't in this array; we just use the array's `filter` method. Then, we can insert all the remaining ones into the episodes database, and call the `resolve` method. If there aren't any new episodes, we'll call the `resolve` method anyway. The last step is to update the `lastUpdated` property on the podcast record.

That's all we need for the `Podcast` class. However, since we expect users to subscribe to more than one podcast, let's make a simple `Podcasts` class to contain that behavior:

```
function Podcasts (id) {
  this.id = id;
}

Podcasts.prototype.all = function () {
  var d = Q.defer();
  pcdb.find({ userId: this.id }, function (err, records) {
    d.resolve(records);
  });
  return d.promise;
};

Podcasts.prototype.get = function (feed) {
  return new Podcast(feed, this.id);
};

Podcasts.prototype.updateEpisode = function (id, update, cb) {
  epdb.update({ id: id }, update, cb);
};

module.exports = Podcasts;
```

When we create a `Podcasts` instance, we'll pass it the ID of the user. Then, the `all` method will return a promise for all of that user's podcasts, and the `get` method will return a single podcast instance. The `updateEpisode` method is just a quick way to update a single episode; we'll only be using this to mark an episode as listened to. Finally, in a true Node.js module form, we end by exporting the `Podcasts` class. That's all we'll need to be able to access from the `server.js` file.

Building a Podcast Application

Speaking of the `server.js` file, let's go back there for a moment. First, pull in your `podcasts.js` file using the following line of code:

```
var Podcasts = require('./podcasts');
```

Then, in the catch-all route, we want to get the podcasts for the current user. Here's the completed version of that route:

```
app.get('/*', function (req, res) {
  if (!req.user) {
    res.redirect("/login");
    return;
  }
  req.user.podcasts = new Podcasts(req.user.id);
  req.user.podcasts.all().then(function (records) {
    res.render('index.ejs', {
      podcasts: JSON.stringify(records),
      username: req.user.username
    });
  });
});
```

If the user is logged in, we can create a property on the user object `podcasts`. This is a new `Podcasts` object, which receives the user ID as the parameter. Then, we get the users' podcasts and send these records to the `index.ejs` file, along with the username we were sending previously.

Preparing index.ejs

We've already created the `login.ejs` template, which will be displayed before a user is logged in. Once the user is logged in, we'll render the `index.ejs` file. Here's what we'll start with:

```
<!DOCTYPE html>
<html>
<head>
  <title> PodcastApp </title>
  <link rel="stylesheet" href="/bootstrap.min.css" />
  <link rel="stylesheet" href="/style.css" />
</head>
<body>
<div class='container-fluid' id='main'>
  <div class='row'>
    <div id='podcasts' class='col-md-3'></div>
    <div id='episodes' class='col-md-3'></div>
```

```
        <div id='episode' class='col-md-6'></div>
    </div>
</div>
<script src="/jquery.js"></script>
<script src="/underscore.js"></script>
<script src="/backbone.js"></script>
<script src="/bootstrap.min.js"></script>

<script src="/models.js"></script>
<script src="/views.js"></script>
<script src="/router.js"></script>
</body>
</html>
```

As we've done in previous applications, we'll be putting all our content inside the `<div id='#main'>` element. This time, however, we'll give it a Bootstrap class: `container-fluid`. It's pretty amazing how, just by applying the right Bootstrap classes, our application becomes reasonably responsive; we don't have to do any extra work. This time, we start with a bit of content in the main `<div>` element. There will be three columns in our application: the first will list the podcasts, the second will list the episodes for a selected podcast, and the third will show the details of an individual episode.

At the bottom, we'll pull in all our script tags; besides the defaults (jQuery, Underscore, and Backbone), we've got the JavaScript components of Bootstrap. This is necessary for the navigation we add later. Then, we have our own three files: `models.js`, `views.js`, and `router.js`.

Creating our models and collections

We'll start with the `models.js` file. There are two types of data we're going to be displaying here: podcasts and episodes. So, we'll have a model and collection for each of these. Let's start with episodes:

```
var Episode = Backbone.Model.extend({
  urlRoot: '/episode',
  listen: function () {
    this.save({ listened: true });
  }
});
var Episodes = Backbone.Collection.extend({
  model: Episode,
  initialize: function (models, options) {
    this.podcast = options.podcast;
  },
```

Building a Podcast Application

```
  url: function () {
    return this.podcast.url() + '/episodes';
  },
  comparator: function (a, b) {
    return +new Date(b.get('pubDate')) - +new
      Date(a.get('pubDate'));
  }
});
```

Our model class is called `Episode`; we give it a root URL and a `listen` method. The `listen` method will mark the episode as listened to, by setting the `listened` property to true and saving the update to the server. You'll recall that, by default, we set `listened` to `false` for every episode when subscribing to the podcast.

Then, the collection class is called `Episodes`. A collection of episodes will need to be associated with a podcast, so we'll get that `podcast` instance from the `options` object passed to the `initialize` method. Also, notice that we're setting a `url` method on the collection. Often, you'll set a `url` method on either the model class or the collection class, but not both. However, we'll need two different URLs here. The collection URL will be used to get all the episodes of a podcast. The model URL will be used when we mark an episode as listened to. The final portion of the collection class is the `comparator`. We want our episodes to show up in the right order, with the newest episodes at the top of the list, so we'll use the publishing dates as our comparison. Normally, we'd subtract value A from value B, but by reversing that, we can get the most recent episode at the top.

The podcast classes are even simpler, as you can see from the following code:

```
var Podcast = Backbone.Model.extend({
  episodes: function () {
    return this.episodes || (this.episodes = new Episodes([], {
      podcast: this }));
  }
});

var Podcasts = Backbone.Collection.extend({
  model: Podcast,
  url: '/podcasts',
});
```

The `Podcast` model class's `episodes` method is rather interesting. As we already saw, each `Podcast` instance will have a related `Episodes` collection. This method will return that collection. What we're doing in this one-line method is returning the `this.episodes` property if it exists. If it doesn't, we'll create it, assign it, and return it, all in one.

[184]

Building the navigation

Now, we're ready to start building our user interface; we can do this by performing the following steps:

1. Open the `views.js` file from the public directory. We'll start with some helper code. You're familiar with the first part, but the `tmpl` function is new. It's just a small helper function that we'll use to get our templates. We'll use this method for almost every view. Here's the code:

    ```
    _.templateSettings = {
      interpolate: /\{\{(.+?)\}\}/g
    };

    function tmpl(selector) {
      return _.template($(selector).html());
    }
    ```

2. Funnily enough, we're not going to use the `tmpl` function for the first view; the first view is the navigation view. Instead of creating a `template` property and choosing a `tagName` property, we're setting the `el` property. We make this property a selector for an element that already exists on the page, and that element will become the element for this view. When we click on the **Add Podcast** link, we'll want to display a form. To display this form, we'll navigate to the `/podcasts/new` route. This is the whole class:

    ```
    var NavView = Backbone.View.extend({
      el: '#navbar',
      events: {
        'click #addPodcast': 'addPodcast'
      },
      addPodcast: function (e) {
        e.preventDefault();
        Backbone.history.navigate('/podcasts/new',
          { trigger: true });
        return false;
      }
    });
    ```

3. Now, we need to create the element with the ID `navbar`, as this view is expecting. A lot of this is just for Bootstrap, but you can see that we have the **Add Podcast** and **Log Out** links. Its code is given as follows:

    ```
    <nav id='navbar' class="navbar navbar-inverse navbar-fixed-top" role="navigation">
      <div class="container-fluid">
    ```

Building a Podcast Application

```
      <div class="navbar-header">
        <button type="button" class="navbar-toggle" data-
          toggle="collapse" data-target="#navbar-tools">
          <span class="sr-only">Toggle navigation</span>
          <span class="icon-bar"></span>
          <span class="icon-bar"></span>
          <span class="icon-bar"></span>
        </button>
        <a class="navbar-brand" href="#">PodcastApp</a>
      </div>

      <div class="collapse navbar-collapse" id="navbar-
        tools">
        <ul class="nav navbar-nav">
          <li><a id='addPodcast' href="#">Add Podcast
            </a></li>
          <li><p class="navbar-text">Logged in as
            <%= username %></p></li>
          <li><a href='/logout'>Log Out</a></li>
        </ul>
      </div>
    </div>
  </nav>
```

Since this is already on the page, we don't have to insert it at any point; we'll just instantiate the router in the class. We'll do this soon, but the screenshot is a sneak peek to what it will look like when we do so:

PodcastApp   Add Podcast   Logged in as andrew   Log Out

One more thing: this navigation bar will be fixed to the top of the screen, so we need to push everything else down a bit so that none of the content is hidden behind it before the user scrolls. It's very simple; open your `style.css` file from the `public` directory, and add the following line of code:

```
body { padding-top: 60px; }
```

Displaying podcasts

The next step will be to display the list of podcasts that the user is subscribed to. We start with the `PodcastListView` class, which will display the collection. Here's that class:

```
var PodcastListView = Backbone.View.extend({
  className: 'list-group',
```

```
    initialize: function (options) {
      this.current = options.current || null;
      this.listenTo(this.collection, 'add', this.render);
    },
    render: function () {
      if (this.collection.length === 0) {
        this.el.innerHTML = "<a class='list-group-item'>
          No Podcasts</a>";
        return this;
      }
      this.el.innerHTML = '';
      this.collection.forEach(this.renderItem, this);
      return this;
    },
    renderItem: function (model) {
      model.set({ current: this.current === model.get('id') });
      var v = new PodcastListItemView({ model: model });
      this.el.appendChild(v.render().el);
    }
});
```

For Bootstrap, we'll add the `list-group` class to the view's element. In the `initialize` method, we'll check the `options` object for a `current` value. If the user has clicked on one of the podcasts in the list to display the episodes, we'll want to highlight that podcast, so `current` will be the ID of the selected podcast (if one is selected). Then, we'll also listen to for new additions to the collection we're displaying. If one is added, we'll call the `render` method again. The `render` method looks for a few different scenarios. If the collection is empty (which it will be, at first), we'll just display **No Podcasts**. Otherwise, we'll clear the element and render each model using the `renderItem` method. The `renderItem` method sets a `current` property on each model; if this model is the current one, it will be `true`; otherwise, it will be `false`. Then, we'll create a new `PodcastListItemView` instance, render it, and append it to the element. Now, we're ready for this view; this is its code:

```
var PodcastListItemView = Backbone.View.extend({
    tagName: 'a',
    className: 'list-group-item',
    template: tmpl('#podcastItem'),
    initialize: function () {
      this.model.episodes().on('count', this.displayCount, this);
    },
    events: {
      'click': 'displayEpisodes'
    },
```

[187]

Building a Podcast Application

```
    render: function () {
      this.el.innerHTML = this.template(this.model.toJSON());
      this.el.href = this.model.url();
      this.$el.addClass( this.model.get('current') ? 'active': '');
      this.displayCount();
      return this;
    }
  });
```

The element for this view is an anchor tag with the `list-group-item` class. We get the `podcastItem` template, which is fairly simple. Add the following code to the `index.ejs` file:

```
<script type='text/template' id='podcastItem'>
  {{ title }} <span class='badge'></span>
</script>
```

In this `initialize` method, we'll get the episodes collection for this podcast model and listen for the `count` event; when it occurs, we'll call the `displayCount` method. But before we write that method, we'll render the view. First, we'll render the template. Then, we'll set the `href` property on this element (remember, it's an anchor); this will be the URL for the podcast instance. If this is the current podcast, we'll add the active class to the element. Finally, we'll call the `displayCount` method. Here's that method:

```
    displayCount: function (evt) {
      var eps = this.model.episodes();
      eps.fetch().done(function () {
        var count = eps.pluck('listened')
          .filter(function (u) { return !u; }).length;
        this.$('.badge').text(count);
      }.bind(this));
    }
```

In this method, we get the episodes collection for the podcast and fetch the data from the server. When it arrives, we pluck the value of the `listened` property from each episode model; this will be an array of Boolean values. Then, we filter out all the `true` values, so we only have the `false` values left. The length of the resulting array is the number of podcasts that have not been listened to. Then, we put that number into the badge element of our template.

One last thing; if you haven't seen the `.bind(this)` trick before, this just keeps the value of `this` inside the function the same as it is outside the function.

Finally, have a look at the `events` property. When this view's element is clicked on, we'll redirect to the model's URL, as follows:

```
displayEpisodes: function (evt) {
  evt.preventDefault();
  Backbone.history.navigate(this.model.url(), { trigger: true });
  return false;
}
```

Creating a layout

With these views in place, we're almost ready to start the router. Open the `router.js` file from the `public` directory. Now, in the previous chapter, we were using Marionette, and it gave us regions and layouts to manage where our views went. We don't have them now, but since they were so useful, why don't we make them ourselves? We can create it with the following code:

```
function Region(selector) {
  this.el = $(selector);
}
Region.prototype.show = function (views) {
  if (!_.isArray(views)) { views = [views]; }
  this.el.empty();
  views.forEach(function (view) {
    this.el.append(view.render().el);
  }.bind(this));
};
```

When we create a region, we'll pass it a selector. Then, the `show` method will take one or more views. If we pass only a single view, we'll wrap it in an array. Then, we'll loop and append each view to the element. Notice that we're calling the `render` method and getting the element for the views here, so we only have to pass the view instance to this method.

If duplicating regions was easy, creating your own layout will be a piece of cake; we will create our layout by using the following code:

```
var layout = {
  podcasts: new Region('#podcasts'),
  episodes: new Region('#episodes'),
  episode:  new Region('#episode')
};
```

Building a Podcast Application

Beginning the router

Now, we are ready to start the router. The following is our `Router` code for the `router.js` file; we can start with this:

```
var Router = Backbone.Router.extend({
  routes: {
    '': 'index'
  },
  initialize: function (options) {
    this.podcasts = options.podcasts;
    this.nav = new NavView();
  },
  index: function () {
    layout.podcasts.show(new PodcastListView({
      collection: this.podcasts
    }));
  }
});
```

When the router is created, we'll accept a `podcasts` collection. We'll also create our `NavView` instance; remember, since the elements for this are already on the page, we don't have to append them. We're ready to take the root route with the `index` method; when that happens, we'll use our `layout.podcasts` region to show a `PodcastListView` instance.

To use this router, let's add another script tag to the `index.ejs` file:

```
<script>
  var r = new Router({
    podcasts: new Podcasts(<%- podcasts %>)
  });
  Backbone.history.start({ pushState: true });
</script>
```

Subscribing to new podcasts

We have all the functionality we need to display podcasts; now, let's create a form to be used when subscribing to new podcasts. As we determined earlier, in our `Podcast` module, all we need to get from the user is the podcast feed URL. So, let's create our `NewPodcastView` class. First, here's the template for this view:

```
<script type='text/template' id='newPodcast'>
  <form class='form-inline'>
    <div class="form-group">
```

```
        <input type="text" placeholder="feed url" class="form-
          control">
      </div>
      <button class='btn btn-primary'> Add </button>
    </form>
  </script>
```

As you can see, it's a simple form with a text input and a button. With this in place, we can now write the actual view:

```
    var NewPodcastView = Backbone.View.extend({
      className: 'list-group-item',
      template: tmpl('#newPodcast'),
      events: {
        'click button': 'addPodcast'
      },
      render: function () {
        this.el.innerHTML = this.template();
        return this;
      },
      addPodcast: function (e) {
        e.preventDefault();
        var feed = this.$el.find('input').val();
        this.$el.addClass('loading').text('Loading Podcast . . . ');
        this.collection.create({ feed: feed }, {
          wait: true,
          success: this.remove.bind(this)
        });
        Backbone.history.navigate('/');
        return false;
      }
    });
```

We'll give the element a list-group-item class and get the template. The rendering is very simple, and we're listening for a click on the button. When that happens, we'll get the feed from the field and replace the form with the text **Loading**. Then, we create a new podcast in the collection of podcasts that we'll associate with this view. The only property we need is the feed. Now, remember that our PodcastListView class will be listening for new models added to this collection. However, we need it to wait until the data has been stored in the server, so it has an ID and episodes to count. So, we'll add the wait option to this create call. Also, upon the successful completion of this request, we'll call this view's remove method to remove it from the UI. Finally, we'll navigate back to the home route (not triggering it, notice, because there's no need; we've just removed the form).

Building a Podcast Application

We're adding the `loading` class to the view's element while the data is being fetched on the server. Open the `style.css` file from the `public` directory, and add the following styling:

```
@keyframes pulse {
  0% {
    background: #fff;
    color: #000;
  }
  100% {
    background: #b81e0d;
    color: #fff;
  }
}

.loading {
  animation: pulse 1s ease-in-out infinite alternate;
}
```

We use a bit of CSS3 here; the element will pulse from red to white while the server is doing its work. Note that I'm using the standard CSS3 syntax here. At the time of writing this book, however, some browsers still require proprietary prefixes, so you'll have to add the code for the browsers you want to support. Of course, there are plenty of tools to assist you with this; Compass (http://compass-style.org/) is a good place to start.

Now, we'll update the router with the route for adding a podcast. First, add the route to the route objects using the following line of code:

```
'podcasts/new': 'newPodcast'
```

Then, we need to write the `newPodcast` method:

```
newPodcast: function () {
  var pv = new PodcastListView({ collection: this.podcasts });
  layout.podcasts.show(pv);
  pv.$el.append(new NewPodcastView({
    collection: this.podcasts
  }).render().el);
}
```

It's pretty simple; like we do in the `index` method, we'll create and render a new `PodcastListView` instance. However, we keep a reference to the view and append our form to it; this way, the form will be displayed like another item in the list.

[192]

The last step in subscribing to podcasts is the server code. We need to manage the POST request that will occur when the user saves a new feed. In the `server.js` file, add the following code:

```
app.post('/podcasts', function (req, res) {
  var podcast = req.user.podcasts.get(req.body.feed);
  podcast.info.then(res.json.bind(res));
});
```

We can use the user's `podcasts` object to get the new podcast by its feed. We wait until the `info` promise is ready, and send the data back to the client. Now, we can successfully subscribe to podcast. Give it a try; start up the application, create a user account, and subscribe to a few podcasts. The result should be similar to the following screenshot:

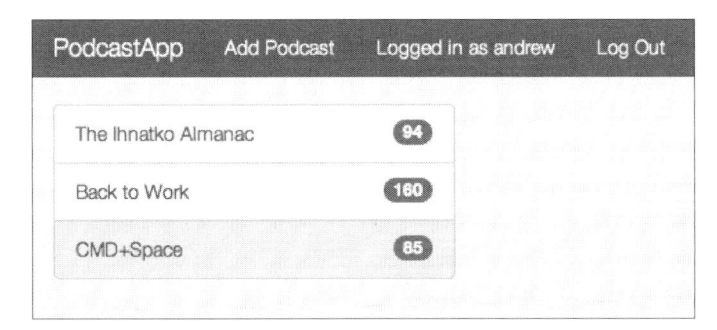

Displaying the list of episodes

Now that we can subscribe to podcasts, let's work on displaying the list of them. We have the `Episode` model and the `Episodes` collection. We'll start with the collection view `EpisodesView`:

```
var EpisodesView = Backbone.View.extend({
  className: 'list-group',
  initialize: function (options) {
    this.region = options.region;
  },
  render: function () {
    this.collection.forEach(function (model) {
      var v = new EpisodeListItemView({
        model: model,
        layout: this.region
      });
```

Building a Podcast Application

```
      this.el.appendChild(v.render().el);
    }, this);
    return this;
  }
});
```

Once again, this element will have the class `list-group`. You'll notice that in the `initialize` method, we expect `region` as one of the `options` object's properties. Keep this in mind, and we'll use it later.

In the `render` method, we loop over the collection and display an `EpisodeListItemView` instance. Notice that we pass `region` along; that's where we'll need it. Let's create this class next:

```
var EpisodeListItemView = Backbone.View.extend({
  className: 'list-group-item',
  events: {
    'click': 'displayEpisode'
  },
  initialize: function (options) {
    this.layout = options.layout;
    this.listenTo(this.model, 'change:listened',
      this.markAsListened);
  },
  render: function () {
    this.el.innerText = this.model.get('title');
    if (!this.model.get('listened')) {
      this.$el.addClass('list-group-item-danger');
    }
    return this;
  },
  markAsListened: function () {
    this.$el.removeClass('list-group-item-danger');
  },
  displayEpisode: function (evt) {
    evt.preventDefault();
    this.layout.show(new EpisodeView({ model: this.model }));
    return false;
  }
});
```

As we've done with our previous list item view, we'll give this one the class `list-group-item`. There's no template here; we'll just set the title of this model as the text for the element. Then, if this episode has not been listened to, we'll add a class to highlight it, marking it as such. In the `initialize` method, notice that we're listening for a change to the `listened` property. When that change occurs, we'll call the `markAsListened` method, which will remove that class so that the view is no longer highlighted.

The last method is `displayEpisode`, which will call the region's `show` method, passing it an `EpisodeView` instance for the model that this view is displaying. This won't just be a title, as we're showing here; it will be the entire model. This is why we're passing the region along. Since we're not changing the URL, we have to change the content of the page right here. So, that's what we do.

There's one more piece for the list of episodes: a toolbar above it. There's only one tool: **Mark All As Listened**, which is a simple button. Its code is as follows:

```
var EpisodesToolsView = Backbone.View.extend({
  className: 'btn-tools btn-group',
  events: {
    'click #mark': 'mark'
  },
  render: function () {
    this.el.innerHTML = "<button id= 'mark' class="btn btn-
      default">Mark As Listened</button>";
    return this;
  },
  mark: function (evt) {
    this.collection.forEach(function (model) {
      model.listen();
    });
    this.collection.trigger('count');
  }
});
```

Again, we start with the `className` property; the `render` method is very simple. In the `events` property, we wait for a click on the `#mark` button. When that happens, we call the `mark` function, which will loop over the collection and mark them all as listened to. Then, we trigger the `count` event on the collection; we listen for this event to occur in the `PodcastListItemView` class, where we'll update the podcast count.

Building a Podcast Application

Notice that one of the classes we're using is the `btn-tools` class. This is one of our own creations, and it's very simple; it just gives our tool bar a little more breathing room on the bottom:

```
.btn-tools {
  margin-bottom: 20px;
}
```

The last step for this is the server component for marking an episode as listened to. Here's the route to add to the `server.js` file:

```
app.put('/episode/:id', function (req, res) {
  req.user.podcasts.updateEpisode(parseInt(req.params.id, 10),
    req.body, function (err, data) {
      res.json(data);
    });
});
```

Now, we're ready to show our list of episodes. In the router of the `router.js` file, add the following route:

```
'podcasts/:id': 'podcast'
```

Now for that `podcast` method, here's its code:

```
podcast: function (id) {
  layout.podcasts.show(new PodcastListView({
    collection: this.podcasts,
    current: parseInt(id, 10)
  }));
  var podcast = this.podcasts.get(id);
  var episodes = podcast.episodes();
  episodes.fetch();
  layout.episodes.show([
    new EpisodesToolsView({
      model: podcast,
      collection: episodes
    }),
    new EpisodesView({
      collection: episodes,
      layout: layout.episode
    })
  ]);
}
```

We first render the podcast list, because it's possible that this page will be loaded directly. Notice that this time we're setting the `current` option so that it will be highlighted in the list. Then, we get the episodes for that podcast from the server. Next, in the `episodes` region, we show the views `EpisodesToolsView` and `EpisodesView`.

To get the episodes from the server, via `episodes.fetch()`, we need another server route, as shown in the following code:

```
app.get('/podcasts/:id/episodes', function (req, res) {
  var podcast = req.user.podcasts.get(parseInt(req.params.id,
    10));
  podcast.update().then(res.json.bind(res));
});
```

We'll get the `Podcast` object, and then call the `update` method to check for new episodes. When that returns, we'll send them to the client as JSON.

With this in place, we can now view a list of episodes, as shown in the following screenshot:

Now, all that's left is displaying individual podcast episodes.

Building a Podcast Application

Displaying episodes

Individual episodes will be displayed in the `EpisodeView` class. Let's start with the template:

```
<script type='text/template' id='episodeView'>
  <div class='btn-group btn-tools'>
    <button id='markOne' class="btn btn-default">Mark As
      Listened</button>
  </div>
  <div class="panel panel-default">
    <div class="panel-body">
      <h1>{{title}}</h1>
      <p>
        <strong>Duration</strong>: {{duration}}
        <strong>Date</strong>: {{pubDate}}
      </p>
      <audio controls='true' src="{{audio}}"></audio>
      {{description}}
    </div>
  </div>
</script>
```

We start with some tools at the top: a **Mark As Listened** button. Then, we show the details for the episode: title, duration, and date. Next comes the `audio` element; this makes it really easy for users to listen to the podcast right in our application. In our case, we only have a single audio source; however, you'll often want to add multiple sources in different formats (MP3, OGG, and so on) when using the `audio` element, for maximum browser and OS coverage. Underneath the `audio` element, we'll display the description, which will be the show notes for that episode. Here's the class:

```
var EpisodeView = Backbone.View.extend({
  template: tmpl('#episodeView'),
  events: {
    'click #markOne': 'listen'
  },
  render: function () {
    this.el.innerHTML = this.template(this.model.toJSON());
    this.$('audio')[0].addEventListener('play',
      this.listen.bind(this), false);
    return this;
  },
```

```
    listen: function (evt) {
      this.model.listen();
      this.model.collection.trigger('count');
    }
  });
```

Most of this view is the standard view code; we get the template, and we render the template with the model data. We also have a `listen` method, which will be called when the user clicks on the **Mark As Listened** button. The one difference is that we can't use the `events` property to listen for the `play` event on the `audio` element because of the way the `audio` element events works with Backbone. So, we get the element and use the `addEventListener` method to listen for that event.

This is the last piece. Now, you should be able to view and play episodes of the podcast. It looks like what is shown in the following screenshot:

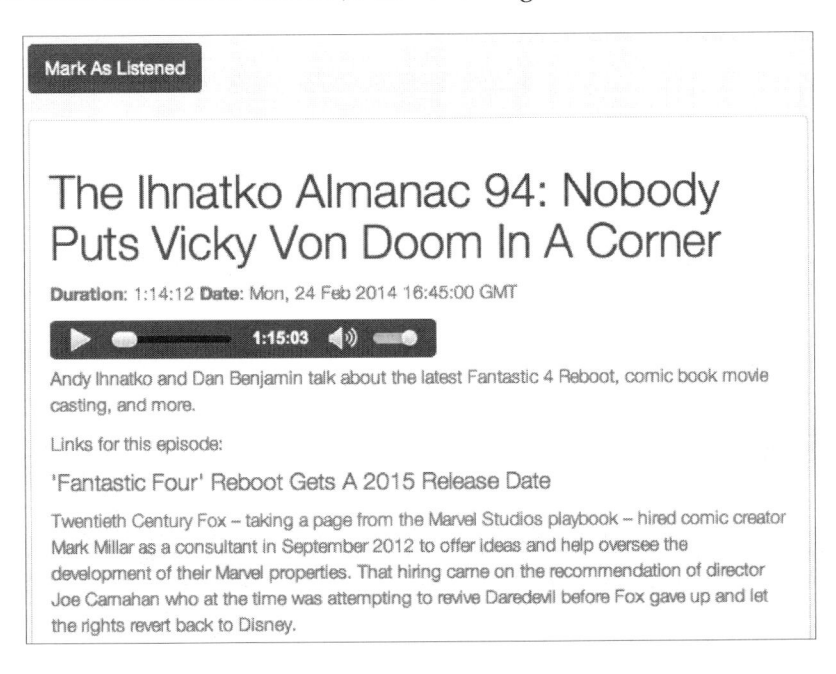

Summary

This brings us to the end of this chapter. A lot of what we did in this chapter was already familiar to you from previous applications, but there were a few nuggets that you shouldn't ignore. The main aspect is the strong server component. It is easy to forget that a Backbone application will always have the server code behind it, and often that code will be much more than a main template being rendered and a bunch of routes that shuttle JSON back and forth. There's often significant logic, data handling, and other details that will be taken care of on the server. As we saw, it's often possible to perform this logic on either the client or the server—we could have captured the RSS feed and processed it in either position. When building your own applications, it's important to make good decisions about where processes take place. It's often much quicker to do something on the client (no request/response to wait for), but you'll probably have more power and ability on the server, so the time delay might be negligible. The decision will be different for every situation, and there often won't be a single right choice.

The other interesting thing we did was recreate some of Marionette's behavior. This serves as another reminder that Backbone is just JavaScript, and there's no reason you can't write your own code to make it easier for you. There's no need to do anything fancy; as we saw, something as simple as our regions and layout can really clean up your router.

Only one chapter left, and that's where we'll have some fun and build a game.

7
Building a Game

We've come to the final chapter of this book, and if I may speak in first-person for a moment, this was my favorite application to build. Everybody loves a game, and if word games are your thing, you'll have fun with this too. Most of the applications we've written so far have been single-view applications; the only screen the user sees is the view that performs the main action of the application. However, full web applications often have other views that aren't the main purpose of the application, but serve to fill it out. We have one or two such views in this application.

So, here are a few of the topics we will cover in this chapter:

- Review all the primary uses of the Backbone components
- Add non-Backbone pages to fill out the application
- Build an app that uses data not provided by the user
- Write (simple) game logic

What are we building?

Once again, we'll start by describing what we're planning the build. It's going to be a word game, modeled after a very simple iPhone game I enjoy, called *7 Little Words* (http://www.7littlewords.com/). Each game (or round, if you will) has seven words that are broken into parts of two, three, or four letters. Your job is to reassemble the words based on the short definitions that you're given. To make it clear, I have no affiliation with this iPhone game, I just like playing it!

However, we're going to take it a little farther than that game does, by assigning different point values to words, and also timing our users. This way, players can compare scores and times to make things a little more competitive.

Building a Game

Here's a screenshot of what the game view of our application will look like when it is finished. At the bottom, you can see the tokens that the user will choose to combine into a word. There's a textbox in the middle that shows the word the user has assembled. Then, they'll click on the **Guess** button to see if the word matches one of the definitions above:

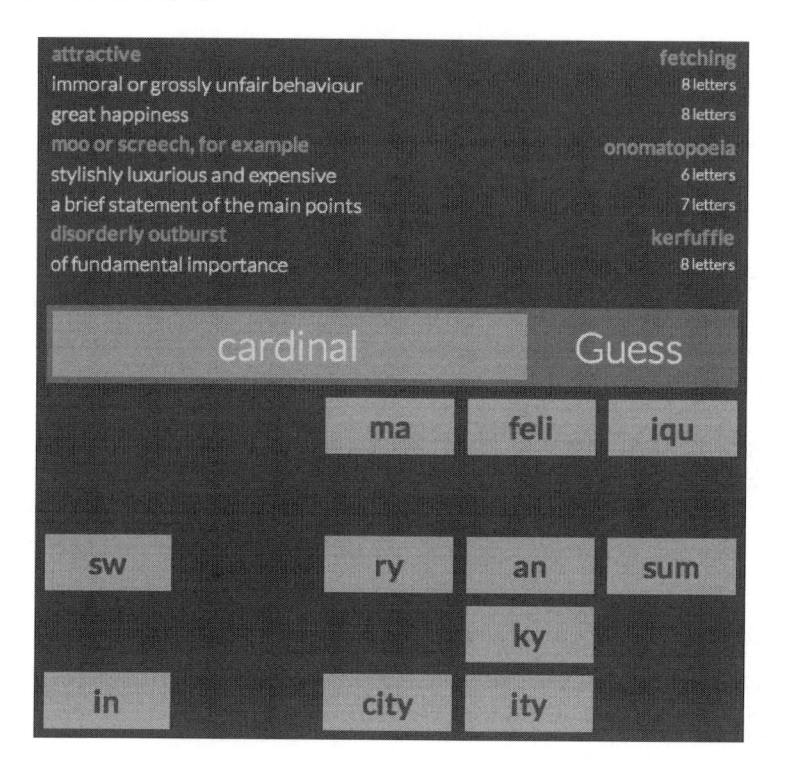

User accounts

We'll start as we did in the last chapter; by adding user account to our basic application. We won't go over the whole process again; you can copy it from the previous chapter's application. There's only one change we have to make. In the `app.post('/create')` route, we create a `userAttrs` object that we store in the database. Users of this application will have three application-specific values to store:

- `score`: This is their highest score
- `time`: This is their lowest time
- `games`: This is an array of the games they have played

Here's the code to create the `userAttrs` object:

```
var userAttrs = {
  username: req.body.username,
  passwordHash: signin.hashPassword(req.body.password),
  score: 0,
  time: 3600,
  games: []
};
```

With this in place, and all the other user account creation code we've previously created, we have the shell of an application, ready to customize.

Templates

Our server-side templates have been pretty basic in previous applications. We've only ever had a single `index.ejs` file, and maybe a `login.ejs` file. However, in a big application, you'll probably have several different server templates. When that's the case, you want to remove code duplication as much as possible. How you go about this is dependent on which server-side template system you use. Since we're using ejs (https://github.com/visionmedia/ejs), we'll do this via **includes**. So, in our project's `views` directory, make a file called `header.ejs`. Here's what goes in there:

```
<!DOCTYPE html>
<html>
<head>
  <title> Tokenr </title>
  <link rel="stylesheet"  href="/style.css" />
</head>
<body>
```

Basic and expected, right? Now, we're also going to have a `footer.ejs` file in the `views` directory, which will close these tags:

```
</body>
</html>
```

Alternatively, you could just remember to add these two lines to the bottom of every template you create that uses the `header.ejs` include (or, if you're hip with the HTML5 lack-of-strictness, leave them out entirely), but I like the symmetry that comes from having both the `header.ejs` and `footer.ejs` files. For example, our `login.ejs` file in the `views` directory, which has both the login and signup forms:

```
<% include header %>
<div id="main">
  <form method="post" action="/login">
```

```
        <h1> Sign In </h1>
        <p><input type='text' name='username' /></p>
        <p><input type='password' name='password' /></p>
        <p><button>Log In</button></p>
      </form>
      <form method="post" action="/create">
        <h1> Sign Up </h1>
        <p><input type='text' name='username' /></p>
        <p><input type='password' name='password' /></p>
        <p><button>Create Account</button></p>
      </form>
    </div>
    <% include footer %>
```

See what I mean about symmetry? We can use the same technique in the `index.ejs` file in the `views` directory, which will start out like this:

```
    <% include header %>
    <div id="main"></div>
    <script src="/jquery.js"></script>
    <script src="/underscore.js"></script>
    <script src="/backbone.js"></script>
    <script src="/models.js"></script>
    <script src="/views.js"></script>
    <script src="/router.js"></script>
    <% include footer %>
```

As you can see, we'll be splitting models, views, and the router into separate files again. This will be especially important in this application because of some of the complex code the models will use. So now that we have a `index.ejs` file in the `views` directory, we can render the index route. In the `server.js` file, this code should be your final route:

```
    app.get('/*', function (req, res) {
      if (!req.user) {
        res.redirect("/login");
        return;
      }
      res.render("index.ejs");
    });
```

Notice that we're not passing any values into the index template; this application won't require anything like that. This might sound strange. Since it is supposed to be a more advanced application, wouldn't you expect it to need more data out of the gate? If your application needs to shuttle a lot of data from the server to the browser, it is sometimes a smarter move not to move the data all at once; it could seriously slow down your load time. A better technique is to load the data when it is needed, and that's what we'll do here. Also, it is possible that you might need the user to make a decision before you know exactly what data you need; this is another reason to delay loading data, and this is true in our case as well.

Creating the game data

Speaking of loading data, the next step is to create the data for our game—the words the users will spell. This is actually the only application in this book that begins with data, instead of only working with the data that users give to the application. The actual raw data will be in the `words.json` file in the root of our project. One of the keys to this being a good game is to have plenty of words to choose from. Here's how the file starts:

```
[{"id":1,"level":3,"word":"anguine","definition":"snakelike"},
 {"id":2, "level":1,"word":"cardinal","definition":"of fundamental
   importance"},
 {"id":3, "level":3,"word":"detersion","definition":"act of
   cleansing"},
 {"id":4, "level":3,"word":"exiguous","definition":"meager"},
 {"id":5, "level":2,"word":"fraternise","definition":"associate
   with"},
```

Of course, every word has an ID. Then, the important properties are the words and definitions. The definition is what the user will see, and the word is what they'll have to piece together. The level is a number between 1 and 3, with level 1 words being the easiest and level 3 words being the toughest. You can write your own list, or download this list from Github (`https://gist.github.com/andrew8088/9627996`).

> During the development of this application, one idea was to use a dictionary API (such as `dictionaryapi.com`) to randomly select words from a much larger database. However, this isn't really practical, because we need a short, crossword-puzzle-like definition, and standard dictionary definitions just don't cut it. Also, most APIs don't have a way of selecting a random word.

Building a Game

Once we have our list of words, we'll need to create the actual database. Add this to the top of the `server.js` file:

```
var _ = require('./public/underscore');
var words = new Bourne('words.json');
```

We also require the Underscore library here; you'll see what we need it for in a moment. We need the very same file that we use on the client side. This won't work for every file; it just happens that the latest version of Underscore (at the time of writing this book, 1.6.0) is written to work on both the client and the server.

Each game played by a user will have eight words; this means that we need to pull eight words randomly, but all of the same difficulty level, from the database. To do this, we'll add a `getWords` function to the server file:

```
function getWords(level, cb) {
  words.find({ level: level }, function (err, records) {
    cb(null, _.shuffle(records).slice(0, 8));
  });
}
```

This function will take a level number and a callback function. Then, we'll get all the words in the database for that level. We'll then shuffle the array of records, using Underscore's `shuffle` method. After we shuffle the array, we'll slice the first eight items off the array and pass them to the callback.

> It should be said that this is probably not an optimal way to get eight random words from most databases. Since I wrote the Bourne database system for small datasets, and it keeps all records in memory, what we do here should be fast. However, there will probably be better ways, depending on the database system you're using.

Now that we have a way of getting the words, we need to create a route for that:

```
app.get('/game/:level', function (req, res) {
  var level = parseInt(req.params.level, 10);
  getWords(level, function (err, words) {
    res.json(words);
  });
});
```

The level for the game is part of the URL. We convert it to a number, and then call our `getWords` function. Once we have the words, we can send them back to the browser as JSON.

Writing the models

Because of the nature of this application, we will have more models than usual. The two obvious ones are the `Word` model and its collection, `Game`. These hardly require explanation. However, remember that we'll split words into parts, which we'll call tokens. For this, we'll have a `Token` model and a `Tokens` collection. These are actually the simplest parts:

```
var Token = Backbone.Model.extend({});
var Tokens = Backbone.Collection.extend({
  model: Token
});
```

Since these are just shells for the chopped-up words, there doesn't need to be much to them. All the primary logic will be in the `Word` and `Game` classes. Let's start with the `Word` class:

```
var Word = Backbone.Model.extend({
  initialize: function () {
    this.set('points', this.get('word').length +
      this.get('level'));
  },
  parts: function () {
    return Word.split(this.get('word'));
  }
});
```

Every `Word` instance will need to be assigned a point value. It's not that tricky; just add the length of the word and its difficulty level. Later, multiply this value with another that's based on time. The other method calls the `Word.split` function, passing it the word. This is where the code gets a little more complex.

However, before we get to splitting up words, notice that the `split` method is a static or class-level method. This isn't something we've seen before in Backbone; but Backbone makes it very simple to add static methods. So far, we've only ever passed one parameter to the `Backbone.Model.extend` method; an object of instance-level properties and methods. However, the method can take a second object, with class properties and methods:

```
Backbone.Model.extend({
  // instance properties
},
{
  // class properties
});
```

Building a Game

This isn't just for models; it works with collections, views, and even routers. So, add a class properties object to the preceding `Word` model; we'll be using it in the next section.

Splitting up words

Randomly splitting the words into tokens is not as easy as you think. We want to do it randomly, so that each time a game is played, a word may be split up differently. We want to split every word into tokens of two, three, or four letters. You might think, then, that we could randomly select one of those numbers. However, we don't really want equal amounts of all three sizes; we'd like fewer two-letter tokens. This requires a weighted random selection, so we first have to write a function for that. The way to represent our weighted options is through an array like this:

```
[[2, 0.2], [3, 0.4], [4,0.4]]
```

Each array within this array has two elements. The first is the value we want to use; this could be a string, an object, or anything. The second value is the chance that this will be the value chosen. As you can see from this array, the value 2 will be chosen 20 percent of the time, and values 3 and 4 will be chosen 40 percent of the time, each. So, here's the function that takes that array as a parameter. Remember to put this in the class properties object of the `Word` model:

```
weightedRandomGenerator: function(items) {
  var total = items.reduce(function (prev, cur) {
    return prev + cur[1];
  }, 0),
    sum = 0,
    list = [];
  for (var i = 0; i < items.length; i++) {
    sum = (sum*100 + items[i][1]*100) / 100;
    list.push(sum);
  }
  return function () {
    var random = Math.random() * total;
    for (var i = 0; i < list.length; i++) {
      if (random <= list[i]) {
        return items[i][0];
      }
    }
  }
}
```

The first step is to add up the percentage values in the arrays. In our case, these values add up to 1, but they don't have to; if they add up to some other value, this will still work. We do this by calling the native reduce method on the array, summing up all seconds elements. The next step is to create a new array, which the weight values sum up as they go along. For example, our weight values are 0.2, 0.4, and 0.4. For these values, we need to create an array like this:

```
[0.2, 0.6, 1]
```

So, we create a `sum` variable and an array called `list`. Then, we loop over the items, adding the value to the `sum` variable, and then pushing that `sum` variable into the `list` array. We now have the array we need. Finally, we'll return a function. The function will start by getting a random number between 0 and the total. Then, we'll loop over the list, checking each item to see whether it is less than or equal to the random number. Once we get a match on that, we'll return the value from the original items parameter, using the same index number. That's all for our weighted random generator. Now, we're ready to use this in the function that splits the word into tokens. This is the `split` function:

```
function split(word) {
  word = word.split('');
  var tokens = [];

  var rand234 = Word.weightedRandomGenerator([[2, 0.2], [3, 0.4],
    [4,0.4]]),
    rand23  = Word.weightedRandomGenerator([[2, 0.5], [3, 0.5]]),
    rand24  = Word.weightedRandomGenerator([[2, 0.5], [4, 0.5]]);

  var w, length;
  while (word.length > 0) {
    w = word.length;
    if       (w >   5) length = rand234();
    else if (w === 5) length = rand23();
    else if (w === 4) length = rand24();
    else              length = w;

    tokens.push(word.splice(0, length).join(''));
  }
  return tokens;
}
```

Building a Game

This function takes a word and splits it into tokens. First, we split the string into an array, and then create an array to hold the tokens. Next, we create three random generators, which we'll need at different points. Then, we have a `while` loop, for when the length of the word is greater than zero. If the length of the word is greater than five characters, we'll use the generator that will return a 2, 3, or 4. If the word is five characters long, we'll use the generator that returns either 2 or 3. If it's four characters long, we'll use the generator that will return either 2 or 4. The final `else` statement will be used if the word is shorter than four characters; we'll use the length of the word.

All of this ensures that the word will be split up into tokens of two, three, or four characters; it also makes sure that we'll never get a one-letter token, by slicing off all but one of the letters. The last step in the `while` loop is to use the word array's `splice` method. This method will mutate the original array, taking those letters out of the array and returning them (this is how the word length changes in the `while` loop condition). Once we've split up the word into tokens, we return the array of tokens. This is the function used in the `Word` class's parts method.

The collection class for this is `Game`. This will start out very simply:

```
var Game = Backbone.Collection.extend({
  model: Word,
  initialize: function (models, options) {
    this.guessedCorrectly = [];
    this.seconds = -1;
    this.score = 0;
    this.level = 1;
  },
  getWords: function () {
    return Backbone
      .ajax("/game/" + this.level)
      .then(this.reset.bind(this));
  },
  tokens: function () {
    var tokens = _.flatten(this.invoke('parts'));
    return new Tokens(tokens.map(function (token) {
      return { text: token };
    }));
  }
});
```

This really is just the start. One of these collection instances will handle much more, but we'll get there. We start by setting the model class for this collection, and then we create the `initialize` method. A collection object will be responsible for tracking time and points, so we give it a `seconds` and `score` property. Since our game will have levels, we also have a `level` property. Then, we have the `getWords` method.

Chapter 7

As we know, we aren't sending a set of words with the initial page load, so this is the method that will do that. This makes an AJAX request to the route we created to send the words. The `Backbone.ajax` method actually wraps the `jQuery.ajax` method. It returns a promise, which we learned about in *Chapter 6, Building a Podcast Application*, here. We call its `then` method, passing it the collection's `reset` method. This method will replace any models in the collection with the array of models passed as a parameter. The `then` method will return the promise object, so we return it. This way, we can perform an action after the words have been loaded.

Finally, notice the `tokens` method; in here, we call the collection's `invoke` method. This method takes the name of another method and calls it on each model in the collection. This will return an array of values; in this case, the values will be an array of tokens, the split-up words. An array of arrays isn't useful, so we'll use Underscore's `flatten` method to flatten the nested arrays into a single array of tokens. Then, we return a `Tokens` collection instance, mapping the `tokens` array into an array of objects.

Writing the tokens view

Now that we have the models more or less in place, we're ready to start writing the actual views. Let's start with something simple: the tokens. We start with the `TokensView` class:

```
var TokensView = Backbone.View.extend({
  render: function () {
    this.collection.tokens()
      .shuffle().forEach(this.addToken, this);
    return this;
  },
  addToken: function (token) {
    this.el.appendChild(new TokenView({
      model: token
    }).render().el);
  }
});
```

Writing this class is very simple. We get the collection of tokens from the game, call the built-in `shuffle` method to shuffle the tokens, and then render them each with the `addToken` method. This method renders a `TokenView` instance and appends it to the element. So that's the next stop – the `TokenView` class:

```
var TokenView = Backbone.View.extend({
  className: 'token',
  events: {
```

```
      'click': 'choose'
    },
    render: function () {
      this.model.view = this;
      this.el.innerHTML = this.model.get('text');
      return this;
    },
    choose: function () {
      Backbone.trigger('token', this.model);
      this.hide();
    },
    hide: function () {
      this.$el.addClass('hidden');
    },
    show: function () {
      this.$el.removeClass('hidden');
    }
  });
```

Each `TokenView` instance will have a class: `token`. The `render` method is pretty basic—it just puts the text of the token in the element. However, notice the first line of the method; we're giving the model a view property that points to this view. This is something we haven't done before; we have never given a model a link to the view that renders it. This isn't always considered a good thing; it's often better to keep a clean separation between the model and the view. However, sometimes this can be a good thing, as we'll see in this case. Either way, it's very easy to do. When this element is clicked on, the `choose` method will be called. This method triggers the `token` event, using the model as a parameter. We've triggered events before, but this is the first time we've used the `Backbone.trigger` method. We can use this to trigger and listen for events globally across all our code. After we trigger the event, we'll hide the view. We have `hide` and `show` views here as well. These add or remove a class on the element to hide or show the token respectively.

Normally, this would be the point where we start the router, so we can render our view and then style it. However, we're going to go a different route this time. Often, when building a more complex application, you're on a roll with whatever you're working on—the views, in our case—and you don't want to switch mindsets. What I'll do in a case like this is put a `script` tag in the `index.ejs` file to test the view we just created:

```
<script>
  var game = new Game();
  game.getWords().then(function () {
    $('#main').append(new TokensView({
      collection: game
```

```
        }).render().el);
    }.bind(this));
</script>
```

It's quick and dirty; we create a `Game` object, get a set of words, and then append a new `TokensView` instance to the page. You should see something like this:

```
tho
ard
summ
lli
card
in
ra
emo
neme
ary
ood
sis
tow
br
ra
umb
al
ent
pen
ple
un
```

If you click on the individual tokens and open your developer tools, you'll see that they get the `hidden` class, just like we coded. Of course, nothing else happens right now, but that's because we don't have anything listening for the `'token'` event. It's a good start, and it's enough to begin the styling. So, open the `style.css` file of the `public` directory. Let's start with this:

```
@import url("//fonts.googleapis.com/css?family=Lato:300,400,700");
body {
    margin: 0;
    padding: 0;
    font-family: lato, helvetica-neue, sans-serif;
    background: #2B3E50;
    font-weight:300;
    color: #ebebeb;
}
#main {
```

Building a Game

```
    width: 540px;
    padding: 0 5%;
    margin: auto;
}
```

We're starting this by pulling in a Google font. There are several to choose from at `https://www.google.com/fonts`; we're going with Lato. On the `<body>` element, we'll set the font, font color, and background. Then, we'll set a width on the main `<div>` element, the one most of our application will be inside. Next, we'll add some styling to our anchor elements:

```
a {
    text-decoration: none;
    font-weight: 700;
    color: #ebebeb;
}
#main a:hover {
    text-decoration: underline;
}
```

All the links will get a bit of styling—no underline, some bolding, and a new color—but only anchors in the main element will get the hover styling. This is because we're soon going to create a navigation bar (outside the main element), and we don't want the links to be underlined when hovered over. Now, we're ready to style the tokens, which we do with this code:

```
.token {
    font-size: 150%;
    font-weight: 700;
    margin: 5px;
    padding:7px 0;
    display: inline-block;
    background:#F0AD4E;
    color: #474747;
    width: 100px;
    text-align:center;
}
.token:nth-child(5n+1) {
    margin-left: 0;
}
.token:nth-child(5n) {
    margin-right:0;
}
.token:hover {
```

[214]

```
    background: #DF691A;
    cursor: pointer;
    color: #ececec;
}
.hidden {
    visibility: hidden;
}
```

We style the token as, basically, an orange block. We space them out evenly; we use the *n*th-child selectors to remove the margin from the outer edges of the other blocks. We add a hover effect to the blocks. Finally, we add the `hidden` class. Now, a refresh of the page should result in something like this:

le	sei	ui	quin	ly
bec	iniq	bu	ripp	lli
oya	ial	ing	ent	om
emo	zure	love	tes	nt
ty	sent			

Looking pretty good, don't you think? Now, we're ready for the next view, the ones that display the clues, that is, the definitions.

Views of the clues

The clues for the words—the definitions—will need to appear above the tokens. The `CluesView` class is pretty simple:

```
var CluesView = Backbone.View.extend({
    tagName: 'table',
    render: function () {
        this.collection.forEach(function (word) {
            this.el.appendChild(new ClueView({
                model: word
            }).render().el);
        }, this);
        return this;
    }
});
```

Building a Game

The clues will be in a table. In the `render` method, we'll loop over the collection, rendering a `ClueView` class for each `Word` model. The `ClueView` class is where all the action takes place. Here's the `ClueView` class's code:

```
var ClueView = Backbone.View.extend({
  tagName: 'tr',
  template: _.template($('#clue').html()),
  initialize: function () {
    Backbone.on('correct', this.correct, this);
  },
  render: function () {
    this.el.innerHTML = this.template(this.model.toJSON());
    return this;
  },
  correct: function (word) {
    if (this.model.get('word') === word.get('word')) {
      this.$el.addClass('correct');
      this.$('.word')
        .removeClass('clue')
        .text(word.get('word'));
    }
  }
});
```

This view will use a table row element, and it's the first view we have that uses a template. To render the template, we'll just pass the JSON version of that model to the `template` function. In the `initialize` method, we listen for the `correct` event to occur. This is the event that will be triggered when the player has correctly guessed one of the words. This is another global event that we'll fire at another location. When it happens, we'll call the `correct` method. This method will receive as a parameter the `Word` model for the correct word. Even though only one word has been guessed, all the `ClueView` instances will be listening for the correct event. So, the first step will be to compare words and to find the right `ClueView` instance. If the model for this view matches, we'll add the `correct` class. Then, we'll remove the `clue` class from part of the template and add the word.

Speaking of the template, add this to the `index.ejs` file in the `views` directory:

```
<script type='text/template' id='clue'>
  <td>{{ definition }}</td>
  <td class='word clue'>{{ word.length }} letters</td>
</script>
```

[216]

As you know, this will go inside our table row element. The first `<td>` element will have the definition. The second will start by displaying the number of letters in the word, as another small clue. As we've seen, when they correctly guess the word, the clue will be replaced with the word itself. Before we check this out in the browser, let's add some styling to the `style.css` file in the `public` directory:

```css
table {
    width: 100%;
}
td:nth-of-type(1) {
    width:75%;
}
.clue {
    font-size:75%;
}
.word {
    float: right;
}
.correct {
    color: #5CB85C;
    font-weight: 700;
}
```

We'll straighten up the `table` element and the first `<td>` cell in each row. When the second `<td>` cell has the number of letters in it, the `clue` class will reduce the font size a little. Then, when the word is correctly guessed, we'll remove that class and add `correct` to the whole `<tr>` element, coloring it and making it bold.

Now, back in the `index.ejs` file, you can render this view in that same quick and dirty way. Replace the content inside the `getWords` callback with this:

```js
$('#main')
    .append(new CluesView({ collection: game }).render().el)
    .append(new TokensView({ collection: game }).render().el);
```

Building a Game

Then, refresh the page. It should look like this:

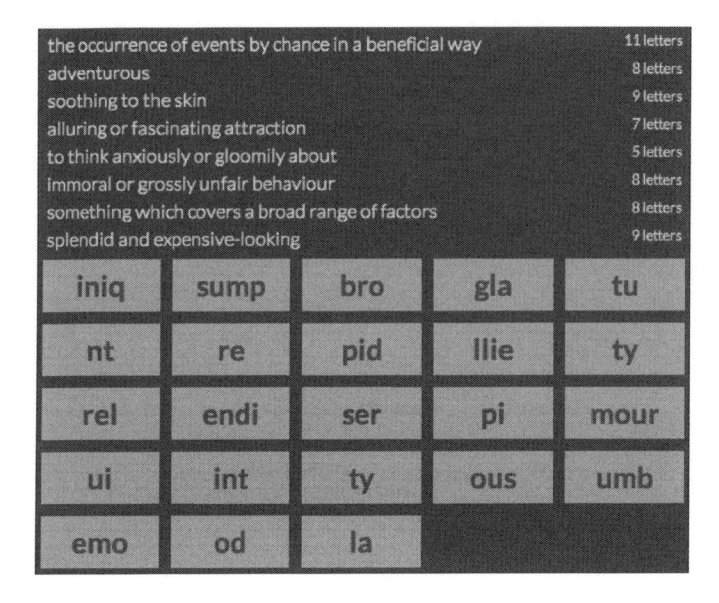

the occurrence of events by chance in a beneficial way	11 letters
adventurous	8 letters
soothing to the skin	9 letters
alluring or fascinating attraction	7 letters
to think anxiously or gloomily about	5 letters
immoral or grossly unfair behaviour	8 letters
something which covers a broad range of factors	8 letters
splendid and expensive-looking	9 letters

iniq	sump	bro	gla	tu
nt	re	pid	llie	ty
rel	endi	ser	pi	mour
ui	int	ty	ous	umb
emo	od	la		

We can't yet see the correct word styling, because we can't yet guess words. That brings us to the next step: the guess view.

Creating the guess view

This will be the longest view in our application, because it's got the most to do. Let's start this one with the template:

```
<script type='text/template' id='guess'>
  <div class='btn text'></div>
  <div id='guessBtn' class='btn'> Guess </div>
</script>
```

It looks simple. The first `<div>` element is where the token text will appear as the player clicks on tokens. The second `<div>` element will be a button; when they click on it, their guess will be "submitted". If the guess is one of the words, it will appear alongside the correct definition. Otherwise, the tokens will reappear with the other tokens. This is the code for the `GuessView` class:

```
var GuessView = Backbone.View.extend({
  className: 'guess',
  template: $('#guess').html(),
  events: {
```

```
      'click #guessBtn': 'guess'
    },
    initialize: function () {
      Backbone.on('token', this.add, this);
      this.currentTokens = [];
    },
    render: function () {
      this.el.innerHTML = this.template;
      this.guessText = this.$('.text');
      return this;
    },
    add: function (token) {
      this.currentTokens.push(token);
      this.guessText.append(token.get('text'));
    }
  });
```

Here's the start; we'll give this element a class called guess, and we'll get the preceding template that we just created. In the initialize method, we'll listen for the token event. Remember, when one of the tokens is clicked on, this event will trigger globally. Here, we catch that event and run our add method. The other thing going on in the initialize method is the creation of a currentTokens property. This will keep track of the tokens the user selects before they actually make a guess. In the render method, we'll get the template (which is just a string in this case, because there's no template data in this view), and then create a property that points to the <div> element we're using as a text field. This property is used in the add method; the method gets the Token model as a parameter. We'll cache the token in the currentTokens array, and append its text to the element.

Before we continue with this, let's style it. You know where to go—the style.css file in the public directory:

```
.guess {
  overflow: hidden;
  margin: 20px 0 5px;
  border: 5px solid #D4514D;
}
.btn {
  background: #D4514D;
  width: 30%;
  cursor: pointer;
  line-height: 50px;
  height: 50px;
  font-size:200%;
  text-align: center;
```

Building a Game

```
    float:left;
}
.btn:hover {
    background: #C04946;
}
.btn.text {
    background: #5BC0DE;
    width:70%;
}
```

Both the inside `<div>` elements have the class `btn`; we'll float them to the left and apply height, width, and coloring. Then, for the one with both the `btn` and `text` classes, we'll adjust the background color and width. When the actual button `<div>` is hovered over, we'll change the background color a bit, as buttons should do.

Now, let's render this view. Back in the `index.ejs` file change the `getWords` callback one more time:

```
$('#main')
    .append(new CluesView({ collection: game }).render().el)
    .append(new GuessView({ collection: game }).render().el)
    .append(new TokensView({ collection: game }).render().el);
```

Open this in the browser and click on a couple of tokens. You should see something like this:

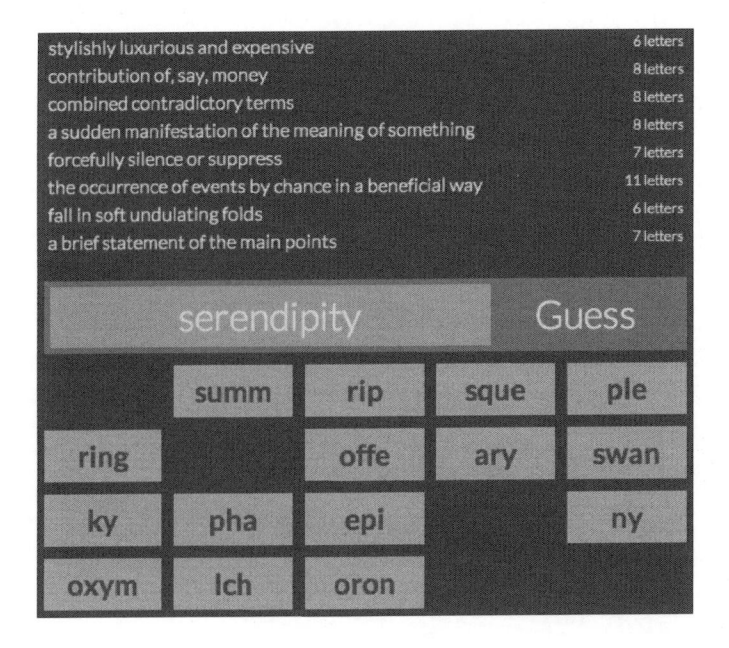

stylishly luxurious and expensive	6 letters
contribution of, say, money	8 letters
combined contradictory terms	8 letters
a sudden manifestation of the meaning of something	8 letters
forcefully silence or suppress	7 letters
the occurrence of events by chance in a beneficial way	11 letters
fall in soft undulating folds	6 letters
a brief statement of the main points	7 letters

serendipity	Guess

	summ	rip	sque	ple
ring		offe	ary	swan
ky	pha	epi		ny
oxym	lch	oron		

After playing with this, you should see two changes we need to make to this view. The big obvious one is that our **Guess** button doesn't do anything. The smaller, design-related problem is that the red border of our `GuessView` class's `<div>` element doesn't change color when the button is hovered over. Since they're the same color, this would be a nice touch. However, we can't use CSS to change an attribute on a parent element when a child element is hovered over. Don't worry, JavaScript is here to rescue the situation. Add these two events to the `GuessView` class's events property:

```
'mouseover #guessBtn': 'color',
'mouseout #guessBtn': 'color'
```

When the button receives the `mouseover` or `mouseout` event, we'll call the `color` method. This method is really simple; all it does is toggle the `border` class on that parent element:

```
color: function () {
  this.$el.toggleClass('border');
},
```

Of course, this means that we'll have to add a `border` class to our CSS file:

```
.border {
  border-color: #C04946;
}
```

Now, let's focus on the more important problem; allowing the player to make an actual guess. We already have the `GuessView` class ready for the click on the **Guess** button. When this happens, we call the `guess` method:

```
guess: function (evt) {
  var results = this.collection.guess(this.guessText.text());
  if (results.word) {
    Backbone.trigger('correct', results.word);
  } else {
    this.currentTokens.forEach(function (token) {
      token.view.show();
    });
  }
  this.currentTokens = [];
  this.guessText.text('');
  if (results.complete)
    Backbone.trigger('completed', this.collection);
}
```

Building a Game

The first step is to check this word against the collection. We do this by calling the collection's `guess` method. We haven't written this yet, but it will return an object with two properties. The first is the `word` property. If the guess is a word in the collection, this property will be the `Word` model itself; otherwise, it will be `undefined`. If there is a `Word` model, we'll trigger the `correct` event, passing along the `Word` model. Remember, the `ClueView` instances are listening for this event. If `results.word` is `undefined`, this means the tokens did not spell one of the words, and they need to be replaced. So, we'll loop over the tokens and call the `show` method on the `view` property that we gave them when rendering those views. In either case, we'll empty the `currentTokens` property and clear the text from the `guessText` property. The last step is to check for a `complete` property on the `results` object. If this is `true`, the player just completed the last word and finished the game. If the game is done, we'll trigger a `completed` event, passing the game object as a parameter.

The last step is to write the `Game` collection's `guess` method. Back in the `models.js` file of the `public` directory, add this method to the `Game` class:

```
guess: function (word) {
  var results = {
    word: this.findWhere({ word: word }),
    complete: false
  };
  if (results.word) {
    results.word.set('correct', true);
    var score = results.word.get('points');
    var mult = 10 - parseInt(this.seconds / 15);
    if (mult <= 0) mult = 1;
    this.score += score * mult;
    results.complete = this.where({
      correct:true
    }).length === this.length;
  }
  return results;
}
```

We start by creating a `results` object with the `word` and `complete` properties. The `complete` property will be `false` by default; for the `word` property, we will search the collection to find a word model that matches the text we passed into this method. The `findWhere` method will return `undefined` if no word is found. However, if a `Word` model is found, we'll give that model a temporary property. We'll set `correct` to `true`. Since the player has just guessed a word correctly, the next step is to update the score. We create a `score` variable; it starts with the basic `points` property on the `Word` model. Then, we need to calculate the multiplier. As we saw earlier, a `Game` instance will have a `seconds` property; soon, we'll see how this will count up.

For now, we'll divide the seconds count by 15, round it with `parseInt`, and subtract it from 10. Then, if that results in a number less than or equal to `0`, we'll reset `mult` to `1`. This way, any correct guesses in the first 15 seconds will get a 10x multiplier, anything in the second 15 seconds will get a 9x multipler, and so on. After 2 minutes and 30 seconds, the multiplier will be 1. Then, we'll increment the `score` property by the word `score` times the multiplier. Finally, we'll compare the number of words with the `correct` property to the total number of words in the collection. If these are equal, `results.complete` will be true, because all the words have been guessed correctly. Finally, we'll return the `results` object.

Now, with this in place, we can refresh the page and actually play our game. Go ahead, give it a whirl! Here's what it should look like:

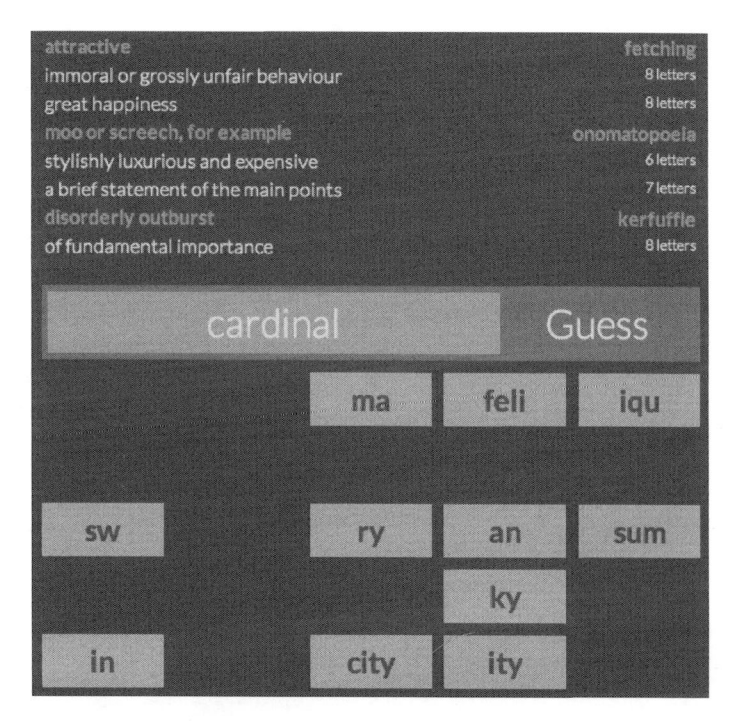

Pretty impressive, don't you think? We can pretty much play our game. However, there are a lot of details to take care of. While we are playing the game here, we aren't actually keeping score yet. So that's the next step.

Building the info view

The next class is for what we'll call the `InfoView` class. This will have both the time counter and the current score. We'll start with the template. Add this to the `index.ejs` file in the `views` directory: we're creating two `<span>` elements: one for the time and another for the points. Here's the code of the template:

```
<script type='text/template' id='info'>
  <span class='timer'> 00:00 </span>
  <span class='points'> 0 points </span>
</script>
```

Now, before we write the view class, we need to add a few more methods to our `Game` collection class. The `guess` method that we wrote earlier keeps track of the player's score. We also want a `Game` instance to track the time. The counter will be inside the game instance, but the `InfoView` class will have to actually show the time. This is the `start` method:

```
start: function (callback) {
  this.callback = callback;
  this.loop();
},
loop: function () {
  this.seconds++;
  this.callback(this.time());
  this.timeout = setTimeout(this.loop.bind(this), 1000);
},
```

The `start` method is what the `InfoView` class will use. It takes a `callback` function as a parameter and assigns it as a property of the instance. Then, it calls the `loop` method. This method increments the `seconds` count, and then calls the `callback` function, passing it the result of the `time` method (that's next). Then, we'll set a timeout for this method to be called again in one second; we have to bind `loop` to `this`, so the value of `this` will remain the same each time we call it. The `time` method just returns the `seconds` count as a nice timestamp:

```
time: function () {
  var hrs = parseInt(this.seconds / 3600),
    min = parseInt((this.seconds % 3600) / 60),
    sec = (this.seconds % 3600) % 60;

  if (min < 10) min = "0" + min;
  if (sec < 10) sec = "0" + sec;
  var time = min + ":" + sec;
```

```
      if (hrs === 0) return time;

      if (hrs < 10) hrs = "0" + hrs;
      return hrs + ":" + time;
    },
```

It's pretty basic math. We can use the division and modulus operators, and the `parseInt` function, to create a time string. So, when the `seconds` count is 42, the string will be "00:42"; 73 will be "01:13". If the time is over an hour (which is unlikely, but possible), we'll add the hour count to the front. This time, string is the value that will be passed to the callback.

Now, let's look at the actual class. We'll give the element the class `info`, and we'll fetch the template. This is the code of the `InfoView` class:

```
    var InfoView = Backbone.View.extend({
      className: 'info',
      template: $('#info').html(),
      initialize: function () {
        this.listenTo(Backbone, 'correct', this.updateScore);
        this.collection.listenTo(Backbone, 'completed',
          this.collection.stop);
      },
      render: function () {
        this.el.innerHTML = this.template;
        this.time = this.$('.timer');
        this.score = this.$('.score');
        this.collection.start(this.time.text.bind(this.time));
        return this;
      },
      updateScore: function () {
        this.score.text(this.collection.score + ' points');
      }
    });
```

The `render` method begins by using the template string, and then creating two properties for the timer element and the score element. Then, we call the `collection.start` method that we have just written. Remember that this method takes a callback that will receive the time string, so, we can just pass it the jQuery `text` method bound to our `this.time` element. This will now count the time for us.

Building a Game

Before we look at the `initialize` method, let's add a little bit of styling to this. Add this to the `style.css` file in the `public` directory:

```css
.info {
  font-size:60px;
  margin: 20px 0;
}
.info span {
  margin-right:40px;
}
```

It's nothing big; we just up the font size and add some margin. Now, add an `InfoView` instance to the quick and dirty test we've been using:

```
$('#main')
   .append(new InfoView({ collection: game }).render().el)
   .append(new CluesView({ collection: game }).render().el)
   .append(new GuessView({ collection: game }).render().el)
   .append(new TokensView({ collection: game }).render().el);
```

Load this in the browser, and you should see something like this:

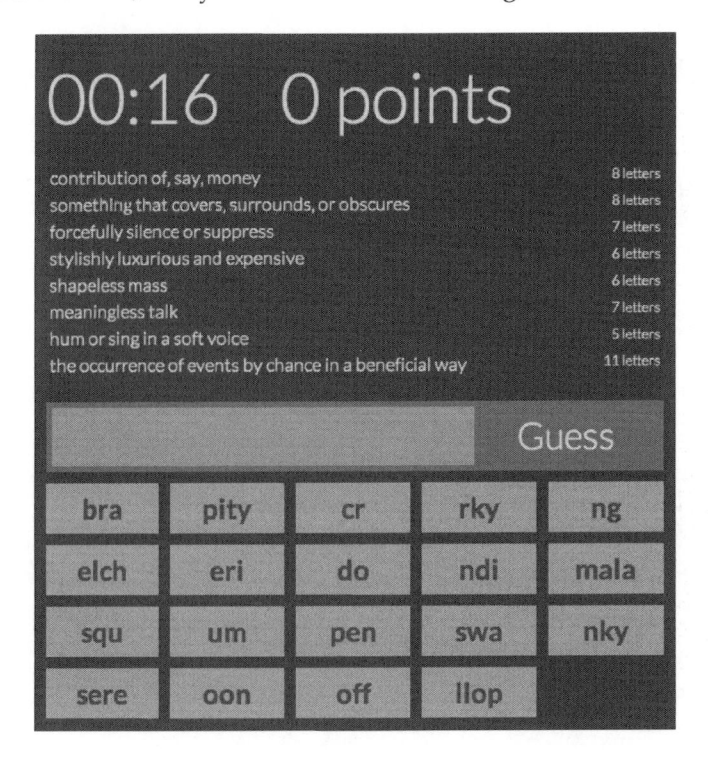

Now, in the `initialize` method, we listen for two application-wide events. When the player guesses a word correctly and the `correct` event is triggered, we'll call the `updateScore` method. As you can see, this will set the text of the score element by using the `score` property that we're updating on the collection object. The other event we're listening for is the `completed` event, which will be triggered when the game is completed. When this happens, we call the `stop` method on the collection object. This method has two jobs to do. First, it must stop the timer, and secondly, it must log the game to the server. This is the last method to add to the `Game` class:

```
stop: function () {
  clearTimeout(this.timeout);
  Backbone.ajax({
    url: '/game',
    method: 'POST',
    data: {
      time: this.seconds,
      score: this.score,
      date: new Date().toJSON()
    }
  });
}
```

When we create the timeout in the `loop` method, we assign it to the `this.timeout` property. In this `stop` method, we can clear the timeout to stop the timer. Then, we store the current game data to the server. Instead of doing this the Backbone way—by creating a model and using an instance of it to send the data to the server—we just use the `Backbone.ajax` method to POST this data to the server. If you'd rather use a model, it's very simple. First, create the model class in your `models.js` file:

```
var GameInfo = Backbone.Model.extend({
  urlRoot: '/game'
});
```

Then, replace the `Backbone.ajax` call with a `GameInfo` instance:

```
(new GameInfo({
  time: this.seconds,
  score: this.score,
  date: new Date()
})).save();
```

Building a Game

We're not actually going to do it this way, because we don't use the `GameInfo` class anywhere else. However, the beauty of these methods is that the server-side code is identical in both cases. Open the `server.js` file again, and add this router:

```
app.post('/game', function (req, res) {
  if (!req.user) return res.redirect('/login');
  var game = {
    time : parseInt(req.body.time, 10),
    score: parseInt(req.body.score, 10),
    date : req.body.date
  };
  req.user.games.push(game);

  if (game.score > req.user.score) req.user.score = game.score;
  if (game.time  < req.user.time ) req.user.time  = game.time;

  users.update({ id: req.user.id }, req.user, function (err, user) {
    res.json(game);
  });
});
```

First, we check to see that the user is logged in; we do this because we need the `req.user` object in this method, and we don't want to get an error. If a user is logged in, we'll put together a game object, with the time, score, and date that we sent from the browser. Then, we'll push that game object into the user's game array. You might recall that the user object has score and time properties of its own; these are for their highest score and lowest time. If the score or time from this game is better than the user's best, we'll update their best results. Finally, we'll store the updated record in the database. Of course, the last step is to return the game as JSON, but we won't really use that on the browser.

Wrapping our views in a GameView class

At this point, for the user to play the game, we are rendering four views. Let's wrap these views up into a single view: the `GameView` class. It is a pretty short view, but it will clean up the code in our router, once we start the router. Here's the code for the `GameView` class:

```
var GameView = Backbone.View.extend({
  render: function () {
    var attrs = { collection: this.collection },
        info  = new InfoView(attrs),
        clues = new CluesView(attrs),
```

```
          guess  = new GuessView(attrs),
          tokens = new TokensView(attrs);

      this.$el.append(info.render().el)
        .append(clues.render().el)
        .append(guess.render().el)
        .append(tokens.render().el);

      return this;
    }
});
```

In the `render` method, we'll create the four views, and append them to the element. We can test this view very easily—just replace the `callback` function code that creates the four views with this single line:

```
$('#main').append(new GameView({ collection: game }).render().el);
```

Nothing will look any different in the browser, and that's exactly what we want.

Starting the router

We're finally ready to begin building the router. As you might recall from the `index.ejs` file in the `views` directory, we pull in a `router.js` script, and so, create a `router.js` file in the `public` directory. Let's start with this:

```
var Router = Backbone.Router.extend({
    initialize: function (options) {
      this.main = options.main;
    },
    routes: {
      'play': 'play',
      'play/:level': 'play'
    },
    play: function (level) {
      var game = new Game();
      if (level) game.level = level;
      game.getWords().then(function () {
        this.main.append(new GameView({
          collection: game
        }).render().el);
      }.bind(this));
    }
});
```

Building a Game

As in our previous applications, the `initialize` method will take an `options` object, which will set the main element for the application. In the `routes` object, you will see that we create two routes. To play the game, we can go to either `/play` or, say, `/play/2`: both routes call the `play` method. This method creates a `Game` collection object; if a level was selected via the route path, we'll set it; otherwise, we'll stick with the default level (level 1). Then, we can get the words and create the `GameView` instance once we have those words.

The next step is to get rid of our quick and dirty test and replace it with the use of our router. In the `index.ejs` file of the `views` directory, this is what the final script tag (the inline script) should look like:

```
var r = new Router({
  main: $("#main")
});
Backbone.history.start({ pushState: true });
```

Now, you can go back to the browser and try the routes `/play` or `/play/3`. You should be able to play the game just as before.

Creating the home view

When a user first comes to our website, we don't want to display the game view right away. Most web applications will have some kind of home view, or welcoming view, explaining the purpose of the application. We could make that a server-side template, but we're going to make it a Backbone view instead. Here's the code of the `HomeView` class:

```
var HomeView = Backbone.View.extend({
  template: $('#levels').html(),
  events: {
    'click a' : 'chooseLevel'
  },
  render: function () {
    this.el.innerHTML = this.template;
    return this;
  },
  chooseLevel: function (evt) {
    evt.preventDefault();
    this.remove();
    Backbone.history.navigate(evt.currentTarget.pathname,
      { trigger: true });
    return false;
  }
});
```

We get the template with the `id` property of `home` from the `index.ejs` file. The `render` method is simple. The `events` object listens for clicks on anchor elements and calls the `chooseLevel` method. We've seen a method like this before; it just prevents the default action—the page refreshing—and uses `Backbone.history` to change the view instead. Finally, here's the template for this view:

```
<script type='text/template' id='home'>
  <h1>Pick a Level:</h1>
  <h2><a href='/play/1'> Level 1 </a></h2>
  <h2><a href='/play/2'> Level 2 </a></h2>
  <h2><a href='/play/3'> Level 3 </a></h2>
  <h1>Or, check out the <a href='/scoreboard'>scoreboard</a></h1>
</script>
```

Let's style the `<h1>` elements a little bit. You know where this goes—in the `style.css` file:

```
h1 {
  font-weight:300;
  font-size:39px;
}
```

Now, we need to use this view in the router. Open the `router.js` file in the `public` directory and add the `index` route:

```
'': 'index'
```

Then, we'll add the `index` function:

```
index: function () {
  this.main.html(new HomeView().render().el);
},
```

Now, you should be able to go to the root route and see this:

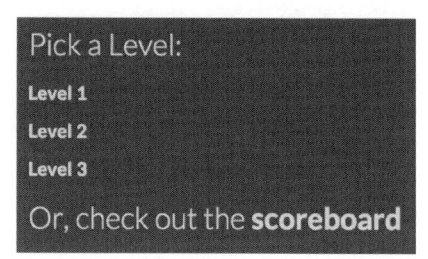

Building a scoreboard

We've already built the primary view for this application. However, every complete web application will have several views that aren't specific to the main purpose of the application, but help round out its usefulness. In our application, this will be a scoreboard view; a place where players can see each other's best time and score. Let's start on the server side this time, in the `server.js` file. Add this route before the catch-all route:

```js
app.get('/scoreboard', function (req, res) {
  users.find(function (err, userRecords) {
    userRecords.forEach(function (user) {
      user.totalScore = 0;
      user.games.forEach(function (game) {
        user.totalScore += game.score;
      });
    });
    userRecords.sort(function (a,b) {
      return b.score - a.score
    });

    res.render("scoreboard.ejs", { users: userRecords });
  });
});
```

We start by getting all the users in the database. Then, we loop over each user, adding a `totalScore` property to each one. We loop over the `games` array for each user and sum up the score for each game, creating the `totalScore` property. Note that we don't actually change anything in the database; we just create a temporary property here. Then, we sort the `userRecords` array; by default, the array's `sort` method will sort alphabetically, so we pass a function here that sorts the users from highest- to lowest-scoring. Then, we'll render the `scoreboard.ejs` template in the `views` directory, passing it the `userRecords` object.

Here is the code of the `scoreboard.ejs` template:

```ejs
<% include header %>
<div id="main">
  <h1> Scoreboard </h1>
  <table class="users">
  <thead>
    <tr>
      <th>Name</th>
      <th>Total Score</th>
      <th>Best Game</th>
```

```
      <th>Best Time</th>
    </tr>
  </thead>
  <tbody>
  <% users.forEach(function(user) { %>
    <tr>
      <td><%=: user.username | capitalize %></td>
      <td><%=  user.totalScore %></td>
      <td><%= user.score %></td>
      <td><%=: user.time | time %></td>
    </tr>
  <% }); %>
  </tbody>
  </table>
</div>
<% include footer %>
```

As with our other full-page templates, we'll open and close with the header and footer includes. Then, we'll create the main element. This element has a table element inside it. We start with a `<thead>` element, with four column headers: the player's name, total score, best game score, and best time. Then, inside the `<tbody>` element, we loop over the user array and add a row for each user. We use one of the EJS's features here: filters. For example, we print the `user.username` property, but we filter it through the `capitalize` filter so that the first letter will be, you guessed it, capitalized. Then, the `user.time` property is a seconds count, so we filter it through the `time` filter to display it as a human-friendly string. However, this isn't a built-in filter, so we'll have to write it ourselves.

Back in the `server.js` file, we first require the `ejs` library that Express uses behind the scenes:

```
var ejs = require('ejs');
```

Then, we have to write the filter function. We can actually just copy and adjust the time method from the `Game` class:

```
ejs.filters.time = function(seconds) {
  var hrs = parseInt(seconds / 3600),
    min = parseInt((seconds % 3600) / 60),
    sec = (seconds % 3600) % 60;

  if (min < 10) min = "0" + min;
  if (sec < 10) sec = "0" + sec;
  var time = min + ":" + sec;
```

Building a Game

```
    if (hrs === 0) return time;

    if (hrs < 10) hrs = "0" + hrs;
    return hrs + ":" + time;
};
```

The last step for the scoreboard is to add some styling to the user's table. Once again, turn to the `style.css` file in the `public` directory:

```css
table.users {
  border-collapse: collapse;
}

.users tbody tr {
  background: #4E5D6C;
}

.users tbody tr td {
  padding: 10px;
}

.users th,
.users td {
  width: 25%;
  text-align:center;
}
```

It's nothing too fancy, but it will do the job. We'll add some padding and color the background, and we're done! Here's the final product:

Name	Total Score	Best Game	Best Time
Andrew	1394	701	00:22
Robert	1209	622	00:16

Scoreboard

Writing the navigation

The next part of our application will pull things together; it is the navigation bar. In previous applications, the navigation has been its own Backbone view, but this is not the case this time. Instead, we'll create a new server-side template just for navigation. We'll be able to use this as an include, as we did with the header and footer templates. So, create the `nav.ejs` file in the `views` directory and put the following code in it:

```
<nav>
  <ul>
    <li><a href="/">Tokenr</a></li>
    <li><a href="/"> Play </a></li>
    <li><a href="/scoreboard"> Scoreboard </a></li>
  </ul>
</nav>
```

It's a basic list; there isn't much navigating to do in our application. But of course, we'll need to add some styling. Here's the last addition to the `style.css` file in the `public` directory:

```
nav {
  margin:0;
  background-color: #4E5D6C;
  overflow: hidden;
  font-size:19px;
}
ul {
  list-style-type:none;
  margin:0;
  padding: 0;
}
nav li {
  display: inline-block;
}
nav li a {
  display: inline-block;
  padding: 10px;
}
nav li a:hover {
  background-color: #485563;
}
nav li:nth-of-type(1) a {
  color: #D4514D;
}
```

Building a Game

This styling creates a nice navigation bar at the top of the page, with a nice hover effect on each link. The last part adds a color to the first item to make it appear like a logo. Now, add this as an include, under the header include of both the `index.ejs` and `scoreboard.ejs` files, like this:

```
<% include nav %>
```

That's it! Here's what it looks like:

Adding new words

Let's add one more feature to our application; the ability to add new words to the word list. We won't allow just any user to do this, only administrators. How exactly can we make a user an administrator? Well, we'll cheat. Open the `users.json` file directly, and add an `"admin":true` property to the user object of our choice. Then, we'll open the `server.js` file; first is the GET route for `/new`:

```
app.get('/new', function (req, res) {
  if (req.user && req.user.admin) {
    res.render('new.ejs');
  } else {
    res.redirect('/');
  }
});
```

If there's a user logged in, and that user is an administrator, then we'll render the new word template. Otherwise, we'll redirect to the root route. Create the `new.ejs` file in the `views` directory, and write this:

```
<% include header %>
<% include nav %>
<div id='main'>
  <form method="post" action="/new">
    <h1> Add a Word </h1>
    <p>Word:</p>
    <p><input type='text' name='word' /></p>
    <p>Definition:</p>
    <p><input type='text' name='definition' /></p>
```

```
    <p>Level:
      1 <input type='radio' name='level' value='1' />
      2 <input type='radio' name='level' value='2' />
      3 <input type='radio' name='level' value='3' />
    </p>
    <p><button>Add</button></p>
  </form>
</div>
<% include footer %>
```

We will post to the /new route when the form is submitted. We have an input element for the word and its definition (we could use a text area here, but an input element will encourage a short definition). Then, we have a set of radio buttons for choosing the level. Since this will post to the same route, we need a POST route on the server side to catch the new word:

```
app.post('/new', function (req, res) {
  if (req.user && req.user.admin) {
    var w = {
      word: req.body.word.toLowerCase(),
      definition: req.body.definition,
      level: parseInt(req.body.level, 10)
    };
    words.find({ word: w.word }, function (err, ws) {
      if (ws.length === 0) {
        words.insert(w);
      }
    });
    res.redirect('/new');
  } else {
    res.redirect('/');
  }
});
```

If there's an admin user logged in, we'll create a word object, w. Then, we'll check the word's database to see if the word already exists; if it doesn't, we'll insert it. Finally, we'll return to the form so that the administrator can insert another word if they want to.

Finally, let's add this path to the navigation, but only when an administrator is logged in. In the nav.ejs file of the views directory, add this as the last list item:

```
<% if (admin) { %>
  <li><a href="/new"> Add Word </a></li>
<% } %>
```

Then, everywhere we call the `res.render` function on the templates that use `nav.ejs` (that's `new.ejs`, `scoreboard.ejs`, and `index.ejs`), we add the `admin` value to the values passed to the template. For example:

```
res.render("index.ejs", { admin: req.user && req.user.admin });
```

If a user is logged in and they are an administrator, admin will be `true`. Otherwise, it will be `false`.

Summary

This brings us to the end of the last chapter. The first big idea we looked at in this chapter is not loading any application data with the initial page load. If your application uses a lot of data, this can often be a good idea. Not only does this shorten the initial page load, but it also prevents you from loading data that the user doesn't need (for example, if the user never uses a specific feature of the application, the data needed for that feature never loads).

The other thing to remember from this chapter is that a Backbone application may not be just Backbone pages. Our scoreboard page is a good example of this. It wouldn't have been difficult to create that page via Backbone—just create a `User` model and a `Users` collection and a couple of views—but since the user records don't really have any client-side relevance, apart from being logged in, we took the simpler route of doing it from the server side. Your web app will likely have other pages too that don't need data: a contact page, an FAQ page, that kind of thing. Don't forget about these details!

Most of what we've covered in this chapter is a review of the primary ways of using Backbone's main components, the model, the collection, the view, and the router. As with anything, the beauty of having a complete understanding of the way something works is that you are then free to bend it in whatever way you choose. Throughout this book, we look at several different ways of doing almost anything in Backbone. If you take only one thing away from it all, let it be this; it's just JavaScript, and there are countless other ways not mentioned here to create patterns of your own. It could be said that programming is just as much about self-expression as anything else, and a skilled programmer isn't afraid to experiment. Here's just one example for the road. What if the `initialize` method of a view class ended by calling the `render` method? Have fun with your Backbone applications!

Index

Symbols

7 Little Words application
  URL 201

A

addComment method 33
addEvent method
  about 122
  writing 120
App.Models.Event class 120
App.module function 139
App.Views.Day view
  about 117
  CreateEvent 117
  DayTable 117
  Details 117

B

Backbone
  calendar app, building 101
  simple blog, building 7
Backbone code, simple blog app 13
Backbone.trigger method 212
bcrypt.hashSync method 40
Bootswatch
  URL 172

C

calendar app
  building 101
  collection class, creating 102-106
  individual day screen, creating 116-130
  model class, creating 102-105
  month view, creating 106-108
  planning 101
  server code, writing 132, 133
changeModel method 127
chat application
  building 135
  chat module, building 158-161
  chat, rendering 161, 162
  CSS, writing 164-166
  layout, building 142, 143
  modules, creating 138-140
  outlining 135, 136
  room, joining 152-158
  router, starting 144, 145
  routes, adding 162, 163
  setting up 136
  Socket.IO 137
  template, preparing 137
  users, creating 140-142
  users, joining 146-152
collection class, calendar app
  creating 102-106
collection class, podcast application
  creating 183, 184
collection class, simple blog app
  creating 13-15
CommentFormView 33
comments, simple blog app
  adding 28, 29
  serving 29, 30
  viewing 30-33
CommentsView 32
Connect library
  URL 41
CreateEvent view 117
CreateEventView class 90

D

DayTable view 117, 118
Day view class 117
deserialize method 39
destroyEvent method 122
Details view 117
displayCount method 188

E

EditEventView class 90
EventView class 72
express.json() 10
express.static() 10

F

file uploads, photo-sharing app
   allowing 48-53
followed users photos, photo-sharing
     application
   displaying 67, 68

G

GLYPHICONS 78

H

Haml
   URL 11
hashPassword method 43
hidden.bs.modal event 82

I

includes 203
index.ejs file, podcast application
   preparing 182, 183
individual day screen, calendar app
   creating 116-130
individual photo page, photo-sharing app
   creating 59-62
initConfig method 73
initialize method 104, 188

J

Jade
   URL 11
JavaScript Templates (JST) Grunt plugin 73
JST.month template 107

L

layout, podcast application
   creating 189
Live Data Dashboard application
   Bootstrap, adding 78
   building 71
   controls, creating 76-78
   CreateEventView class, building 80-83
   event records, editing 89-94
   events, sorting 96-98
   events table, creating 84-88
   implementing 94, 95
   models, creating 74, 75
   planning 72
   precompiled templates, setting up 72-74
   record, deleting 88, 89
   router, starting 78, 79

M

Marionette
   URL 136
model class, calendar app
   creating 102-106
model class, podcast application
   creating 183
model class, simple blog app
   creating 13, 14
Moment
   URL 160
moment constructor 104
moment method 104
MongoDB 9
month view, calendar app
   creating 106-108
   day cells, building 112-115
   week row, building 108-111

N

navigation, photo-sharing app
  creating 45-48
navigation, podcast application
  building 185, 186
nodemon package 8
nodemon server.js command 8
Node.js packages
  q 175
  xml2js 175

O

Object.keys method 149

P

parse function 177
parseString function 177
Passport
  URL 38
passport.authenticate function 42
path.join() method 10
photo-sharing app
  cookieParser method 41
  creating 37
  file uploads, allowing 48-53
  followed users photo, displaying 67, 68
  individual photo page, creating 58-62
  multipart method 41
  navigation, creating 45-48
  passport.initialize method 41
  passport.session method 41
  photos, sending from server to client 54, 55
  profile pages, creating 55-58
  session method 41
  urlencoded method 41
  user accounts, creating 37-44
  users, following 62-67
photos, photo-sharing app
  sending, from server to client 54, 55
podcast catcher 169
podcast-listening application
  building 169, 170
  collection class, creating 184
  episodes, displaying 198, 199
  EpisodesView, displaying 193-197
  index.ejs, preparing 182
  layout, creating 189
  model class, creating 183, 184
  navigation, building 185, 186
  new podcasts, subscribing 190-193
  podcasts, displaying 186-188
  podcasts, storing 174-181
  podcasts, subscribing 174-181
  router, starting 190
  user accounts, building 170-174
PodcastListView class 186
PostListView class 17
post, simple blog app
  creating 26, 27
  viewing 23-25
PostsListView class 18, 19
processName function 74
profile pages, photo-sharing app
  creating 55-58
public folder, simple blog app
  creating 12

Q

q
  URL 175

R

removeEvent method 122
renderItem method 187
req.login method 43
resolve function 180
res.render method 11
router, podcast application
  starting 190
router, simple blog app
  creating 20-22

S

serialize method 39
server code, calendar app
  writing 132, 133
showComment method 60
showDetails method 127
showUser function 59

simple blog app
  app-specific code 13
  building 7
  collection class, creating 13, 15
  comments, adding 28, 29
  comments, serving 29
  comments, viewing 30-34
  model class, creating 13, 14
  post, creating 26, 27
  post, viewing 23-25
  public folder, adding 12
  router, creating 20-23
  server, starting 9-11
  setting up 7-9
  template, creating 11, 12
  test, performing 15
  views, using 19, 20
  views, writing 16
Socket.IO
  about 137
  URL 135
strategy method 39

T

template, simple blog app
  creating 11

U

updateEpisode method 181
update method 180
user accounts, photo-sharing app
  creating 37-44
user accounts, podcast application
  building 170-174

V

views, simple blog app
  PostListView 17, 18
  PostsListView 18, 19
  using 19, 20
  writing 16

W

word game
  building 201, 202
  clues views 215-218
  game data, creating 205, 206
  guess view, creating 218-223
  home view, creating 230, 231
  info view, building 224-228
  models, writing 207
  navigation, writing 235
  router, starting 229, 230
  scoreboard, building 232-234
  templates 203, 204
  tokens view, writing 211-215
  user accounts 202
  views, wrapping in GameView
    class 228, 229
  words, adding 236-238
  words, splitting up 208-210

X

xml2js
  URL 175

[PACKT] open source
PUBLISHING
community experience distilled

Thank you for buying
Backbone.js Blueprints

About Packt Publishing

Packt, pronounced 'packed', published its first book "*Mastering phpMyAdmin for Effective MySQL Management*" in April 2004 and subsequently continued to specialize in publishing highly focused books on specific technologies and solutions.

Our books and publications share the experiences of your fellow IT professionals in adapting and customizing today's systems, applications, and frameworks. Our solution based books give you the knowledge and power to customize the software and technologies you're using to get the job done. Packt books are more specific and less general than the IT books you have seen in the past. Our unique business model allows us to bring you more focused information, giving you more of what you need to know, and less of what you don't.

Packt is a modern, yet unique publishing company, which focuses on producing quality, cutting-edge books for communities of developers, administrators, and newbies alike. For more information, please visit our website: www.packtpub.com.

About Packt Open Source

In 2010, Packt launched two new brands, Packt Open Source and Packt Enterprise, in order to continue its focus on specialization. This book is part of the Packt Open Source brand, home to books published on software built around Open Source licences, and offering information to anybody from advanced developers to budding web designers. The Open Source brand also runs Packt's Open Source Royalty Scheme, by which Packt gives a royalty to each Open Source project about whose software a book is sold.

Writing for Packt

We welcome all inquiries from people who are interested in authoring. Book proposals should be sent to author@packtpub.com. If your book idea is still at an early stage and you would like to discuss it first before writing a formal book proposal, contact us; one of our commissioning editors will get in touch with you.

We're not just looking for published authors; if you have strong technical skills but no writing experience, our experienced editors can help you develop a writing career, or simply get some additional reward for your expertise.

Backbone.js Cookbook

ISBN: 978-1-78216-272-8   Paperback: 282 pages

Over 80 recipes for creating outstanding web applications with Backbone.js, leveraging MVC, and REST architecture principles

1. Easy-to-follow recipes to build dynamic web applications.
2. Learn how to integrate with various frontend and mobile frameworks.
3. Synchronize data with a RESTful backend and HTML5 local storage.
4. Learn how to optimize and test Backbone applications.

iPhone Game Blueprints

ISBN: 978-1-84969-026-3   Paperback: 358 pages

Develop amazing games, visual charts, plots, and graphics for your iPhone

1. Seven step-by-step game projects for you to build.
2. Cover all aspects from graphics to game ergonomics.
3. Tips and tricks for all of your iPhone programming.

Please check **www.PacktPub.com** for information on our titles

Backbone.js Patterns and Best Practices

ISBN: 978-1-78328-357-6   Paperback: 174 pages

A one-stop guide to best practices and design patterns when building applications using Backbone.js

1. Offers solutions to common Backbone.js related problems that most developers face.

2. Shows you how to use custom widgets, plugins, and mixins to make your code reusable.

3. Describes patterns and best practices for large scale JavaScript application architecture and unit testing applications with QUnit and SinonJS frameworks.

Jasmine JavaScript Testing

ISBN: 978-1-78216-720-4   Paperback: 146 pages

Leverage the power of unit testing to create bigger and better JavaScript applications

1. Learn the power of test-driven development while creating a fully featured web application.

2. Understand the best practices for modularization and code organization while putting your application to scale.

3. Leverage the power of frameworks such as BackboneJS and jQuery while maintaining the code quality.

4. Automate everything from spec execution to build; leave repetition to the monkeys.

Please check www.PacktPub.com for information on our titles

Made in the USA
San Bernardino, CA
18 September 2014